NEW SCIENCE LIBRARY

presents traditional topics from a modern perspective, particularly those associated with the hard sciences—physics, biology, and medicine—and those of the human sciences—psychology, sociology, and philosophy.

The aim of this series is the enrichment of both the scientific and spiritual view of the world through their mutual dialogue and exchange.

New Science Library is an imprint of Shambhala Publications.

General Editor   Ken Wilber
Consulting Editors Jeremy W. Hayward
                   Francisco Varela

WAKING UP

Overcoming the Obstacles to Human Potential

Charles T. Tart

An Institute of Noetic Sciences Book

NEW SCIENCE LIBRARY
SHAMBHALA
Boston
1986

New Science Library

An Imprint of
Shambhala Publications, Inc.
314 Dartmouth Street
Boston, Massachusetts 02116

9 8 7 6 5 4 3 2 1

First Edition

Printed in the United States of America

Distributed in the United States by Random House
and in Canada by Random House of Canada Ltd.

Library of Congress Cataloging-in-Publication Data

Tart, Charles T., 1937-
  Waking up.

  Bibliography: p.
  Includes index.
  1. Subconsciousness. 2. Self-perception.
3. Conflict (Psychology)—Prevention. 4. Happiness.
I. Title.
BF315.T34 1986   158′.1   86-11844
ISBN 0-87773-374-0

"I Think Continually of Those Who Were Truly Great," copyright 1934
and renewed 1962 by Stephen Spender, is reprinted in Chapter 15 from *The
Selected Works of Stephen Spender* (New York: Random House, 1964) by permission of Random House, Inc.

The quotation from Daniel Goleman in Chapter 22 is reprinted by permis-
sion from the *Newsletter*, Association for Transpersonal Psychology, P.O.
Box 3049, Stanford, CA 94305, from Daniel Goleman, "Early Warning
Signs for the Detection of Spiritual Blight," *Newsletter*, Summer 1985, p. 11.

CONTENTS

ACKNOWLEDGMENTS

This book is dedicated to all who seek more understanding of themselves and others, and who wish to awaken from the narrow and twisted dream called "ordinary consciousness."

I am especially indebted to G. I. Gurdjieff and his students, whose writings and practices were the central stimulation for this book.

The idea for this book originated with Henry Rolfs of the Institute of Noetic Sciences. Henry has had a long-standing interest in Gurdjieff and was looking for someone to undertake a modern interpretation of Gurdjieff's work when he sought me out. I have had a similar interest for many years. Henry and the Institute of Noetic Sciences proceeded to provide generous financial support that gave me the time to write this book, for which I am very grateful.

My students Christie Atkinson-Meyers, Etzel Cardena, David Gabriel, and John Price were especially helpful in suggesting clarifications and expansions of an earlier draft of this work, and my wife, Judy, provided the indispensable support and encouragement (as well as much editorial assistance) needed to create this book. Special thanks are also due to David Daniels, Henry Korman, Claudio Naranjo, Kathy Speeth, and others who taught me much about the Gurdjieff work.

I am pleased that this book is to be part of a new series originated by the Institute of Noetic Sciences. The Institute is a pioneering research and educational organization that has contributed greatly to our understanding and acceptance of a larger and richer appreciation of human potentials. It is a membership organization whose work is supported in part by members' contributions. If you are interested in learning from and supporting the Institute's activities, you may write to it at 475 Gate Five Road, #300, Sausalito, CA 94965.

INTRODUCTION

The purpose of this book is to help you find what you think you already have, namely free will, intelligence, and self-consciousness.

I expect you to find this idea preposterous.

I shall provide information to demonstrate that your will is largely a mechanical reaction based on your conditioning, that your intelligence is severely limited compared to what it could be, and that there is no true self controlling your life from a state of genuine self-consciousness. Then we can consider what to do about this situation. You can be far more than you are now!

To demonstrate the problem succinctly at the start, do the following exercise. Look at the sweep second hand or the digital readout of seconds on your watch. Note the time. Now use what will you have and resolve that for the next five minutes you will pay full attention to the movement of the second hand or every change of the digital display while simultaneously being aware of your breathing, and that you will not think about anything else.

If you cannot use your will and awareness to do this simple, emotionally neutral exercise, what can you do in the real stress of real life? If you maintain continual awareness of the seconds display and your breathing without thinking of anything else for the next five minutes, you have an extraordinary ability to concentrate. Concentration isn't enough, though, as this book will show.

Try the exercise *now,* before reading on.

With the threat of nuclear annihilation hanging over the world, we all agree that establishing foundations for permanent peace is our most important task. The psychological and spiritual aspects of that task are more important than the more obvious political and economic aspects, for without firm psychological and spiritual foundations, our so-called practical tasks, the political and economic actions, will not be effective.

Recently I heard a great spiritual leader, the Dalai Lama, talk about promoting world peace. I was very moved by his lecture, for he spoke from his heart as well as his mind. He stressed the many ways that external conflicts between people and nations stem from internal conflicts within ourselves, rather than arising only from external sources. We have to work on the external reasons for conflict, but if we want lasting external peace, we must work for it from a solid, inner foundation of personal peace.

There were several other speakers at this meeting. Immediately following His Holiness's talk, a woman commented from a feminist perspective on peace. She spoke of the way women have been mistreated in our own and other cultures, the ways in which war is a masculine activity that hurts women, and the need for women to use their power to stop war. Her analysis of the way sexism supports war opened new understandings to me. Intellectually, I agreed with all the points she made. They were clear, incisive, and very practical.

Emotionally, though, it was a different story. "Illogically," I found myself growing increasingly angry at her and everything she represented. My wife felt the same way, as did every other person in the audience with whom we later spoke. I was disturbed at feeling angry, as I knew it was both irrational and contrary to my own positive feelings toward feminist perspectives.

Through self-examination I realized that while the conceptual content of what she said was fine, indeed noble, the emotional tone of her talk was angry and aggressive, and aroused an automatic emotional opposition. Conditioned emotional reactions were aroused in spite of intellectual acceptance. She illustrated, unfortunately, His Holiness's main point. If you don't have peace within yourself, your attempts to create peace in the outer world can backfire, and may create even more hostility than if you hadn't done anything. This book is about the unconscious aspects of our selves that destroy our chances for real peace.

The fact that I and others automatically grew angry illustrates another aspect of the horror of the human situation, of course. We are far too automatic; indeed, we are automatons, another point this book will focus on.

Our discussion of the human condition will center on a central but seldom accepted or understood idea: we are "asleep," compared with what we could be. We are dreaming. We are entranced. We are automatized. We are caught in illusions while thinking we are perceiving reality. The woman who spoke after the Dalai Lama's talk was asleep, dreaming, entranced, unaware that parts of her self contradicted and sabotaged other parts. Her condition is our condition. We need to awaken to reality, the reality of the problems caused by our fragmented selves, so we can discover our deeper selves and the reality of our world, undistorted by our entranced condition.

This book is about waking up, a necessary step to create the foundation for inner peace as well as greater effectiveness in the world. It is about the psychological and cultural processes that create inner conflict, delusion, needless suffering, and hostility in us, that unnecessarily divide us from others, that deepen our sleep. Few of us may be in a position to have a decisive influence on world peace, but the cultivation of our own inner resources can create peacefulness and effectiveness in action in ourselves and the people we come into contact with, and this can spread. As we attack those near us less and care for them more, we start to have an effect on the kinds of political processes that need enemies for hidden psychological reasons. It is my hope that furthering the creation of inner peace in people will contribute to outer peace in the world.

THE INNER LIGHT

William Wordsworth in his "Ode: Intimations of Immortality" aptly described an all too common human condition. The personal recognition of this condition can be very depressing, or can start a journey of discovery:

> There was a time when meadow, grove and stream,
> The earth and every common sight
> Did seem to me
> Appareled in celestial light,
> The glory and the freshness of a dream.

There was a time, a state, in our childhood, when there was a vitality, a freshness, a zest, a longing for and loving of beauty that could make the earth a heaven. Light is a good metaphor for it, a metaphor that is literally true in some ways. Unfortunately, the light we once experienced gets covered over and seems lost. Reverting to an adult perspective, Wordsworth laments:

> It is not now as it hath been of yore.
> Turn whereso'er I may,
> By night or day,
> The light which I have seen
> I now can see no more.

No one likes this sense that something precious has been lost. Indeed, your personal loss of the light is also a loss to everyone else. You want to do something about it. The recognition of loss can be depressing, and/or can start you on a journey of growth. As adults we sometimes have brief glimpses of the light, which motivates us to seek it.

Many of the searches tried eventually lead to disappointment. You can drown out the voice of discontent by living harder, for example, striving for the ordinary kind of *more*: more money, more power, more sex, more fame, more excitement, more glamour. You can dull the recognition of emptiness with alcohol or other drugs. You can turn bitter and attack the world that has taken something precious from you, even if you don't know exactly what you have lost. Too often we resent and attack those who seem to have the light, for they remind us of our emptiness. You can try to console yourself with some religion that tells you all will be well in some future state, but the now remains empty.

Or you can look within to seek the light.

There are many paths available for seeking the light within. To start, you have to recognize that there is something precious within to be found, in spite of our culture's pressure to keep us externally oriented, looking for happiness by being consumers of external goods. You have to continually struggle against the social current, of course: people who go within are dangerous and unpredictable, so society distrusts, discourages, and often punishes them.

The paths have led some people to happiness, some to disappointment, some to mild delusions, some to insanity. Some paths are powerful, some may have been effective in the past but no longer work, and some are dangerous. Some are merely fantasies about paths; some are dangerous neuroses disguised as paths. All genuine paths require courage: courage to buck the social tide, courage to see yourself as you really are, courage to take risks. Progress on any genuine path is a gift to us all, as well as a gain for yourself.

This book is my sharing of some understandings that have helped me see why we are cut off from the light, and a sharing of some tools that have helped me and others see enough glimpses of the light to travel toward it. My understandings are a combination of my professional psychological knowledge and researches with the results of my personal search through several traditional spiritual paths.

My previous books have been scientific studies. Although many of the ideas I will present have scientific backing from modern psychology, the search for the light cannot limit itself to what has been scientifically researched to date: science is too young, too specialized, too narrow as yet, and it may never be able to deal with some of the most important aspects of human life. Deeper meaning in life must be found *now*, without putting off the search in the vague hope that science will make it all easy some day. Thus I write this book primarily as a fellow seeker of the light, secondarily as a psychologist.

I have also deliberately avoided the scholarly style of using numerous references to back up every point: I want you to test the things I say in your own experience, not to be impressed by distant authorities. Indeed, the material in this book must be grasped in an experiential way, as knowledge about your own being. A more scholarly style might produce intellectual conviction about what happens in other people, but if that were all that reading this book produced, I would be disappointed.

My engineering background will also show in this book, for it is a "nuts and bolts" approach. I am all for beautiful and transcendent goals, but I want to know as specifically as possible how things work. You will find much detail on our problems that allows specific actions to be planned for correcting them.

The way I present here is not The Path: God forbid that I ever think I have found an exclusive franchise on truth! I doubt that there is any one path for all people. Different types of people profit from different types of path, even though the ultimate goal is the same.

I don't know how practical the particular path I have followed is for everyone. I know how useful it has been to me, though, and since there must be many other people who are like me in important ways, what I understand of this path may be helpful to them. It may be particularly useful for those who can't or don't want to retreat from ordinary life, as it is based on a path that stresses being in the world but not of it.

G. I. GURDJIEFF

Of the several paths I have explored, the one called the Fourth Way, presented in the West by George Ivanovitch Gurdjieff, has been the most helpful to me. My interpretation of and additions to it are the organizing core of this book.

Gurdjieff was a seeker after the light. Born in Alexandropol in the Caucasus, somewhere between 1872 and 1877, he traveled through the East at the turn of the century, when such travel was a heroic undertaking. He studied with Christians, Muslims, Indians, Tibetans, and secret groups, looking for the core of spiritual truth he was convinced was hidden under the degenerated external forms of conventional religion.

He found an enormous amount of theoretical and practical knowledge that was largely unknown in the Western world. He wanted to share what he had found, and he was intelligent enough to understand that he couldn't transport his understandings in a wholesale fashion. What made sense for Easterners of a certain culture might not be effective in contemporary Western society, so he worked on developing a system adapted to Westerners living in the first half of our century. Gurdjieff died in 1946, but his work is still carried out by many people.

Gurdjieff intimated that the core of his work was based on the deliberate efforts of a secret school of wise men, a school some have claimed to be the mythical Sarmouni Brotherhood. I find this idea appealing, as I want to believe that there are advanced and wise people who are trying to help the rest of us evolve. We certainly need them! I do not know if there are such secret schools of the wise, and for our purposes in this book, it doesn't matter. As a psychologist with both practical and theoretical knowledge of the human mind, and as a person who has learned a little in my attempts to seek the light, I know that Gurdjieff's formulations of the human condition and many of his techniques for working on oneself are accurate, ingenious, and effective. That is what makes them worth sharing.

After Gurdjieff's death, various groups grew up to foster his ideas and work. As is unfortunately typical, most of these groups tend to think that they have the "real" teaching and that the other groups are, at best, well-intentioned imitators who waste people's time or, at worst, charlatans who harm people under the guise of liberating them. Gurdjieff's work does lend itself to abuse, as we shall discuss in Chapter 22. I try to avoid getting entangled with disputes about this kind of doctrinal purity, though, and I make no claim to purity in presenting Gurdjieff's ideas myself.

This book is centered on my understanding of Gurdjieff's psychological ideas. I have added to them when I think my ideas or modern psychological findings are useful. I have not dealt with some of Gurdjieff's ideas, especially his cosmological ones, either because I don't trust my comprehension of them or because I am not sure of their validity. Gurdjieff was a genius, but geniuses can be wrong about many things, just like the rest of us. If you find the ideas and techniques in this book useful in your personal quest for the light, good. Then you may wish to go on to other writings by or about Gurdjieff: Appendix A provides some direction. In the end, though, we can never be given knowledge by others; we can only be stimulated. We must develop our own knowledge.

Take the ideas and practices in this book as stimulation. If they resonate with something in you, try them out. Do they fit in your personal experience? Do they expand your understandings? Do they need modification? Are they appealing to the better or worse sides of your personality? Should some be rejected? As Gurdjieff emphasized, you should *believe nothing* about his teachings or, for that matter, my version of them. If the ideas and practices appeal to you, be open to them until you feel you have a basic understanding, and then test them. If they work for you, build on them and go on.

A man whose life was rather dull and unhealthy began to become aware of his condition and decided that he wanted to grow beautiful flowers and nutritious vegetables in his yard. He wasn't sure how to go about it, so he went to a local store and looked around. There were packs of seed with marvelous illustrations of beautiful flowers and nutritious vegetables on them, and boxes and jars of fertilizers. Naturally these seemed just what he wanted.

As he was preparing to buy them, a friend who was somewhat wiser happened by and asked him what he was planning. After listening, the friend, who had seen the man's yard, was compelled to give him some advice: "Your ultimate aim is very good, but I've seen your yard. It is already fertile and is overgrown with flourishing weeds. You won't need seeds and fertilizer for a long time; you need information on recognizing weeds and tools for thoroughly digging them out. If you use seeds and fertilizer now, the weeds will flourish even more and the flowers and vegetables will be choked out."

I would prefer to write about just the flowers and nutritious vegetables, but, as an old weed grower, I have learned about the importance of weeding. This book is about looking for the light, but much emphasis is put on recognizing and dealing with the weeds of sleep, trance, defenses, and the like that use up our energy and choke out our deeper side. I am sorry that so much of this book will focus on the causes and exact nature of human foolishness and suffering, but the aim is to prepare for cultivation of the light. I believe the material in this book can be useful to anyone seeking truth, whether scientist or mystic. All of us have a lot of weeding to do.

This book is divided into three main sections. The first briefly deals with the nature of enlightenment and the possibilities of drawing on resources from many states of consciousness for our full evolution. The second is a detailed discussion of weeds, the automatisms and defenses that limit us. The third is about weeding techniques and some of the results that may occur.

There is an inner light, an inner peace, that can be found. There is an awakening of your mind possible that will indeed make ordinary consciousness seem like a state of sleep. It will make you more, not less, effective in the ordinary world, and allow you to give more genuine attention, care, and compassion to others. I have tasted it, not just thought about it. I know it leads to an inner peace that facilitates an outer peace. I am happy to share what I can of this knowledge with you.

Part One

Possibilities

I

States of Consciousness and Enlightenment

This book is about enlightenment and states of consciousness, about methods for pursuing an important aspect of enlightenment, and, particularly, about the obstacles that keep us in an unenlightened, ignorant state.

The terms *states of consciousness* and *enlightenment* are new to our culture. Although personal experimentation with altered states of consciousness and a desire for enlightenment are now important in some people's lives, the ideas associated with these terms are seldom clear. Indeed, there is an unnecessary mystification clinging to them that interferes with our growth and understanding, so this chapter will be devoted to clarifying what we mean by *states*, by *altered states*, and by *enlightenment*. This will set up a general perspective on our possibilities. It will also give an overview of the obstacles to full realization of our potentials that will be helpful to us as we become involved in the detailed understanding of obstacles to enlightenment that the next part of this book deals with.

In this chapter I will deal with three main ideas: What do we mean by enlightenment? What are altered states of consciousness? In what ways can altered states be used for growth toward enlightenment, or be part of enlightenment?

STATES OF CONSCIOUSNESS

Let us start by sharpening our use of the term *state of consciousness*. There is a common but unhelpful use of the phrase to mean whatever one is experiencing at the moment. Thus, when you eat a cookie, you are in a "taste of cookie" state of consciousness. If you then think about some financial problem, you are in a "financial" state of consciousness, and so on. This is too broad for the term to be useful. For precise scientific use, I proposed in my book *States of Consciousness* that we reserve the term *state* for *major* alterations in the way the mind functions.[1]

For example, if I ask you, "Are you experiencing a nighttime dream right now, just dreaming that you are reading this book, but soon you'll wake up at home in bed?," I would not expect you to say yes. Actually, I've occasionally had someone raise his[2] hand when I've asked this in large lectures, but such people want to play word games. If I ask such a person whether he is willing to bet me fifty dollars that he will wake up in bed from this dream in five minutes, he admits that he certainly knows he is not dreaming.

What I'm illustrating is that we make commonsense distinctions about states. There is usually a *pattern* to our mental functioning that we can examine and then classify. If you examine the pattern of your mental functioning at this moment, it doesn't feel like the pattern you usually call dreaming. It feels like the pattern you call waking or ordinary consciousness. The difference is quite clear, and for the vast majority of us, dreaming is discretely different from waking.

To be more precise, in my systems approach to understanding altered states, I defined a *discrete state of consciousness for a given individual* (individual differences are very important) as a unique *configuration* or *system* of psychological structures or subsystems. The parts or aspects of the mind that we can distinguish for analytical purposes (such as memory, evaluation processes, and the sense of identity function) are arranged in a certain kind of pattern or system. The pattern or system is the state of consciousness. The nature of the pattern and the elements that make up the pattern determine what you can and cannot do in that state. In dreaming, flying by an act of will is possible. I wouldn't want to say it is totally impossible in consensus consciousness, but it certainly isn't easy!

A state of consciousness is a dynamic process; aspects of it are constantly changing in their particulars even while the overall pattern remains recognizably the same. The particular content of my last few thoughts, for example, has been different from thought to thought, but all my thoughts are obviously occurring as parts of a pattern I call my ordinary consciousness. I sometimes think of a state as being like a juggler throwing several balls around and around in a circle: the balls are always moving, but the pattern they form stays circular.

The pattern of a state of consciousness deliberately maintains its integrity in a changing world. "The structures operative within a discrete state of consciousness make up a *system* where the operation of the parts, the psychological structures, . . . stabilize each other's functioning by means of feedback control, so that the *system* [the discrete state of consciousness] maintains its overall pattern of functioning in spite of changes in the environment"[3]. If I were physically present with you now and suddenly clapped my hands, you would be startled. There would be a change in the environment and your momentary internal mental functioning, but you probably wouldn't suddenly go into some sort of "trance," attain enlightenment, pass out, or anything like that. Your state of consciousness maintains its integrity in a changing world.

A state is an *altered* state if it is discretely different from some baseline state we want to compare things to. Since we usually take ordinary waking consciousness as our standard of comparison, a state such as nocturnal dreaming is thus an altered state. Other well-known examples of altered states are the hypnotic state, states induced by psychoactive drugs such as alcohol, states centered on strong emotions such as rage, panic, depression, and elation,[4] and states induced by meditative practices.[5]

My personal interest in altered states began when I was a child. For as far back as I can remember, my dream life was real and vivid. My parents, being quite normal for our culture, taught me that dreams were not real and that I needn't pay attention to them, but my direct experience contradicted this typically Western point of view. How could people dismiss such real aspects of life? Why did I forget my dreams so readily? How could I improve the quality of my dream life? One question especially intrigued me: I could fly in dreams by a certain act of will; why couldn't I make that same act of will work in waking life so that I could fly here?

THE POWER OF ALTERED STATES: HYPNOSIS

My childhood interest in dreams was one factor in my choosing to become a psychologist, and many of my early research projects involved dreaming. The altered state that most impressed me early in my research career, though, was hypnosis, and it can serve briefly to illustrate the enormous power that altered states have to change what we perceive as reality. (We will look at hypnosis in detail in Chapter 9, as it tells us much about the problems of ordinary consciousness.)

In inducing hypnosis I would sit down with a volunteer who wanted to be hypnotized. We were presumably both normal people. With our eyes we presumably saw the same room around us that others saw; with our ears we presumably heard the ordinary and real sounds in the room. We smelled what smells were there and felt the solidity of the real objects in the room.

Then I began to talk to the subject. Researchers give the style of talking the special name of "hypnotic induction procedure," but basically it was just talking. The subject was given no powerful drugs, was not in a special environment, had nothing external done to his brain—and yet in twenty minutes I could drastically change the universe he lived in.

With a few words, the subject could not lift his arm. With a few more he heard voices talking when no one was there. A few more words and he could open his eyes and see something that no one else could see, or, with the right suggestion, a real object in plain sight in the room would be invisible to him.

Another suggestion and the subject would have a dream, sometimes as vivid as or more vivid than his nighttime dreams. Another suggestion and the subject would forget the present and be five years old, feeling and acting as he did at that age. Another suggestion and he would not remember what happened while he was hypnotized after he woke up.

A sense as basic as pain could be abolished. In spite of the number of times I have seen it, a test procedure we called "anosmia to ammonia" still amazes me. I would tell a subject that he could no longer smell anything. Then I would hold a bottle of household ammonia an inch under his nose and ask him to take a good sniff. The smell of ammonia is not only a strong smell, it is an extremely painful sensation, as if your nostrils were set on fire. A talented hypnotic subject would take a deep sniff, while I winced. No reaction. No tears would form in his eyes, and he wouldn't jerk his head away or show any other reaction. "Did you smell anything?" "No."

For those readers inclined to refresh their memory of the smell of ammonia, I would advise starting with a *very small* sniff!

Our commonsense view is that we live in the real world and perceive it essentially as it is. The book in your hands is real, it feels solid because it is solid, you see the words because they are really there. Yet this commonsense reality can disappear as a result of a few minutes of talking. The book in your hands could disappear altogether, it could feel soft instead of hard, and the English words could turn into gibberish. Can we, then, really take the commonsense wisdom of ordinary consciousness for granted?

WHAT IS ENLIGHTENMENT?

A part of my mind is highly amused that I plan to write about the nature of enlightenment. What presumption! Isn't enlightenment something possessed and understood only by superhuman beings? What in the world can a Western psychologist have to say about it?

As I will elaborate later, many of the most important aspects of enlightenment are nonverbal in nature. Words cannot capture the essence of this knowledge. Further, enlightenment involves certain kinds of knowledge, *state-specific knowledge*, that cannot be adequately comprehended in our ordinary state of consciousness, a point that I will also elaborate upon later. Here we are, right now, using words in our ordinary state of consciousness. It certainly is silly, in one sense, to use words about enlightenment. Nevertheless, words in our ordinary state can be useful in thinking about enlightenment, *especially if we are careful not to confuse the words with the realities.* With this caution in mind, let us go on and consider some aspects of what enlightenment is, and later see how altered states fit in with it.

To begin with, I find it helpful to think about enlightenment as a *continuum* of development rather than an all-or-none state. Just seeing it as a totally-incomprehensible-to-us end point, with no intermediate steps, does make it difficult to talk about, and difficult to do anything about. Compared to the rest of us, a pilot is enlightened about flying airplanes, but he didn't get that way in a single magical act; he studied for a long time, moving along a continuum from being completely unenlightened about flying to knowing more and more about it. When we think about enlightenment on a continuum, we can see it as a process, not just a final state.

Within this overall continuum of enlightenment there are "jumps," though, created by the functioning of altered states, and this is where state-specific knowledge becomes important.

The phenomenon of state-specific knowledge is important in understanding why complete enlightenment must involve access to altered states of consciousness. In a particular state of consciousness you may have access to and/or deeper understanding of certain kinds of knowledge that you cannot adequately comprehend in other states of consciousness. Thus, if you cannot enter a certain state, you can never fully understand certain things. Insofar as these items of state-specific knowledge are important, your life without them is impoverished: you have to settle for partial and often distorted understanding of them based on others' descriptions.

Consider a person with no musical training or talent hearing a symphony for the first time. It may have a strong emotional impact on him, and afterward he may tell his friends that the symphony was beautiful or deeply moving or full of sound. That sort of description is like someone else telling you that in an altered state "I directly experienced the Infinite Love at the core of the universe!" It's impressive-sounding but not very specific or useful if your goal is to reproduce the sounds of the symphony.

Now consider a trained musician hearing the same symphony. In addition to being moved by it, the musician can describe it (at least to other musicians) in quite precise terms of notes, keys, and movements, and even write it out in a musical notation so precise that other musicians can re-create the symphony almost exactly as it was originally played. The musician has far greater understanding (of a specialized kind) of the symphony than the untrained listener. The musician's knowledge is analogous to state-specific knowledge. Similarly, the person who has directly experienced certain kinds of knowledge in an altered state has much more understanding of it than the person whose mind has never functioned in that mode. Reading a retrospective philosophical analysis of a mystical experience of union with the universe, for example, may be intellectually stimulating, but it hardly provides a new foundation for your life the way the experience of union probably did for the person who had the actual experience.

For our purposes in this chapter I will focus on state-specific knowledge that is useful, without raising questions about its validity. As a practical consideration, though, we should keep in mind that just because something seems obviously true in some altered state doesn't mean that it necessarily is. Any kind of knowledge, whether from consensus consciousness or some altered state, should be validated against other aspects of our knowledge whenever possible. Appealing delusions occur in all states.

BASIC GIVENS

There are certain things I will take as givens for our discussion of enlightenment, even though each could be explored at length in some other context.

Awareness Is

First, awareness is. Our basic ability to have experiences, to know that we are, to be aware of things, has never been satisfactorily explained in terms of anything else. Current Western science likes to assume that awareness will be explained as an aspect of brain functioning, reduced to "nothing but" some action of the brain, but this assumption is an item of current faith and fashion, not good science. Indeed, science itself can be seen as one among many derivatives of the action of awareness, such that we wouldn't expect the part ever to be able to explain the whole.

We may never be able to explain awareness, but we can be aware: that is an axiom.

Consciousness Simulates the Environment

Second, consciousness, by which I mean that enormously elaborated, habituated, conditioned system of perception, thought, and feeling which we normally experience as our mind, has, as one of its primary functions, the simulation of the environment. Consciousness, particularly its perceptual aspects, creates an internal representation of the outside world, such that we have a good-quality "map" of the world and our place in it.

Most of you have seen pictures of flight simulators. These are devices for training pilots. You can train a pilot by having him read some instructions and then putting him at the controls of a real airplane. It's a fine system, but costly. If he makes a mistake, the plane crashes. No more pilot-trainee, no more plane. Instead of risking life and plane, you can have him enter a special room that looks from the inside just like the cockpit of the plane he is training for. When he operates the controls to start the simulator's "engines," he hears the sound, feels the vibration, and sees the appropriate meters reading out rpm, temperature, oil pressure, and the like. He sees a runway and airport ahead of him when he looks out the simulator's "cockpit window," the scenery moves when he "taxis" the plane, and so on. It's just like piloting a real plane as far as sensory perception and feedback go, with one important difference: when a fatal mistake is made that crashes the plane, you get CRASH displayed on the "cockpit window" instead of a dead trainee and a destroyed airplane, and the trainee can go on to practice again.

Scientific knowledge of brain functioning and the psychology of perception have created a very useful model of reality as being like living in an extremely complex and sophisticated simulator. Consciousness is seen as being inside the brain. Consciousness per se has no *direct* access to the world around us (ignoring the reality of extrasensory perception, as conventional scientists do), but only to processes inside the brain. These brain processes take the information that our senses provide us about the world and create a simulation of that world, just as the machinery of the flight simulator creates a simulation of being in an airplane. What we visually "see," then, is not the actual light that struck our eyes but a pattern of neural impulses that was initiated by the light that struck our eyes.

This brain simulation is our major tool for coping with ordinary reality, and it is important that the simulation be accurate. Insofar as this simulation model is useful, the degree to which the simulation is accurate is an aspect of enlightenment. The degree to which the simulation is a poor representation of external reality and the degree to which we mistakenly identify the simulation, experienced reality, with actual reality are important aspects of lack of enlightenment. Note carefully that the reality we are concerned with simulating accurately is not necessarily the same as what society defines as real, a point I will come back to many times.

We Have a Basic Nature

Third, we have a basic nature, an *essence*. To be human is to have characteristics, potentials, limits. We are not mountains or dolphins or gorillas or angels; we are people. I will not attempt to define what that basic nature is here. It is vitally important, however, not to confuse what our ultimate nature actually is or might be with what we currently think it is or what we have been told it is.

We Have an Acquired Nature

Fourth, we have an acquired nature. Whatever our basic nature is, it has been subjected to an enormous amount of shaping, bending, conditioning, indoctrination, development, and repression in the course of enculturation. In the course of our being made into normal people, fitted into our particular culture's image of what normal is, our basic nature has been selectively cultivated. Our perception, our thinking, our emotional feelings, our assumptions and intuitions, and our behaviors have all been strongly molded. Our ordinary consciousness is not "natural," but an acquired product. This has given us both many useful skills and many insane sources of useless suffering.

It is a great mistake to confuse our acquired nature, the product of our cultural and personal histories, with our basic nature. Most people do make this confusion and thus cut themselves off from many basic human possibilities. We will look at the processes by which our acquired nature suppresses our basic nature in subsequent chapters.

To keep the acquired, semi-arbitrary, conditioned nature of our ordinary consciousness before us in the rest of our discussions, I shall no longer use the phrase *ordinary consciousness*, with its connotations of naturalness and normality. I shall substitute a technical term I introduced some years ago, *consensus consciousness*, as a reminder of how much our everyday consciousness has been shaped by the consensus of belief in our particular culture.[6]

THE TOOL ANALOGY

We can now consider the question of what enlightenment is by means of an analogy.

A carpenter is a person who has to solve a variety of problems in the physical world by using tools to build, repair, and maintain things. A good carpenter, one who is competent at a variety of jobs, has many tools available and knows how to use them. He has hammers, saws, rulers, squares, nails, chisels, and so forth. He uses the saws to cut, not to hammer; the hammers to drive nails, not to chop through boards. A poor carpenter would be one who doesn't have the necessary tools to do the job, or who can't improvise adequately from the tools he does have. A poor carpenter could also be one who has the necessary tools but doesn't know how to use them properly, or, for whatever reasons, *won't* use them properly.

These two dimensions of adequacy in carpentry, having the right tools and knowing how to use them properly, are analogous to two major dimensions of enlightenment. The tools are like the skills, including access to various altered states, available to you. For now we will define each tool as being a particular altered state, or as state-specific knowledge and skills that are available only in a particular state of consciousness. The ability to use each tool intelligently and properly, in accordance with its inherent characteristics, is the degree of enlightenment shown within a particular state of consciousness.

Thus there are these two independent dimensions of enlightenment for any person. What states are available to him, with their particular characteristics, talents, and costs? We will call that the *available-state* dimension of enlightenment. *Within* any of these states, how intelligently does he understand and use the characteristics of that state? We will call that the *within-state* dimension of enlightenment.

A person may be relatively enlightened on one of these dimensions and not on another. Like a carpenter with only a few tools, he might be "stuck" in consensus consciousness, with no access to altered states. A good carpenter would use his few tools skillfully, though, and analogously a person who is stuck in consensus consciousness might be mature, intelligent, and enlightened in the way he uses the mental qualities he has. He is relatively enlightened within that one state, but unenlightened in terms of access to other states.

Another person might be like a sloppy carpenter, having access to many tools but using them poorly. I have certainly known people who could enter many exotic altered states, but whose unintelligent and neurotic behavior showed they weren't very enlightened in any of them.

Let us look more closely at the qualities we would expect of within-state enlightenment.

QUALITIES OF WITHIN-STATE ENLIGHTENMENT

Focusing Awareness as Desired

Basic awareness is the ultimate essence of any state of consciousness, so within-state enlightenment would include the ability to focus awareness as desired, within the limits of the natural capacity of that state. Such limits should be found by effort, not by preestablished beliefs that might artificially limit the capacity. Ideally any aspect of the state, or the world as perceived in that state, could be focused on, brought to awareness. Since initial awareness is usually the prerequisite for using any particular capacity, this ability to focus awareness volitionally sets the stage for the use of our talents.

Focusing Awareness as Needed

An ability to focus awareness as needed by the survival and growth needs of the person is also vital. You might desire, for instance, to focus on a pleasing aspect of a situation you are in, such as the taste of a good meal you are eating. But if there is a potentially dangerous aspect of the situation, you had better perceive *it,* even if it is unpleasant and you would rather be aware of pleasant things. The lurking figure outside the window may frighten you and spoil your meal, but you are more able to do something constructive in this situation if you know about the figure than if you keep it out of your conscious awareness. Giving priority to more basic needs over less important desires is a quality of within-state enlightenment.

Undistorted Perception/Simulation

Undistorted perception/simulation of the world, within the inherent limits of the state, is another important quality of within-state enlightenment. In consensus consciousness or a drug-induced state, for example, the nature of the human eye sets some ultimate limits on what can be visually perceived, but the constructed nature of visual perception after the initial stimulation of the eye can vary greatly in its accuracy. Seeing people as threatening when they are friendly, for example, can lead to treating them in a hostile manner and evoking a consequent reaction, all of which is unenlightened and leads to useless suffering.

Recognition of Current State

I am not sure that there is any one state of consciousness that offers totally unlimited and undistorted perception of the world around us or modes of thinking and feeling that are optimal for all situations. Every state that I know of seems to offer perceptual, cognitive, and emotional advantages in some respects and disadvantages in other respects. Thus recognition of the state of consciousness you are currently in, knowledge of its advantages and disadvantages, leading to optimal use of that state, is another important quality of within-state enlightenment. This leads to another quality of enlightenment that applies to the available-state dimension as well as the within-state dimension of enlightenment, namely *recognition that the state of consciousness you are currently in may not be useful for handling the life situation you are currently facing.*

QUALITIES OF AVAILABLE-STATE ENLIGHTENMENT

Suitability of Current State

The recognition that you are in a state that may not be useful, or at least not optimal, for dealing with a current situation is important. You might be called upon, for example, to help settle an argument between lovers, but you are in a state of unresolved rage from an earlier, unrelated personal encounter with someone else. A state of rage might be highly useful for saving your life in certain situations where you are attacked, but its characteristics do not include the calm sensitivity about hurt feelings between lovers that is required to help them remember their basic love after their argument.

Ability to Change State

If you recognize your current state and understand it enough to know it is not a good one for dealing with your current situation, you could try to *postpone action until you happen to be in a more appropriate state.* This is a second quality of available-state enlightenment. A more active form of this quality would be *knowing what state is optimal for the situation you are currently in and knowing how to end your current, inappropriate state and induce the optimal one.*

Modifying Current-State Knowledge with Altered-State Knowledge

A third quality of enlightenment on the available-state dimension is that you not only have as clear an understanding as possible of your basic nature as it manifests in the state you are currently in, but you have at least some recognition that this knowledge, no matter how clear and convincing it seems, is only a partial view that needs to be supplemented by the knowledge available to you in other states. Thus *knowledge and action in any particular state must be tempered by the knowledge gained in other states of consciousness.*

For example, I may be in a state of rage, and as I get the advantage of my opponent, it is perfectly natural and reasonable, given my state, to want to destroy him completely. Further, I know I will enjoy destroying him; it will be one of the greatest pleasures of my life! That is the inherent logic of a state of rage.

There may be an inhibition of my urge to destroy. It may be checked by the emotional conditioning of my superego, for example. Such a check may be desirable from a social point of view, but it is a relatively unenlightened kind of inhibition: the superego is conditioned in us by others, not the result of our own choosing, a point that will be elaborated in later chapters.

Realistic inhibition may occur by recalling, probably from consensus consciousness knowledge, my fear of the consequences of my planned destructive action. More enlightened control may also occur if, while in my state of rage, I recall other states in which I could experience or have experienced kinship with my opponent, and states in which I could feel or have felt compassion for him. Then I may use my will (assuming it is strongly developed enough, another point we will consider at length later) to terminate my state of rage and enter into a more appropriate state, a state judged more appropriate to my deeper self, *given my values as known and manifested across several states of consciousness.* If I cannot voluntarily end the state of rage at will, I can at least keep myself from acting wholeheartedly on the basis of my current rage.

To more fully illustrate this kind of available-state enlightenment, suppose you are in a state where you are very compassionate, but you are dealing with someone who is enraged. The enraged state may be available to you: you could use instinctive emotional reactions to the other's rage as an induction technique[7] to enrage yourself, if you thought that would be the optimal state to deal with the enraged individual. Or you can draw on your personal memory of what it is like to be enraged to understand more fully the enraged person you are dealing with, even though you don't allow yourself to go into an altered state of rage yourself, and then act compassionately in a more effective way because of this available-state enlightenment.

This ability to recognize what state you are in and draw on relevant knowledge from other states, as well as having the ability to enter those other states if you desire, implies some aspect of consciousness, of our basic awareness, that transcends any particular state we are in at the time. The nature of that quality is of profound interest, and understanding and cultivating it are a prime focus of this book.

DISCRIMINATING BASIC FROM ACQUIRED NATURE

A fourth quality of the available-state dimension of enlightenment is that access to multiple states of consciousness allows sharper discrimination between our basic and our acquired nature. The bulk of the conditioning and shaping of our acquired nature, our enculturation, took place in consensus consciousness or in some emotional state that is ordinarily accessed from consensus consciousness. Part of the enculturation process works to convince us that the acquired characteristics of enculturation are actually natural, so it can be very difficult to see these things when we are in a state of consensus consciousness. Sometimes being in some altered state (with its inherently different feeling and thinking functions) gives an alternative view that is like an outside perspective on yourself. Then you may see the conditioned, restrictive quality of consensus consciousness or of some emotional states. This kind of insight may be sufficient to dissolve the conditioning in the other state, or may at least form a basis for focused work on the blocking conditioning.

Potentials versus Developed Qualities

A fifth quality of the available-state dimension of enlightenment involves a realistic assessment of your capacities, including the fact that some may only be potentials at present, requiring development. A mode of thinking, feeling, or acting experienced in a particular state may need considerable work to become robust and usable in that state, or for you to learn to transfer any or all aspects of that ability into some other state, such as consensus consciousness.

An experience of great compassion in a meditative state, for example, may seem to carry over into consensus consciousness, making you feel like a very enlightened being, until someone insults you. The feeling of compassion is immediately replaced by anger. This kind of discrimination between developed reality and potential is particularly important when there is excessive attachment to an altered-state experience, such that you want to believe that you have made the envisioned qualities a permanent and functional part of yourself.

Now that we have looked at some of the qualities of enlightenment, let us return to its primary use: diminishing suffering.

ENLIGHTENMENT DIMINISHES SUFFERING

Much of our suffering is useless: it is unknowingly created by us through unenlightened, unintelligent use of our human capacities. We misperceive the external world and our own deeper desires and nature, act in a way that is contrary to the realities of our situation, and then reap the unpleasant consequences. Within-state enlightenment leads to more realistic perception of the world and ourselves: consequently we can engage in more effective action that can eliminate much useless suffering.

Although not well recognized in Western psychology, many aspects of our suffering occur in and/or result from various altered states, particularly emotional states, as well as in consensus consciousness. We think of emotions as part of consensus consciousness. This is usually true for weak feelings, but not for strong ones. We try to deal with the consequences of strong emotions with our understanding of consensus consciousness, but often do not succeed because the principles governing these strong emotions are those of the altered state induced by the emotion, not those of consensus consciousness.

By understanding the nature of altered states, we can relieve suffering in those states: the remedy for suffering in some particular state is often specific to that state. Our attempts to apply a remedy suitable to some other state lead to frustration and more suffering. For example, fear may trigger an altered state and consequent maladaptive behavior in a person. He spends many hours with a psychotherapist trying to get at the root of this fear. But the hours with the therapist are in consensus consciousness, while the heart of the fear is in experiences only fully accessible in the altered state of fearfulness, so the therapy proves only partially effective.

The alternative perspectives on our selves offered by altered states can allow work on both negative and positive aspects of our ordinary selves that might not otherwise be possible to us. Perhaps most important, the direct experiences of values and modes of knowing not available in consensus consciousness may be able to transform us in ways that consensus consciousness "knowledge about" can never do. The unitive

experience that we are all one is just an abstraction for most of us in consensus consciousness, but it is direct knowledge for those who have
experienced it in an altered state. The relief from suffering that comes
from a direct knowledge that the universe is meaningful is far more profound than any other kind of specific-problem-oriented relief.

OUR UNENLIGHTENED REALITY

I have sketched a rather grand picture of human possibilities here. Our
enlightened human being has a large number of states of consciousness
readily available. Faced with any situation in life, he intelligently assesses
it in his current state of consciousness, using all the resources available in
that state. This includes a memory that the current situation might look
different from the perspective of one or more altered states, which intelligently tempers assessment and action in his current state. Indeed, he
may decide the situation could be better handled in some particular altered state, so he takes a minute to change states and now handles the
situation even more effectively with the new mental/emotional/
intuitive tools available.

How often are we like that? Typically we meet life in consensus consciousness or in some emotional state that was not initiated by our
conscious choice. Typically we do not use that state as effectively as it
could be used—we see this in hindsight rather than know it at the time—
and we frequently do and say things that we later regret and that create
unnecessary suffering for ourselves and others. In spiritual language, we
have lost the power, reality, and purity of our full nature; we have gone
through some kind of Fall from grace, so we live life in a narrow, con-
stricted, unhappy way.

It could be so different *if* we were more enlightened. Why do we fall
so short of our possibilities? What is the nature of our "fallen" state?
The next part of this book is about the reasons we are entranced instead
of enlightened.

Part Two

Problems

2

God and Reality

There is no God but Reality.
To seek Him elsewhere
Is the action of the Fall.[1]

3

Automatization

Man is a machine.
—G. I. GURDJIEFF

One of the most upsetting and insulting remarks made by Gurdjieff was his statement that man is a machine. Machines are noisy, dirty, mindless things that repeat some stupid task endlessly, are controlled by others, and eventually break down and are destroyed: surely *I* am not like that!

This idea is quite troubling to most people, and they deny vehemently that they are like machines, much less *are* machines. This is most interesting from a psychological point of view. If the idea that you are a machine is truly nonsensical, why should it be so upsetting? Depth psychology has shown us that things that people deny strongly often have a component of truth to them. Unfortunately, Gurdjieff was right: for practical purposes, we *are* machines in multitudes of ways we fail to recognize. We should be upset.

Academic psychology also sees man as a machine, but seldom states the idea so baldly as Gurdjieff did. Introductory psychology courses routinely teach students that the goal of psychology is the understanding of human behavior, an understanding that is validated by the prediction and control of behavior. In principle, if you knew everything about a person's genetic and biological makeup and all of the psychological events in his personal history, he would be absolutely predictable. You could make statements like the following: "Smith is a biological type 1376 with a general psychological history of type 242, modified by personal history events X, Y, and Z. Therefore when a man of type A says 'How is the project coming?,' under conditions M, N, and Q, Smith will blush, say 'Fine,' and have a twelve-second fantasy about rowing a boat on a lake." That is just what would happen.

Absolute control would follow from such a high level of predictability. You would just set up the circumstances necessary to produce the response you wanted.

The fact that the idea that we are so mechanical, predictable, and controllable is upsetting is one of the reasons academic psychologists seldom spell it out clearly. How can you ask for support and respect from someone if you tell him you think he is just a machine? Indeed, how can you respect yourself, since you are also a machine? Much of the current controversy about sociobiology arises because that discipline is too clear about our machinelike qualities. Gurdjieff wasn't looking for ordinary, mechanical social support. He wanted to deliberately shock people so there would be an opportunity to start the work of going beyond being a machine. Academic psychology doesn't recognize the possibility of waking up and going beyond the mechanical, so it soft-pedals its dehumanizing philosophical foundations to itself as well as to others.

By studying machines, we can learn about ourselves. By fully recognizing and studying our machinelike qualities, however, it is possible to take a step no other machine can take: we can become genuinely human and transcend our machinelike qualities and destiny.

The idea of studying ourselves as machines can be very useful. Like any statement, the assertion "Man is a machine" is only an analogy, but it can give us a unique perspective on ourselves if seriously worked with. Until recent times, however, there has been a technological limitation on fully using this method. Ordinary machines, even complex ones, are so obviously mechanical, limited, and stupid when compared with human life that our ability to see ourselves mirrored in them is limited. We can see analogies with some very rigid habits, perhaps, but we feel so much more intelligent and subtle than machines. We can watch an irrigation pump turning round and round, pushing water from a canal into a ditch, and perhaps see some similarities to parts of our lives. Some of us continually take in pieces of paper at one end of our desks and push them out to the other end, for instance. But I believe I am so much more subtle than this machine that the analogy cannot go far. Or can it?

RUNNING ON AUTOMATIC

I consulted one of my spiritual teachers about my concerns over the best way to present Gurdjieff's ideas about man being a machine. We had the following dialogue:

TEACHER: So, Charley, what's your problem?

ME: I'm wondering how best to use a machine analogy in presenting Gurdjieff's ideas.

TEACHER: So you've come to me because you are wondering how best to use a machine analogy in presenting Gurdjieff's ideas?

ME: Yes.

TEACHER: Are you sure?

ME: That's my most immediate concern.

TEACHER: So what seems to be the problem?

ME: I'm worried that readers will be discouraged too quickly and not go on to learn what's really valuable.

TEACHER: How long have you worried that readers will be discouraged too quickly and not go on to learn what's really valuable?

ME: Ever since I started this book. Gurdjieff is hard on people.

TEACHER: So what does this suggest to you?

ME: Maybe I should soft-pedal the unflattering parts?

TEACHER: You sound somewhat uncertain.

ME: Yes, I have something very valuable to share with people, but I don't want to turn them off to it and throw away their chance of learning.

TEACHER: So you don't want to turn them off to it and throw away their chance of learning?

ME: Right.

TEACHER: I see.

ME: What should I do?

TEACHER: Why do you ask?

ME: I'm looking for guidance.

TEACHER: Do you think it's normal to be looking for guidance?

My teacher demonstrates some of the qualities we think of as uniquely human. She was more concerned with my motivations and feelings on this issue than with the simple overt content of my concern, something I have found in several master teachers.

My "spiritual teacher" here is also teaching a powerful and rather unpalatable lesson. My teacher's name is Eliza. "She" is a computer program. Not even a sophisticated program running in a huge computer, but a small program running in my home computer. To add insult to injury, Eliza was written as a tongue-in-cheek comment, to illustrate the inadequacy of attempts to simulate human intelligence on a computer, especially in a subtle area like psychotherapy. The program has worked better than its designer thought, however, and some people now like their computer "therapists" and say they benefit from their dialogues with them. The higher reaches of human intelligence are certainly beyond any computer simulation, but much of what passes for ordinary intelligence is not.

A person may appear to be acting intelligently and consciously, but he may be mechanically "running on automatic." By mistakenly thinking he is really conscious, he blocks the possibility of real consciousness. This is why it is so important to understand what Gurdjieff meant in saying that man is a machine.

Gurdjieff constantly emphasized that almost all human misery results from the fact that our lives are automatic, mechanical affairs. You (your behavior, thoughts, and feelings) are the *effect* of external and historical causes, rather than the *cause*, the initiator of desired actions. The horror of this fact is that we do not have to be machines, yet we are, too much of the time.

What does it mean to be a machine? How do we become automatic, mechanical? We'll approach this idea by designing a machine to perform a useful task, starting with a very dumb or mechanical machine and working toward a more intelligent one. As we add various aspects of intelligence to our machine, we can both understand better what intelligence is and see Gurdjieff's point that, unfortunately, we do not need any genuine consciousness to pass for normal by many ordinary social standards. The analysis is long, fascinating, and unpleasant, but will, I hope, lay a foundation for eventually transcending being a machine.

A VERY DUMB MACHINE

Imagine that we are in a warehouse. Uniformly sized square boxes come into the building on a conveyor belt. They are all oriented the same way on the belt and spaced at even intervals. For some reason we don't want to hire a person to pick the arriving boxes off the end of the belt. We would like a machine to lift each box off and put it on another belt, the output belt, which will take it to a storage area.

What we need is a sort of crane, something that will lower a pair of grippers, tighten the grippers so that they grab the box, lift the grippers, swing them just the right distance over to the output conveyor belt, lower the grippers, and then open the grippers so that the box will be carried away by the output conveyor belt. Our machine should then lift the grippers, swing the crane back to the input belt, wait for the fixed length of time it takes for the next box to arrive, and then repeat its nine-step transfer cycle. We'll call this our first-generation crane.

This first-generation crane can do useful work. It is also, unfortunately, quite prone to malfunctioning, as it has no mechanical intelligence to cope with possible changes in its situation. Our crane runs on an absolutely fixed cycle, no matter what happens in its world. Suppose the spacing between boxes is disturbed by something up the line and becomes too long or too short. The grippers will close on empty air and move nothing at all to the output belt, while the boxes fall off the end of the input belt.

SENSORY INTELLIGENCE

We can add a small amount of "sensory intelligence" to our crane by allowing it to sense its environment and have the results of that sensing control its behavior. Instead of its transfer cycle running mechanically over and over again, for example, let's define the start point of its cycle as lowering its grippers over the input conveyor belt, and the end point as returning to its waiting position above the input conveyor. At its end point the crane stops, waiting for a new start signal.

If we now install a sensing switch at the end of the input conveyor belt, we have the beginnings of rudimentary sensory intelligence. We give it a sense of touch, the kind of sense that was one of the very first that life had to evolve. When a box actually reaches the end of the belt, it pushes on the switch and turns it on. This sends a start signal to the crane, and it lowers itself and begins the transfer cycle. It is no longer important that the boxes be spaced absolutely regularly on the belt, for the transfer cycle won't begin until a box is in the correct position to be picked up and transferred. Our second-generation crane, with its rudimentary sensory intelligence, is smarter than our first-generation crane.

Now we can define one of the qualities of intelligence: it is *responsive*. Intelligent behavior is initiated as a result of sensing that an appropriate situation actually exists in the organism's environment, instead of automatically assuming that the situation is appropriate. One of the problems of people when they function as machines is that they do not always exhibit this characteristic of intelligence.

THE COMPLEXITY OF THE WORLD

The increase in mechanical intelligence of our crane is very small, for it is sensing and responding to only one possible change in its environment, irregular box spacing. Many other changes could cause malfunctioning and sometimes destructive behavior. Consider a second possible change: suppose the output belt stops running: the crane will swing the next box into the previous one, which is still sitting there, and we'll end up with boxes all over the floor, possibly damaged from their fall.

A third possible unplanned event: suppose our crane gets out of adjustment and swings too far. Boxes will be dropped on the floor on the far side of the output belt. If someone is working on the far side of the output belt, the dropped boxes may cause an injury.

We can increase the mechanical intelligence of our crane here in the same way as we did before by making it more "aware" of its environment. We can put a movement sensor on the output belt and wire it to send a stop signal to the crane if the output belt stops moving. We can go further and have the crane send a stop signal to the input conveyor belt to avoid a pileup of boxes on it. By adding an increase in sensory intelligence for one specific need, we gain some intelligence that can be used for other things. As we shall see when we examine Gurdjieff's ideas on self-observation and self-remembering, adding sensory intelligence in our lives is of enormous benefit.

As for the crane swinging too far, we can divide our crane operation into two cycles instead of one. The first will be the picking up of a box and swinging it toward the output belt; the second cycle will be the lowering and releasing of the box and returning to the start position. Now we can install a sensing switch above the output belt, so that when the crane is in the right position above the belt, it hits the switch: this ends the first cycle. The crane stops swinging and starts the second lowering cycle. Our crane is four times as intelligent as it was originally, for it will respond to the actual spacing of the incoming boxes, stop if either the input or the output belt malfunctions, and not swing too far if it gets out of adjustment.

ADJUSTING TO A GOAL

So far our third-generation crane's mechanical intelligence is of an all-or-none variety. The box has or has not hit the start switch; the output belt is or is not moving; the crane has or has not swung to just the right position to lower its box over the output belt. But suppose one of the boxes is turned at an angle on the input conveyor belt. Will the angled side of the box properly press on the start switch to start the crane's lifting cycle? Will the grippers hold securely? Might they damage the box or drop it after picking it up?

If the box is turned just a little, none of these problems will occur, but they will if it's turned too much. How much is too much? Is too much the same for each potential problem? We need mechanical intelligence that can deal with something more complex than an all-or-none situation. We need mechanical intelligence that has a memory of a goal, senses its environment for *degrees* of deviation from that goal, and then makes fine adjustments in its behavior to compensate for those deviations that might interfere with attaining its goal.

All-or-none, black-or-white perceptions and responses are a major problem in human life, of course. Someone makes a slighting remark to you and your adrenaline begins flowing, your muscles tighten, your body prepares for fight or flight, and you feel very threatened, angry, or anxious. Yet it was only a small verbal slight; no bodily response was called for. We overreact or underreact too often, whereas we need to react in correct proportion to the reality of the situation.

This kind of mechanical intelligence for discriminating degrees of change has been programmed into computer-controlled machines to a limited degree. To enable our crane to detect and handle turned boxes, we could add a television camera looking down on the box from above. The output of the camera is digitized in a computer, and a program then extracts the square shape of the top of the box, regardless of the angle it is at with respect to the belt. This shape is compared against information about the defined shape for a box in the computer's memory: the computer "recognizes" the box. This also locates the box for the computer.

Our fourth-generation crane's discrimination and control program now computes the angle that the box is turned away from the standard position it should be in. By fitting our crane with rotatable grippers, controlled by the computer, it can now rotate the grippers so that it grips it squarely and securely. Then it rotates the grippers to bring the box back to the alignment it should have had. Now it can go on with transferring it to the output conveyor belt.

RIGIDITY VERSUS INTELLIGENCE

There is a second way of dealing with the problem of turned boxes that does not require increasing the mechanical intelligence of our crane. We could design the belt so it was exactly the width of the boxes, with a raised track along the side. Then boxes would have to stay squarely aligned on the belt, or they wouldn't be carried along it to the crane.

We pay a price for this kind of solution, though. If we ever wanted to change our product line to something in smaller boxes, they would be able to get turned along the belt, reintroducing our problem. If we wanted to make a product that needed larger boxes, they wouldn't fit on the belt. For these cases we would have to rebuild our conveyor belt, which might be a costly process.

The two directions we can take for solving the problem of turned boxes represent two general directions that people have followed in trying to increase efficiency and reduce errors. As one direction, we can put more and more restrictions and limits on what can happen, make the situation more and more rigid, try to prevent problems from happening in the first place. Applying this approach to human activities, we can pass more laws, write more detailed rule books, establish more customs, paint more "No U-Turn" signs, and so on, to cut down the variability in human behavior that can create problems. "Well-behaved," "predictable," "rigid," "mechanical" people make the system run more smoothly: choose your favorite adjective. At its extreme, nothing is required of people other than following the rules. And, as the old joke says, "Everything that is not required is forbidden!" The rules are external environmental rules (like "No U-Turn" signs) or internalized psychological rules ("Decent people never even think of doing X"). For best results, both kinds of rules need to be backed up by rewards for following them and punishment for violating them, as well as by the strength of mindless habit.

The alternative direction is trying to increase the general intelligence of people so they will do the sensible thing on their own initiative. For example, I will sometimes drive diagonally across a near-empty parking lot to save time, rather than follow the marked lanes: most of the people I meet doing the same thing avoid running into me, even though there are no specific legal rules (I hope!) for diagonal driving across parking lots. A few weeks ago I was nearly run into by people driving recklessly across a parking lot, but, of course, I immediately classified them as *un*intelligent!

If we want a smoother, more efficient, less dangerous world, then, one direction we can take is to make people more like machines, machines with lots of mechanical intelligence. You can also spend great effort and use lots of resources in designing the world so that it is mechanically impossible to violate the rules. Many parking lots now have concrete dividers or green belts that prevent you from driving diagonally across them when they are empty. The other direction is to increase genuine intelligence, including the discovery and cultivation of the uniquely human aspects of intelligence that are not mechanical.

The unfortunate truth about people is how machinelike we can become. Gurdjieff observed how mass forces in cultures tend to make people more mechanical; we will look at these forces in detail in other chapters. Right and wrong ways are set up and rules to implement them are established. Goodness then becomes a matter of following the rules.

The problem with trying to create a rule to cover everything is that reality frequently gets more complex than rules can handle, or changes faster than the rules change. Yet many people keep mechanically following the rules, feeling virtuous about it but actually destroying themselves and others.

GOING ON AUTOMATIC

We could use a person such as you to perform the functions we have had to devise an intelligent crane to do. You can see when a box is actually on the conveyor belt, even if the spacing varies, and reach out and pick it up properly even if it's turned. You can lift it over to the output belt and put it on properly. You can see whether the two belts are still running properly, and turn off the input belt if the output belt stops. You have the qualities we defined as the start of mechanical (and human) intelligence: you remember the goal, namely, transferring intact boxes from belt one to belt two; you sense your environment to detect a variety of things that might interfere with the goal; and you make adjustments in your behavior to compensate for environmental changes that would interfere with attaining your goal.

How long will you remain intelligent on this job?

When you first take the job, it will be somewhat interesting. Exactly what is it you need to do? What is the most efficient way to do it? After a while (minutes? hours?), though, the job is thoroughly mastered and you are bored. You are overqualified for the job. Now what?

You find that you don't need to pay very close attention in order to do a good job. In fact, you can let your mind wander, you can daydream, plan what you'll do after work, wonder if you're being paid enough for this job, converse with a co-worker on another line, and so on. You will, without consciously trying, have *automated* yourself, let a good part of your sensing and judgmental capacity become mechanized, so that you perform like a machine, an *automaton*. If your daydreams, thoughts, and conversations are more entertaining than transferring boxes, you will be happier than if you paid attention to a present you find boring. Since you are no longer paying very much conscious attention to the job, it may seem to require much less effort, an apparent bonus of automatization.

The ability to set up some limited part of our sensitivity and intelligence so it automatically performs some fixed task with little or no awareness on our part is one of humanity's greatest skills—and one of its greatest curses.

THE COSTS OF AUTOMATIZATION

In the simple example given above, automatization seems desirable. It makes you happier. If your mental activities unrelated to the job are used for, say, planning to improve other areas of your life, you are even being more efficient. You have more sensing and intellectual capacity than you need to perform the job efficiently, so you use only as much as you need and devote the rest to furthering your own ends.

If the intelligent use of surplus mental capacity were the only or typical result stemming from automatization, being automated would not be a problem in human life. Problems occur when reality changes but your automated responses carry on, and/or when the automated responses have (automated) emotional satisfactions associated with them.

When you have an automated response pattern, it means that you have a very specialized type of attention. A situation occurs that fits an internalized representation of the situation, a representation that is a stereotype. The stereotype can be a box on a conveyor belt, a stranger's physical appearance, a verbal statement, a certain smell, whatever. It is close enough to some previously automated aspect of attention that *the stereotype is "perceived" and the stereotype is mistaken for the reality*. Your automated reaction then follows. If the actual situation is importantly different from the stereotype, your automated reaction may be inappropriate.

The Panhandler

An example: you have just parked your car and are walking down the street when a man starts walking toward you, obviously getting ready to say something. You're thinking about something you plan to buy in a store down the street, but part of your attention goes to the man. He is raggedly dressed and needs a shave. A part of your mind immediately "perceives" him as a panhandler, a type of person who makes you nervous and angry. This is actually a stereotyping, as there are other people who could be raggedly dressed on a city street and intending to say something to you, but the stereotype is activated and with it your automated reaction to panhandlers. A look of scorn crosses your face and you deliberately turn away, dismissing him before he can speak. Automated fantasies about your superiority as a person who earns his own living may run through your mind, and/or thoughts like "Why doesn't the government do something about people like him?"

It could be that way, but in the reality I have set up for this example, the man was a college professor on his day off. He was dressed in his oldest clothes, as he was working on his car and had come uptown for parts. He saw oil dripping out rapidly from under your parked car and was going to warn you about it. Your look of scorn and immediate dismissal make him instantly angry. "Screw you!" is his immediate reaction, and he turns away. Later, when you drive away, your engine burns out. Automated perception, automated feelings, automated behavior, automatic disaster. You didn't see that reality was different from your stereotype, and you had an emotional investment in it (feeling superior) that made it even more rigid.

Mechanical intelligence can often be useful for utilitarian purposes, but it is dangerous in a changing and complex world. The mechanical, automated stereotypings we know of as racism, sexism, and nationalism, to use just three examples, are enormously costly. Automatized perceptions, emotions, thoughts, and reactions to one situation frequently get associated with the automatized perceptions, emotions, thoughts, and reactions to other situations, so we can be lost for long periods—a lifetime in the most extreme cases—in continuously automated living.

Automatization is a major obstacle if you are trying to awaken from your culturally imposed trance. If you can awaken, however, automatization can become a useful tool as long as it is kept track of from a more awake level of consciousness. We are indeed machines, far too often, but we needn't be.

In the next chapter we will increase the mechanical intelligence of our crane even more and examine the human parallels.

4

Evolving Intelligence

The discussion will get rather detailed in this chapter, but I ask you to bear with me. We will be looking at machine parallels to human functions that are usually automated, glossed over, and out of consciousness. They need to become more conscious as part of awakening.

In the last chapter we endowed a machine, our crane, with rudimentary intelligence. In its fourth generation of evolution, it could sense several types of changes in its environment and make appropriate compensations in its behavior to meet its goal, namely transferring boxes from one conveyor to another.

To achieve an ability to respond to *degrees* of change, rather than just all-or-none changes, we added a computer, a rudimentary centralized brain, to our crane. As long as we have the processing power of a computer, let us make our fifth-generation crane go through an evolutionary leap that comes closer to the kind of intelligence we see in humans.

To use the stimulus of handling greater complexity as a spur to evolution, let's have our input conveyor belt bring along a variety of boxes to be transferred to one of three output conveyor belts, depending on the type of box. Different products from the factory need to be stored in different areas of the warehouse. The fifth-generation crane thus becomes a crane/sorter, a decision maker rather than just a transferrer of boxes. People usually have to choose among multiple possibilities, rather than always respond the same way to the same stimulus. Indeed, we often prefer decision making that challenges us.

The boxes can be of different sizes and contain different products. Some of these products are light and delicate, some are heavy and rugged. The heavy boxes with rugged products in them need to be tightly held by the grippers, lest they slip out and fall. That same grip applied to the light boxes, though, would crush them, so the strength of the grip must be adjusted to the type of box.

As before, the spacing and orientation of the boxes on the input conveyor belt vary: some are properly aligned; some are turned at odd angles. Sometimes there is a long time interval before the arrival of the next box; sometimes several of them are jammed together.

UNEXPECTED EVENTS

We wouldn't like to hire a worker who got so totally absorbed in his job that he didn't notice unanticipated but vital changes and so failed to react to them. We've already dealt with one of the output conveyors stopping; suppose it starts running backward? Suppose there is a fire in the warehouse, endangering human life and other equipment? Suppose someone walks into the area where the crane swings? Suppose so many boxes arrive in a brief time span that the crane/sorter can't keep up with transferring them? Suppose the power to the crane/sorter fails and boxes start piling up on the conveyor? If our fifth-generation crane/sorter is to take a leap forward in intelligence, it must respond to these events.

NEW SENSES

Our first evolutionary step is to add new senses to our crane/sorter. Several of these needs can be met with simple all-or-none-type sensors. Our output conveyors must be fitted with sensors that detect not only whether they are running, but whether they are running in the proper direction. A sensor to measure high temperatures would serve as fire detectors. A simple voltage sensor would measure whether power is available to the crane.

Dealing with various sizes and orientations of boxes is more difficult. Our fourth-generation crane used a television camera above the input conveyor belt, coupled to an analysis program that found the edges and shape, such that it could recognize a box, its orientation, and its location. To do this, it had to consult an internal memory that defined what a box looked like in a television picture.

How should we handle boxes of different sizes (and thus weight and fragility)? For simplicity, we'll program the computer's box analysis program to assume (as people usually do) that these three things are perfectly correlated: little boxes are always light and delicate; bigger boxes get progressively heavier and more rugged. The box analysis program can then instruct the gripper to exert very little force on small boxes and progressively greater force on larger boxes.

As long as our computer is big enough to run a box size analysis program from the input from a television camera, let's use a second camera to scan the area around the crane that we don't want a person to enter. The image from this second camera must be analyzed to indicate when a person is present. We can simplify this analysis considerably. We don't have to know whether it's a man or a woman, how tall he or she is, or what color clothes he or she is wearing. Indeed, we don't even really need to know if it's a human being. If *anything* moves into the restricted area, we want our intruder analysis program to detect it and stop the crane.

There is a problem here, though. Something regularly enters and moves around in our restricted area, namely the crane itself. We don't want the crane/sorter's control computer stopping the crane every time it detects itself. A basic intelligence function of life is to recognize itself, to discriminate self from not-self. We might eat ourselves otherwise! Our intruder analysis program must analyze the television image such that it recognizes the shape and motion of the crane, as distinct from any other shape moving into the restricted area. The stop-the-crane command is then issued only when a noncrane shape is detected.

Since our crane/sorter must put different boxes on different output conveyor belts, the box analysis program must not only perceive a box, it must classify it into one of several categories. For simplicity, we will let it do this solely on the basis of size.

YOU CAN'T DO EVERYTHING AT ONCE

We are asking our fifth-generation crane/sorter to do quite a few things. It must concurrently (a) watch for boxes on the input conveyor belt, (b) perceive the size and orientation of each box, rotate its gripper to match the orientation of the box, lower the gripper over it, (c) grip the box with an amount of force related to the size of the box, lift the box, (d) classify the box as to type and direct the crane to move it toward the appropriate output conveyor, (e) rotate the box so that it will be aligned on the output conveyor belt it is intended to be transferred to, (f) position the box over the output belt, (g) lower the crane arm, open the grippers, (h) raise the arm, and (i) return to the waiting position over the input conveyor belt. Simultaneously, it must be ready to shut the conveyors down and/or stop the crane moving and sound an alarm if (j) there is a fire, (k) an intruder enters the restricted zone, (l) any of the three output conveyor belts stop or run backward, or (m) power to the crane is lost.

It seems very complicated. One of the results of trying to develop more intelligent machines, though, has been to make us aware of how much we take for granted about our simple actions.

Shutting any of the conveyors down stops production, so this action should not happen unnecessarily. Thus, stopping the input conveyor if any of the output conveyors stops or runs backward could be further elaborated so that the computer shuts the input conveyor belt down only if it perceives a box on it that must go onto the malfunctioning output conveyor. Meanwhile it could sound a maintenance alarm to get the broken conveyor fixed, which might happen before a box intended for it came along.

The above task requirements would not be too demanding if we had unlimited capacity in our computer for programs and memory. People don't have unlimited capacity, though, nor do computers. While you could hire many workers to watch minute parts of the task simultaneously, or buy a very big computer, there are economic considerations: you don't want to spend more money than absolutely necessary. Practically, then, our computer's "attention" must be split among these tasks in a way that optimally meets our goals, given its limitations.

It takes the computer a finite amount of time to monitor any one of its senses, and a finite amount of time to compute what to do about what it detects. Further, our computer only does one thing at a time, so it will have to spend some time on one task, then go to the next task, then the next task, and so forth. Its progression through the set of these tasks and back to its start is its operating cycle. Do we let it spend all the time it needs on each task, an equal amount of time on each task (too much for some, too little for others), more time on important tasks, or what?

PRIORITIES AND VALUES

The priorities the computer gives to various tasks are a mechanical analogue of human *values*. Without getting into detailed considerations of emotions yet, we can observe that something you value can be identified by some combination of the amount of time it gets your attention and/or the priority given to it to interrupt other activities when the situation is appropriate. I spend a lot of time reading books, for example, which shows that I value reading. Further, I don't like to have people talk to me if I'm reading an interesting book. If you interrupt to tell me, "The house is on fire!," though, I'm quite glad you did! I value my and my wife's lives and saving my home from destruction, more than my absorption in a book.

Let us give our computer control program values in the form of time allocations and priorities.

Suppose it takes one-tenth of a second for the crane/sorter's computer to check each sensor. We have eight sensed inputs (fire, intruder, belts 1, 2, and 3 running, and belts 1, 2, and 3 each running in the correct direction). If we assigned equal value to knowing about the condition that each sensor detects, we would program the computer to check each one in sequence. We would have an eight-step operating cycle for sensory checking. If all these inputs were OK, the crane/sorter could check for an incoming box (a ninth 0.1-second operation) and, if it was there, begin its sorting and transferring task. If there is no box coming in, it can start checking its eight sensed inputs again. Such an operating cycle will repeat over and over until a box is detected.

The detection of an input box in step 9 leads to sorting and transferring it. Let's say this takes 9.1 seconds before the crane returns to its ready position over the input conveyor belt, for a total cycle of 10 seconds to scan all the sensory inputs, transfer a box, and be ready to once again check for fire, intruders, and the like.

Implicit Values

Because the transfer of a box takes 9.1 seconds, while the sensory check cycle takes 0.9 seconds, we have implicitly assigned values to our crane sorter, values of a rather materialistic sort. We can state them, in anthropomorphic form, this way:

> First Commandment: If there is no work to be done (no box to be sorted and transferred), protect human life and the machinery by devoting one-ninth of your time to checking for a fire, and another one-ninth of your time to checking for an intruder in the potentially dangerous crane movement zone.

Second Commandment: If there is work to be done (sorting and transferring a box), give less priority to protecting human life. Protect human life and the machinery by devoting one one-hundredth of your time (0.1 second every 10 seconds) to checking for a fire, and another one-hundredth of your time to checking for an intruder in the danger zone.

In the last decade we have become increasingly aware that sometimes what seem like simple technological strategies and solutions are often value decisions. The less we recognize that they are complex like that, the more future trouble we create through our blindness. It is probably most wise to assume that *all* plans as to how to do things, not just those involving technology, implicitly embody values, consciously and/or unconsciously.

The automation of our thinking, perceiving, and feeling processes that we looked at in the last chapter helps to keep us blind to what we are doing. A situation is stereotyped as "engineering decision" or "technical problem," and we then tend to perceive our preconceptions about the situation to the exclusion of the actual reality of it.

We could describe our fifth-generation crane/sorter as being reasonably responsive to dangerous situations when it has no work to do. When it is busy, though, it gets lost in its work for a long time and loses touch with outside reality. The parallel with many human actions is all too clear.

We could increase the value our crane/sorter puts on protecting human life by modifying the program for the transfer cycle. As it is, once the crane has sensed a box coming in, it pays no further attention to its environmental sensors until it has completed the transfer, an action that takes much more time than checking the environment. We can reprogram the transfer program to check the intruder detector between various steps within the transfer cycle. Now our crane/sorter doesn't get so deeply lost in its work; it has better "reality contact" with the reality we, its makers, value.

Values Have Costs

Note that we pay a price for the crane/sorter's extra protection of human life. Before we added this extra intruder checking to the transfer cycle program, it and the environmental checking cycle took ten seconds to complete. If the boxes came in fast enough, we could sort and move one every ten seconds. With the addition of extra checking steps, our whole cycle now takes longer, so we can't be as productive. Do we value human life enough to make our production cycle less efficient? Is the chance of a human entering the restricted area high enough to be worth lowering productivity, or are we overprotecting against a very unlikely event?

Our crane/sorter has now evolved to adapt to handle several possible changes in its environment. It can be more efficient in acting in accordance with its preprogrammed values, namely correctly transferring boxes in an efficient manner, while protecting human life and the warehouse's machinery. Would an intelligent nonhuman observer, which had no a priori prejudices that life and intelligence should be organically based, perceive our crane/sorter as a somewhat intelligent animal? Would this observer attribute consciousness to it? Might a human worker doing the same task as the crane/sorter be perceived as totally equivalent?

5

Operational Thinking

An essential characteristic of intelligent life is that it seeks to protect its own life and well-being. This goal of self-preservation usually has priority over almost all other goals. To evolve our fifth-generation crane/sorter to its sixth-generation embodiment, we must give it a self-preservation instinct. This is not as straightforward as it seems, for there are compromises to be made. As Gurdjieff recognized, our involvement in other aspects of life, especially as it is unconscious, often interferes with the proper functioning of our self-preservation instinct.

SELF-PRESERVATION INSTINCT

Our fifth-generation crane/sorter is a physical device. It has moving parts, and moving parts wear out. We can give it as high-quality parts as is economically justifiable, taking the cost of replacement into account, but given the way it's made, we want to maximize its life. A short life means high replacement costs, and frequent stoppages for repair means lost production as well as extra costs.

To simplify, let's assume that the main source of wear is in the bearings of the crane that support the load. No matter how well a bearing is made there is always some friction. Friction creates heat as well as wearing away the bearing. Heat dries out the lubricant in the bearing and so creates more friction, which creates more heat, and so on, in a vicious cycle. To get long life from a bearing, you don't want to get it very hot. If it is heating too rapidly, you should stop using it for a while until it cools.

MECHANICAL SELF-PRESERVATION INSTINCTS

Our fifth-generation crane/sorter has no goal of self-preservation and has no way of knowing if its bearings are too hot or wearing too rapidly. If a box comes along, it is transferred, hot bearings or not. Although it has evolved a fair amount of intelligence, it is entirely at the mercy of its environment. If you know what's happening in the crane/sorter's environment, you can predict exactly how it will respond. The adjective *mechanical* describes it perfectly well, both in a technically accurate sense and in the pejorative sense of "stupid."

There are mechanical, rigid ways we can prolong the life of our crane/sorter's bearings. Just turning the crane off permanently would give its bearings enormous life but would totally disrupt productivity. Running it constantly until it failed would maximize productivity for a while, but then the high cost of repairs and the long down time would wipe out the short-term gain in productivity. Adding a simple timer to cycle its power on for five minutes, off for five minutes, and so on, would give it lots of cooling-down time. It would also interrupt production every five minutes, which is a very high price to pay for longevity. How can we give the crane a new kind of intelligence that will maximize both production and equipment life as much as possible?

Let us take several steps to prolong the life of our crane/sorter's bearings. First, we'll give it a temperature sensor that continuously measures how hot the bearings are. Second, we'll give its computer brain information to store about the relation of bearing failure to bearing temperature. This would consist of information like "At 200 degrees the bearings fail 20% faster than normal; at 250 degrees they fail 80% faster than normal; at 300 degrees they fail 225% faster than normal." This is *external* knowledge, someone else's knowledge about bearing failure that is programmed wholesale into our crane/sorter's computer.

Third, we will program it with values to prolong its own life and to maximize production. Such a value or operating rule might be "Stop the crane and input conveyor belt immediately if the bearing temperature exceeds 300 degrees and wait until it falls to 200 degrees before starting again." These are our values, but, with our absolute power to program, they become the crane/sorter's values. With its new self-preservation instincts, the crane/sorter has evolved to its sixth generation.

If you are becoming a little uncomfortable about the idea of programming values into something or someone, your discomfort is quite appropriate. As we shall see later, this was done to you in massive ways.

Finally, we'll give our sixth-generation crane/sorter's computer a whole new ability in addition to its new bearing-temperature sense and its new knowledge, namely that of *simulating its world and computing, simulating better ways of operation*. This last talent is another major evolutionary step and will produce the seventh-generation crane/sorter.

CREATING AND ORGANIZING A BODY OF EXPERIENCE

Learning from experience is a hallmark of intelligence. So our computer must start storing information about events that have happened to it in its past, our analogue of experience.

What are the experiences in our crane/sorter's life?

Detecting intrusions into the danger zone
Detecting fires in its environment
Sensing the presence of boxes, their orientation, and their size
Transferring boxes
Detecting when input and output conveyors stop or run backward
Nonoperating times, when the crane/sorter has been shut down for repair

Now it will have another sensory input, sensing the temperature of its bearings.

Organizing Experience with a Time Sense

To begin to organize its experience, we must give our computer another absolutely essential sense, though, a *time sense*. By installing an internal clock and calendar, the computer can remember that a particular kind of event happened at a particular time, such as "Size 3 Box transferred to Output Belt Number 3 at 4:15:22 P.M. on July 14, 1985." or "Shut down to repair bearing failure, 2:10:22 P.M. to 8:10:22 P.M., 6 hours exactly, March 10, 1986."

Now we have a body of experience to draw upon. This experience is already located in space, as a particular operation of the crane/sorter always means it is in some particular spatial position. Now it is located in time also.

TIME TO THINK

Since we would like to get good performance from the least expensive computer possible, we didn't buy a really big computer for our crane/ sorter. If we had, it could think about its past experiences while simultaneously carrying out its primary function, classifying and transferring incoming boxes. We don't need that much computing capacity: most of the time the overall character of the environment changes rather slowly, so we only have to think about it occasionally. There are occasions when there is a long time interval between incoming boxes, and those times can be used for thinking about things other than immediate tasks. Thus our smaller, less expensive computer will be adequate.

We wouldn't want such thinking to interfere with box sorting and transferring, though. Having boxes fall on the floor because the crane/ sorter's brain is busy thinking is a costly path to improving its operation. It must be interruptible thinking, thinking that can, as it were, be put on hold.

Now we have spare time for thinking when the demands of the environment are low (no incoming box). Even if thinking is interrupted, its results to that point can be stored and the thinking process can be taken up later from where it left off. (This is better than some ordinary human thinking, which, if interrupted, must be started again from scratch!)

LEARNING FROM EXPERIENCE

To learn from experience requires that: (a) you have past experiences stored; (b) the stored past experiences are organized, such as by being located in space and time; (c) you can call up selected experience memories; (d) you can logically compare and operate on these called-up memories, what the psychologist Piaget called operational thinking; (e) you have some set of values to rank the desirability of the various outcomes you can envision through operational thinking; (f) you can store the results of your operational thinking, the insights and outcomes; and (g) you can change your future behavior as a result of the stored insights and outcomes.

Operational Thinking

Operational thinking is one of the highest abilities of the human mind. It consists of the ability to create images or other mental representations of reality. The images may be sensory or abstract or symbolic. Then you can manipulate or play with those representations in order to answer questions of the "What would happen if . . . ?" variety in the space of your mind. The manipulations of these images may follow some formal system of logic (there are many) at one extreme, be random or illogical, or be alogical or intuitive at the other extreme. This is often much safer than finding out "What would happen if . . . ?" in reality. For example, what would happen if you jumped off a rock that was twenty feet high?

You could find out by doing it. You could also draw on your stored experiences about how hard you land as you jump from various heights. I've jumped from two feet off the ground: no problem. I've jumped from four feet; I land harder, but it's not too big a deal. I've jumped from six feet high, and the landing is very hard. I have to be very careful to avoid injury, and I wouldn't do it unless it were really necessary. I've never jumped from any greater height, but I can employ operational thinking and image that a twenty-foot drop would be so much more intense that I would probably injure myself badly. Therefore I will not jump from twenty feet. Operational thinking has saved me from a bad injury.

Operational thinking also allows us to be more efficient and to invent new ways of doing things. Suppose I want to install a wall bookcase on an unusually shaped space on a wall. I could build or buy a lot of bookcases of different sizes and shapes, hold each one up to see how it fitted, then return or destroy those that didn't fit. That's a lot of work and expense. Instead I visualize how different styles and sizes of bookcase would look and find a good solution. Measurements of the space available add to my visualization and thinking. Deciding to build a bookcase, I visualize the various steps of the job and what tools are needed for each. Now when I go out to my shop I should be able to get all of the tools I need in one trip, instead of making many trips.

I'll usually forget some tool, of course. Operational thinking may *feel* as if it's perfect (an important flaw we'll consider later), but in retrospect we often see how we left something out or jumped to a wrong conclusion. But it is exceptionally powerful, and giving operational thinking to our crane/sorter is an enormous leap up the evolutionary ladder for it.

We will program our crane/sorter's computer to do operational thinking in its spare time, when it's not moving a box and doesn't see one coming down the line.

Rechecking Old Knowledge

One of the kinds of operational thinking we will program will test the adequacy of the computer's stored knowledge. Earlier we programmed it with some externally obtained information on the relationship between bearing failure and bearing temperature. We also programmed it with the external value to maximize crane life while keeping up the highest possible productivity.

As the crane/sorter works over the years, it will have a number of experiences of its bearings failing and will duly record these events and the times they happened. It also will have a mass of stored data about the temperatures of the bearings. In its spare time, it can think about these facts by computing the actual relationship between various aspects of temperature (such as average temperatures, peak temperatures, or the length of heating and cooling cycles) and the times between bearing failures. Which is the best predictor of bearing failure? Is some combination of these measures a better predictor than any one alone? How do these computed relationships compare with the stored external knowledge and operating rules originally given it about these relations? Is the discrepancy great enough to decide to alter or reject the original external knowledge? Would this produce an overall improvement in productivity? As a result of such operational thinking, it may alter its operating cycle, either creating longer rest periods for bearings cooling if the bearing failure rate has been too high, or creating shorter rest periods (and consequent higher productivity) if the bearings actually hold up better than expected.

HIERARCHIES OF VALUES

Notice that we have given our crane/sorter the ability to change one of its operating rules, a rule about shutting down if the bearing temperature goes over some certain value, in order to attain the programmed goal/value of prolonging crane life while maximizing productivity. We have not, in this particular operational thinking program, given it the ability to even question, much less change, the externally given goal/value of maximizing productivity and prolonging crane life.

We humans also have apparently unalterable values. It is impossible, for example, for an ordinary person to kill himself by holding his breath. The biologically given, built-in value of survival takes precedence over our ability to modify our breathing patterns.

Only a few values are *absolutely unalterable*, though. Values are usually hierarchical: I want to do A and B, as long as it doesn't interfere with C and D. The operational thinking program for maximizing productivity and prolonging crane life is not absolute, for example. Early in the evolution of our crane/sorter we programmed in two higher values, namely that the equipment must be stopped and an alarm sounded if there is a fire or if a person enters the restricted danger zone. Stopping the equipment and sounding an alarm to save a human life is absolutely higher in the value hierarchy than maximizing production. At least these values take priority if we are in the part of the operation cycle where a considerable portion of the crane/sorter's time is devoted to checking for fires and intrusions.

But suppose we have not programmed the crane/sorter's computer to check its senses while it is thinking about improving itself. We can describe this as a flaw, if we wish to continue the value of giving absolute priority to protecting human life. Many of us have this kind of flaw. We get lost in our thinking and don't notice what's happening in the world around us, sometimes putting ourselves at great risk as a result.

We can also describe this apparent flaw as a *state-specific value*, for its priority is dependent upon the state (sensing or thinking) of the crane/sorter. As discussed in Chapter 1, some human values are indeed state-specific.

Our seventh-generation crane/sorter has evolved to the point where it illustrates one of the most important characteristics of human consciousness: our brains simulate our world. We shall explore this point in the next chapter.

6

Living in the World Simulator

Our seventh-generation crane/sorter has become quite intelligent. It has goals and values. It senses its environment and responds to events relevant to its goals, such as sorting and moving boxes in order to be productive, or stopping the crane if a person walks into the danger zone in order to preserve human life. It has a sense of self-preservation in that it tries to minimize wear on its bearings. Indeed, our crane/sorter even transcends the rigidity of action usually associated with machines, for it remembers and organizes its past experience, simulates its environment in its brain, and occasionally works out new, more effective ways of functioning that optimize attainment of its goals.

Although we don't want to attribute real consciousness to our crane/sorter, let's pretend that its computer brain is conscious for the sake of discussion. Now we can ask the questions "What *is* its consciousness?" and "What is it conscious *of*?"

At ordinary levels of discussion, the answer to what is its consciousness is straightforward: it is the pattern of electrical impulses operating in a particular set of circuits, its computer brain. The specific functioning of the computer brain at any instant is a matter of where electrical impulses are, what circuits they are activating, at that instant. Computation, thinking, consists of the movement of electrical impulses into different patterns in the computer's circuits. Any state of the computer, any "sensation" or "thought" in it, can be specified and understood *exactly* by the distribution of electrical impulses in the computer's circuits. For the computer, consciousness *is* its electrical state.

As to what the computer brain is conscious *of*, the answer is again straightforward: it is conscious of electrical impulses. It does not see a box on the incoming conveyor belt, for example, for boxes do not travel through the scanning television camera into the computer; only electrical impulses do. The box, entering the field of vision of the camera, causes a pattern of electrical impulses to be produced and sent to the computer, and it is this pattern which the computer is "conscious" of. The computer has no *direct* perception of anything in the real world, but only of electrical patterns that are associated with and caused by events and objects in the real world. A fire in the plant, as a second example, is not red or hot or dangerous or beautiful: it is only a certain pattern of electrical impulses coming from a fire sensor. The computer's simulation of its environment (its "images") and its computations (its "thoughts") are nothing more than patterns of electrical impulses.

This austere view of what a computer's consciousness would be like is almost identical to the contemporary scientific view of human consciousness.

Suppose you are looking at a fire. You experience it as red in color; you feel the heat from it on your skin. If the fire is threatening you or your possessions, you perceive it as dangerous. In another situation and mood you perceive it as beautiful. These seem like direct perceptions of external reality, but our modern understanding of brain functioning tells us that it is not really direct, but mediated by many intermediate processes, each one of which can alter the nature of what we perceive.

Take the experience of the fire being red. We believe we understand the physical world well enough to be certain that the fire is emitting electromagnetic radiation. Some of this radiation is in a vibratory range that can stimulate the human eye, so radiation in this range is called light. Light of a particular frequency does not have any attributes of color; it is just light vibrating at that particular rate. In the most accurate description, it is just electromagnetic radiation: calling it "light" is talking about light in relation to human beings.

This electromagnetic radiation passes through the lens of your eye. The lens can impose limitations on your perception; it won't pass the faster rate of electromagnetic radiation we call ultraviolet, for example. There are no significant problems with passing the radiation from the fire that will later be called red light, though.

The radiation strikes special structures on your retina, the cones, which are responsible for color vision. The energy of the light stimulates electrochemical changes in the cones, such that the particular frequency of the light hitting the cones sends out a particular pattern of electrochemical impulses, nerve impulses, that travel up special nerves from the eye to the brain. The brain modifies these nerve impulses in complex ways that we don't fully understand, and, in what is the biggest mystery of all, the final pattern of electrochemical impulses in the brain results in our perception/experience of the fire being red. *It is the structure and activity of the brain and eyes that create the experience of red, rather than red being a property of the outside world.*

You have probably seen those oddly colored computer-processed photographs taken by special Earth-sensing satellites. Water may appear as shades of red, vegetation as shades of blue, bare earth as shades of green. Such photographs are usually labeled "false color" photographs. But there is nothing false in an absolute sense about these colors. Computer processing of photographs involves just the same kind of *arbitrary* simulation of the outside world as your brain carries out. Your brain could just as well, and just as usefully, construct fire as the experience of green or blue instead of the experience of red. The construction/ simulation process enables us to survive in the world when there is a regular, dependable correspondence between some feature of the outside world and your constructed perception of it. As long as ordinary fires were always green, that would be fine.

The colors in a computer-processed photo, then, are not false colors in any profound sense; they are simply not simulated, constructed, to the usual human visual system standards. The redness you directly experience when looking at a fire is an arbitrary construction of your brain. Hotness could be constructed by the brain so that it would be experienced with the sensations we now think of as coldness. As long as the relation of the experience of coldness to objects and processes associated with higher temperatures in the outside world held constant, so that you knew things that felt cold would burn you, it would be just as useful to our survival as the present experience of hotness being associated with high-temperature objects.

Similarly, the dangerousness or the beauty of the fire you see are arbitrary constructions of your brain, not direct properties of the outside world. Indeed, these two examples involve even more complex construction/simulation activity on the part of the brain than redness or hotness, for emotional evaluation of the outside world, as beautiful or dangerous, has now been added to the construction/simulation of the object itself. We can see a fire as a fire and then separately decide it's dangerous or beautiful, but often we instantly see a dangerous fire or a beautiful fire. What we are *directly* aware of, then, are the constructions/simulations of our brains, not outside reality itself. This is the sense in which we live "in" a world simulator.

Living in a world simulator, then, means that what we think are direct perceptions of the physical world are arbitrary constructions of our brains, not the things themselves. Our apparently direct experience of the world is actually indirect.

If this were all that living in the world simulator meant, it would not be a great problem. Perceptions could be taken for granted in everyday life: whatever the real physical nature of fire, whether it makes me itch, shiver, or feel cold or tense or relaxed or elated, I nevertheless have learned that fire can burn and so I will treat it carefully. If I am curious about the nature of the outside world in and of itself, I can employ scientific instruments and procedures to learn about its properties that are not adequately represented in my (arbitrarily constructed) sensory perceptions. Unfortunately, living in the world simulator has much more important meanings.

EMOTIONAL AND PSYCHOLOGICAL CONSTRUCTION OF PERCEPTION

If perception involves a complex, active construction of a simulation of reality, why aren't we aware of the construction process? Or of the effort involved in constructing it? When I turn my head to the right I instantly see a bookcase. There is no moment of ambiguous shapes and colors, no effortful feeling of comparing these with past knowledge and deciding that a bookcase is the best construct I can make of these particular shapes and colors. My experience is that I instantly see a bookcase.

The difficulty in realizing that perception is an active construction is that the work readily becomes automated, and then we don't sense the effort. Nor does it take any appreciable time. Early in our lives, as infants, we had to work at constructing perceptions, but that was long ago and is now forgotten. We occasionally have experiences of ambiguous perceptions today: What is that shape in the dark? Could it be a bush? A crouching person? An animal? Ah, it's a parked motorcycle, viewed end on! Now that you see it as a motorcycle, it is difficult to see it again as a bush or animal or crouching person. Such experiences should alert us to the constructed nature of perception, but they are so rare compared to the instant recognition of things in our automated perception that they have little impact.

A striking example of the construction and automation of perception comes from a classical psychological experiment. A pair of special goggles is put on a subject. Prisms in these goggles invert the visual field both vertically and horizontally so that what was up is now down. The floor is above you, the ceiling below. What was on your left is now on your right, and vice versa. To describe the subject's reaction as confusion is to put it mildly. Moving about is especially difficult, and some subjects feel nauseated. Your lifetime store of visual and motoric simulations of the world and their relation to it are now wrong in major ways.

The inverting goggles are worn for days or weeks. Initially the subject must make perception and movement a *conscious* act instead of letting them run on automatic. His automatized reactions do not work. If he sees an object that he wants and it is obviously to his left, he must move in the direction his body thinks is right, for example.

After a few days, though, amazing things happen. Things no longer look upside down! He can reach directly for things without any calculations of where right and left really are. An entirely new set of perceptual simulations has been constructed and automated. It feels as if he perceives reality directly, as it is, the same feeling he had before donning the inverting goggles.

When the goggles are finally removed, after this new adaptation, the world is suddenly upside down and reversed! Conscious compensation for left and right is again required. After some visual experience, though, the old, "normal" pattern is reestablished. Because the old simulation pattern is so thoroughly learned, its reestablishment takes much less time than it took to establish new simulation patterns when the goggles were put on. The old simulation pattern is just as arbitrary as the new one, of course.

A less drastic example that you can try for yourself involves reading. You read right side up, and when you turn a page upside down it makes no sense. You can examine individual letters and words upside down and figure them out, but it is slow and difficult compared to ordinary reading: you will see how the perception of meaning, ordinarily automatic, is an active, effortful process in this case.

Try reading upside down for a page or two. Surprisingly, psychological experiments have found that many people can work up to almost normal reading speed within a page or two. After the initial work, automatization of the perceptual simulation/construction process can be surprisingly fast.

Reading itself is a good example of the constructed nature of perception. Studies of eye movements show that we do not look at every word. Instead our eyes jump several words at a time, about four times per second. Our visual acuity is such that we can really only see one word clearly at normal reading distances, so we see one word and have a vague impression of features around it, such as long spaces indicating the end of a paragraph. If we have a general sense of what we are reading, this is adequate. Our minds construct the sense of what the words in between the fixated words should be.

When the topic changes, we can't do this and have to look at more words within the line. If we don't, we may get a wrong sense of what's been said. Indeed, we often keep up our wide scanning in reading and go on for a while before we begin to realize that we don't really understand what we're reading and must go back and reread in more detail. How many times do we fail to realize that we've lost the correct sense of what we're reading and go away with a distorted impression? This is one of the prices of automating perception.

This construction of what we read, with only partial perception of what's actually there, is one of the reasons that proofreading is so difficult, especially for something we've written ourselves. We know what should be there and so *perceive our expectations instead of what's actually there*. The distortion of perception in proofreading, a distortion usually based on cool, intellectual expectations only, is small compared to what happens when emotional expectations and desires become active.

PERCEPTUAL DEFENSE

The reality of unconscious processes, mental or emotional processes that affect us and yet lie outside conscious awareness, is widely accepted in modern psychology. A specific form of unconscious processes, known as perceptual defense, has not been generally accepted, in spite of good experimental evidence for it. The haggling over the reality of perceptual defense has been so intense that I have suspected the idea is being actively resisted. It is too clear a reminder of how mechanical we are.

Perceptual defenses are a form of defense mechanism that works to keep us unaware of events in the outside world that would arouse unpleasant or unacceptable emotions in us. The effect was first noticed experimentally in some studies of perceptual thresholds. If a word is flashed very briefly on a screen, what is the minimal time exposure, the threshold, for conscious recognition of it?

If the flash is extremely brief, say a hundredth of a second or less, you will see only a flash of light, without even perceiving the overall patterning of the letters, much less recognizing them. If it is long, say one-quarter of a second or more, you will readily perceive the word. If you start with flashes too short for recognition and slowly increase the duration of the flashes until correct recognition occurs, the length of flash required is the threshold value.

Factors like the length and familiarity of a word will affect the threshold of recognition. Long, unfamiliar words will have higher thresholds than short, familiar ones. What researchers also noticed was that emotionally charged words, especially those that might create personal conflict in the subjects, had higher thresholds than words of similar length and familiarity that had no threatening emotional connotations. In research on college student subjects of three generations ago, who would usually not have a secure sexual identity in those more sexually repressed times, *fuck*, for example, would generally have a higher threshold than a word like *flex*.

An alternative explanation for these higher thresholds was not that they took greater stimulus intensity (longer flashes) to perceive but that the social unacceptability of the words made the subjects more reluctant to voice them until they were quite certain. Further research showed that this accounts for part of the delay, but there is still a perceptual defense factor. More direct evidence for perceptual defense comes from the fact that physiological reactions associated with emotions, like quick changes in the electrical resistance of the skin, can sometimes be seen when emotionally threatening words are presented that are well below a subject's conscious perception threshold.

Psychologists concluded that there are three stages in perception. There is first an initial perception/recognition outside of consciousness. This is followed by a stage involving discrimination of the potential emotional threat of the stimulus. If the stimulus is classified as threatening at this second stage, an influence is exerted on the mind to raise its threshold for the third step of the process, conscious perception of the stimulus.

This raising of the threshold applies to stimuli that bring up topics that the person generally defends against by not dealing with them. For those who have a more active style of defense (see Chapter 13, "Defense

Mechanisms") there may be a *lowering* of the threshold for relevant stimuli. For others, or even in the same person at different times, there may be a distortion of the stimulus so that what is consciously perceived is different enough from the actual stimulus to be less threatening.

In terms of our world simulator model, perceptual defense is an understandable phenomenon. A particular stimulus pattern, already modified to some extent by the physical structure of the senses, reaches the brain. There, learned processes go to work to construct a simulation of this aspect of reality. As part of creating an appropriate construct/ perception/simulation, memory data about this kind of particular stimulus are drawn on. In the case of perceptual defense, the memory data include information that this is emotionally threatening in a certain way. This calls up more memory data about how these kinds of emotional threats are handled. If the defense style is to try to avoid noticing such threats, then the simulation of this stimulus is constructed in such a way as to be less noticeable to consciousness. And/or the simulation is altered—we could say "distorted" in terms of resemblance to the initiating stimulus—so that the final simulation, what consciousness will perceive, represents something else. This something else resembles the original stimulus but is not identical to it. So *fuck* may become just a flash of light with indistinguishable features, or the simulation/perception may become *flock* or *duck* or *tuck*. As long as the stimulus is not too intense, not well above threshold, the simulation process can carry out this sort of altered, distorted construction.

All this discussion of simulation may create a feeling that there is something unreal about a simulation. Yes, there is in one sense. In terms of what is perceived, though, the simulation in our mind *is* reality. The person you clearly see crouching in the shadows is a perfectly real perception, is your reality at the time you perceive it, even if you later realize that it was a misperception, a poor simulation of a bush in the dark. In this model, the reality we live in is the simulation.

We can now see an important aspect of Gurdjieff's statement that man is not awake. In a nighttime dream we see a whole world of things that are not present in reality, but we mistake it for reality. By contrast (we think), in our waking state we perceive reality. But what we perceive is a simulation of reality.[1] If the simulation is seriously distorted, yet we mistake it for reality, we can be accurately described as being in a kind of waking dream, not really awake.

In our examination of parallels between an intelligent machine and human behavior, the topic of emotion has inevitably crept in, even though it has no exact mechanical parallel. It is now time to look at emotions more closely.

7

Emotions

Emotions are a puzzle to our rational minds. We love them, we hate them. Life would be meaningless without them, and they can ruin life. We try to stimulate them and control them, and some we try to avoid altogether.

Our evolved crane/sorter is quite different from a human. It has no features that resemble emotions. A person might feel proud and elated if he's accomplished a lot, or feel depressed knowing he's ill and slowly dying. But we can't picture our crane/sorter "feeling good" when it has moved a lot of boxes efficiently or saved a life by stopping its crane when a human entered the danger zone. Nor can we picture it as "feeling depressed" if its bearings are wearing out too frequently.

SIMULATION OF EMOTIONAL BEHAVIOR

We could program our crane/sorter's computer brain to act externally as if it felt such emotions. After a period of high productivity it could blow a cheerful whistle, or it could get balky and inefficient after a period of low productivity, but why would we want it to do that? Neither action contributes to optimal attainment of its goals. Indeed, the whistle uses energy, and energy costs money. Having the crane perform in a balky, inefficient manner further cuts productivity.

In people the story is quite different. Emotions can serve a purpose and drastically affect performance. When you feel good about the work you are doing, you will probably do it longer and more efficiently than you otherwise would. Negative emotions are a mixture. They may worsen your performance or sometimes improve it: if you get angry when your job isn't coming out right, for example, you may put more energy into it and get it done.

EMOTIONS AS ENDS IN THEMSELVES

Emotions are strong motivators of external behavior. They are also pleasant or unpleasant in and of themselves, regardless of their link to external circumstances. We can feel good or bad whether or not we have an external reason for feeling that way. Because emotions are also ends in and of themselves, we often try to create good feelings and avoid creating bad feelings regardless of our external circumstances. This lack of necessary connection to external circumstances for emotion creates possibilities and pitfalls for our human minds that do not exist for our crane/sorter.

Suppose our crane/sorter has just computed a new strategy for increasing productivity and decreasing the wear on its bearing. It runs the new pattern in its simulated world of past experience and finds that it is indeed a much more efficient strategy, so its operating programs are changed to reflect the new strategy. The crane/sorter does not *feel* anything about this, though: no pride of accomplishment, no pleasure at being clever, no satisfaction of a job well done. It goes back to performing its sensory check cycle, waiting for the next incoming box. The next box comes along and is handled according to the new strategy. After sufficient time, as new experience has accumulated, the new strategy will be evaluated for its effectiveness in the real world of boxes and conveyor belts, and then modified, rejected, or retained. All this is passionless and objective.

If you were a new worker doing this job, though, you would feel elated when you thought of a more efficient way to do your job. In fact, the *feeling* of being clever and competent would come with the first insights into how to work better, before you even checked whether it actually worked. The feeling of insight is usually emotionally rewarded immediately: we all like to feel clever. Even if the insight turns out to be false and so later disappoints you, you still had the original good feeling that went with the insight. Further, if the insight does not work out when you try it in practice later, you may become angry: why isn't this damn world cooperating with your brilliant understandings!

The crane/sorter experiences no pleasure at its insights and no disappointment or anger when the insight fails to work out. If it works better than the old way, it's adopted. If not, recompute.

Advantages of Emotions

The ability you have to experience feelings in this job may work to your advantage. Since you like to feel clever, you may spend a lot of time thinking about ways of improving things even if you are not required to do so. Feeling clever is its own reward. Being clever might also get you an external reward. Since you don't like to feel disappointed, the failures of your thinking may spur you on to more clever thinking than you would otherwise do, so increasing your chances of eventual success. The carrot and stick of good and bad feelings are a powerful motivator.

Emotional Triggering by Simulations

In nonhuman animals, we believe that emotions are almost exclusively linked to external events. Fear or anger is felt if the animal is threatened, pleasure when something pleasant happens, and so forth. In contrast, one of our greatest human abilities, and greatest curses, is our ability to create *simulations* of the world (and of our own internal state), imaginary projections and ideas about reality. Animals may simulate their world to some degree, but I am sure we humans do it on an enormously greater scale. These simulations, whether or not they accurately reflect the world, can then trigger emotions. Emotions are a kind of energy, a source of power. What happens when you add power to a simulation of reality, particularly if it is an inaccurate simulation?

When you *think* of, or simulate, a better way to do your job, the positive, rewarding, reinforcing feelings you get from that can be just as powerful as or more powerful than positive feelings generated by your actual situation in the world. When you *worry* about, think about, what could go wrong, the fear or distress or anger or depression resulting from that can be just as powerful as or more powerful than the negative feelings generated by actual events. *Your imaginings can have as much power over you as your reality, or even more.*

Back in your job as a human crane/sorter, the power that emotions add to your simulations of your world might inspire you to do a good job and improve your performance, or your emotions can ruin your performance and you.

Suppose you're just getting a good idea about improving your job and a box comes along on the incoming conveyor belt, interrupting you. The crane/sorter would just store its computations done up to that point, attend to the task of sorting and moving the box, and then come back to its computations and continue where it left off the next time a slack period in incoming boxes allowed it to. You, on the other hand, may lose your train of thought and have a hard time getting it back. You may get angry at the box for interrupting you just as you were figuring things out. It may not be "logical" to get angry at an inanimate object like a box, but we do things like that quite often. Indeed, if you're angry enough at being interrupted, you may work off steam by grabbing the box with too much force and damaging it, or by letting some boxes just pile up until *you* feel like moving them.

Emotions and Fantasied Satisfactions

Suppose you've had what seems a brilliant idea for improving your performance. Your personality makeup may be such that you want to hold on to this idea and the emotional satisfaction that goes with it. Yet there's an insecurity in your personality makeup from past frustrations: you don't want to risk trading your feeling of satisfaction for disappointment by actually trying it out. Reality is nasty: it may not work according to your wonderful idea, so it's best to stay with the feeling of brilliance in your mind, in your world simulation. Indeed, one of Gurdjieff's basic false personality types, called Ego Plan in a later teaching supposedly coming from the same source,[1] has a strong tendency to do just this. Better to continually dream about wonderful, brilliant improvements in the world than deal with the world itself. So you continue working the old way, which may not be very efficient, but have a little smile on your face, knowing how brilliant you are.

Suppose you take your bright idea and try it out. Unfortunately there is a complication you hadn't thought about, so the new strategy is worse than the old. If the crane/sorter tries a new strategy that clearly doesn't work, it simply goes back to the old way until its operational thinking computations suggest a better way to try out. The new way is again evaluated, and accepted or rejected solely on the basis of its actual effectiveness in the real world. But in your case you may be angry that your insight didn't work. There's something wrong with the world, not with you or your idea. Or your perception may be distorted so that you don't quite see that your new way is worse. Since you're emotionally attached to your new way, of course you think it works better!

The simulation programs designed for the crane/sorter have a clear criterion for accepting or rejecting any particular simulation. Given the crane/sorter's values and goals, do the strategies created in simulations increase or decrease optimal attainment of them? Any simulated strategy that increases attainment is "good" and gets tried out, without the interference of emotions.

To a large degree our human plans ought to be judged, both by ourselves and others, by the same criterion. Given our values and goals, do new strategies created by operational thinking, by simulation, increase or decrease optimal attainment of our values and goals in reality? In addition, though, simulations can arouse emotions so that you *feel* good or bad, and this can drastically affect what you do in addition to (often in spite of) the simulations' adequacy in dealing with the real world.

With the addition of emotions, we lose our ability to further understand human reactions by parallels with our crane/sorter model, as something distinctly human has been added. Our emotions can, however, be quite automatized and function as mechanically as any machine, a point we shall discuss many times in this book. We can be emotional machines.

We have barely begun to touch on emotions and have focused on their negative rather than their positive side, but we will return to them in several subsequent chapters, particularly Chapter 14, where we consider the idea of people being "three-brained" beings, with emotion potentially being just as intelligent in its sphere as intellect is in its. We have the potential to be emotionally competent, perhaps even to be emotional geniuses, and to have the light and vitality return to our lives. To modify Wordsworth:

> The light which I once saw
> I now will see once more.

And will see with the full resources and sensitivities of an adult.

Now we shall consider some of the specifically human dimensions of our state of sleep.

8

Conditioning

One of the most fundamental psychological processes is conditioning. While we tend to think of it as applying mainly to lower organisms, it is actually very pervasive, even if not consciously recognized, in our ordinary lives.

CLASSICAL CONDITIONING

Psychologists distinguish two forms of conditioning, based on how the conditioning procedure is carried out.

Classical or Pavlovian conditioning was first demonstrated by Ivan Pavlov in 1927. When food was presented to a hungry dog, it salivated. The food in this case was called the unconditioned stimulus, and salivating was the unconditioned response. Salivation is a natural, automatic response to the sight and smell of food, a reaction to make the chewing and digestion of the food easier.

Now the experimenter rang a bell (called the conditioned stimulus) a second or so before presenting the food. Dogs do not normally salivate at the sound of bells, but after a number of conditioning trials, ringings of the bell followed by food, salivation occurred to the sound of the bell alone. Salivation had become a conditioned response to the conditioned stimulus, the sound of the bell. Almost any kind of sensory stimulus can be conditioned to elicit salivation.

The commonsense interpretation of classical conditioning is that an association has been formed in the dog's brain: the bell is followed by food. The anticipation of food activates the appropriate brain area, and salivation results. The sequence of expectation and response becomes automated.

INSTRUMENTAL CONDITIONING

The second form of conditioning is known as instrumental conditioning. In classical conditioning, the conditioned stimulus is paired with the unconditioned stimulus (and thus the consequent unconditioned response) regardless of what the animal being conditioned does. Pavlov's dogs could bark, whine, yawn, blink their eyes, whatever, but shortly after the bell was sounded the food was presented. In instrumental conditioning, the animal must behave in a certain way, make a conditioned response, in order to receive a reward. *Conditional response*—no work, no pay—would be a better term, but *conditioned response* is the standard term.

A typical instrumental conditioning procedure might consist in putting a hungry rat into a box containing a lever protruding from one wall. Such a box is commonly known as a Skinner box. The rat will look for food but not find it. Eventually, as part of exploring the environment, it may push on the lever. A switch connected to the lever activates a feeding mechanism and a food pellet is released into a feeding tray. The rat eats it.

Pushing levers is not normal rat behavior. The environments rats evolved in did not contain levers connected to feeding devices, so it is accidental that the rat pushes the lever. It may not push the lever again for some time, and then apparently by accident, but again it is rewarded by food. Eventually the rat pushes the lever more and more: it learns the connection between lever pressing and food. The conditioned response becomes pushing the lever. The unconditioned response, the reward, is eating. This kind of conditioning is called instrumental because the conditioned response is instrumental in achieving a reward.

The reward in instrumental conditioning can be the avoidance of unpleasant stimulation. A rat could be put in a box with two sections of metal grid floor. When a red light on the box wall comes on, the left side of the floor will become momentarily electrified a few seconds after the light comes on. If the rat is standing on it, it receives an unpleasant shock. It can learn a conditioned instrumental response, though, namely moving to the right-hand side of the box when the light comes on. Its reward is now the avoidance of the shock.

Instrumental conditioning is very much like what we ordinarily call learning. In the above example it is easy to imagine that the rat learned that a red light coming on meant that an unpleasant event would soon happen on that side of the cage. Since it did not like unpleasant events, it moved.

With classical conditioning, however, there is more than simple learning involved. The dog may have learned that the sound of the bell would be followed by food, but it did not then have a choice to salivate or not. The salivation, the conditioned response, was automatic. A classically conditioned response has a mandatory quality about it, a compulsiveness, that is very powerful.

REWARDS FROM THE BRAIN'S PLEASURE CENTER

One of the most dramatic forms of instrumental conditioning can be demonstrated after electrodes are implanted in the pleasure centers of the brain of an experimental animal. If a lever switch is now connected to an electrical device that stimulates this pleasure area, the animal will learn to press the lever. Indeed, it will learn to press it as continuously as possible. Animals have been known to work their paws raw pressing the lever, ignoring food and water beside them in spite of their hunger and thirst, ignoring a sexually receptive mate. Direct stimulation of pleasure centers in the brain can be *very* reinforcing!

Simulations of reality, whether realistic or not, can also trigger emotions that in turn affect the brain's pleasure centers. We can become conditioned to distort our simulations of reality in ways that make us feel good. Since apparent unpleasant feelings often have a hidden secondary gain of feeling good underneath, as was discovered in studies of psychopathology, simulations of reality that seem to make us suffer may have a hidden payoff, a point we shall explore later.

Conditioning of either variety can take place very rapidly, sometimes in a single trial. This is especially true if the unconditioned response elicits strong emotions. While initial conditioning can be to a quite specific stimulus, the conditioned response can also generalize, so that situations less and less like the original one evoke the conditioned response. In humans conditioning is often not overtly observable, as it is a thinking and feeling response that has been conditioned to certain situations. Such a response may not result in an obviously observable behavior, yet is just as important, for it automatically steers our mental and emotional processes and keeps us from awakening.

EXTINCTION

The conditioned association between the formerly neutral conditioned stimulus and the conditioned response is formed by the deliberate pairing of the conditioned stimulus and the unconditioned response. Suppose we now break up that pairing, continuing to present the conditioned stimulus, but no longer following it with the unconditioned stimulus?

The process is called extinction. At first the conditioned stimulus will continue to elicit the conditioned response. Then it will elicit it only occasionally, and finally not at all. The conditioned response has been extinguished.

HUMAN CONDITIONING

What does conditioning have to do with human beings? With *your* life?

I was once trying to explain the great importance of conditioning in human development to students in one of my Awareness Enhancement Training programs. Judging from the expressions on their faces, they didn't seem to think this had any personal application to their lives. Conditioning was some abstract thing that experimental psychologists did with rats in Skinner boxes, not part of everyday life. To bring the point home, I carried out the following demonstration of classical conditioning in people.

I first explained what I was going to do, including the fact that it might be somewhat unpleasant, even if educational, and then asked for volunteers. Everyone volunteered to take part. I had the students divide into pairs. One person was given the role of "conditioner," the other of "conditionee." I explained that I would occasionally make an unusual sound that was to become the conditioned stimulus, by slapping two metal rulers together. The conditioners, standing behind their conditionees, were to wait about one second and then lightly slap the conditionee on the cheek and say "Bad boy!" or "Bad girl!," whichever was appropriate, whenever they heard the sound of the rulers. The slap was to be strong enough to sting, but not strong enough to do any actual physical damage. The slap and scolding were the unconditioned stimulus. The pain of the slap, and any earlier conditioned unpleasant feelings in response to being called a bad boy or girl, constituted the unconditioned response.

I then struck the rulers together every once in a while, randomly varying the interval between soundings so that no obvious rhythm would develop. I wanted the conditionees to become conditioned to the unusual sound, not the time interval.

After a dozen or so conditioning trials, it was obvious that most of the conditionees were conditioned. I could see them flinching in anticipation of the coming slap.

I then introduced a variation to make the conditioning more thorough and to simulate ordinary life more closely. Psychological research has found that if the conditioned stimulus is always paired with the unconditioned stimulus, learning is quick, but extinction is rapid. To make the conditioning last much longer and to slow extinction after the initial conditioning, the organism should be put on an intermittent reinforcement schedule. You continue to present the conditioned stimulus, but you only occasionally and unpredictably pair the unconditioned stimulus with it. That is, the conditioned stimulus is sometimes followed by the unconditioned stimulus, sometimes not. This greatly enhances the strength of the conditioning.

I instructed the conditioners that from now on, whenever they heard the sound of the metal rulers, they should not always slap the conditionee and say "Bad boy!" or "Bad girl!," but do it intermittently and unpredictably. We then carried out another dozen conditioning trials.

By now the conditionees were flinching involuntarily whenever the rulers clapped together. Indeed, those who could see me were closely watching the rulers in my hand, and slight movements of my hand often produced flinching. The conditioning was complete.

Feelings of the Conditionees

I put down the rulers and asked the conditionees how they felt. My students had been together for many sessions and had developed feelings of mutual trust and an ability to share their feelings, so more honest reports were given than would usually occur in a formal experimental situation. Aside from a surface intellectual interest, the reports were quite negative. "Anxious." "Fearful." "I can't keep my eyes off of those damn rulers!" "I feel like crying."

As we discussed our reactions in greater depth, it became clear that the slap on the cheek was startling, but the scolding ("Bad boy!" "Bad girl!") and the pairing of the scolding with the slap were far worse. Memories of childhood punishments came back, and the scolding became *real*: some of the conditionees began to *feel* like bad children. They developed strong, unrealistic emotional feelings toward their conditioners. "She doesn't like me!" "He *has* to like me in spite of having to punish me for being bad!" In psychoanalytic terms, the conditionees were developing transference feelings toward their conditioners, unrealistically projecting onto them the kinds of childhood feelings they had toward their parents.

Quite aside from the specific conditioning occurring, a fear response to the sound of the rulers, the conditioning process was interfering with the conditionees' reality contact. Their simulations of reality, especially their simulations/perceptions of their conditioners, were becoming distorted. Our parents and teachers and peers often played the role of conditioners in the course of our development, and our peers do so today.

The discussion also brought out the involuntary nature of conditioning. Conditionee after conditionee made some remark to the effect that he intellectually knew it was illogical to flinch and become agitated at the sound of the rulers slapping, especially when the reinforcement schedule became intermittent, but he couldn't stop. Conditioning is not all-powerful, but it can often overcome our will. If we can't admit to ourselves that our will isn't strong enough to overcome something, it is then tempting to rationalize that we don't really care about overcoming it anyway; it's easier to go along with the flow.

Feelings of the Conditioners

We also explored the feelings of the conditioners. Two basic reactions occurred, often mixed together. One reaction was distress at what they were doing. "I felt terrible each time I slapped him." "It made me remember being punished by my mother." "I had to force myself to do this, it seemed so cruel." But because they had the sanction of authority (the leader instructed them to do it as part of their "growth"), all the conditioners performed their job.

The second basic reaction of the conditioners, quite contrary to most expectations, was finding they liked the job of being conditioners. "I felt important and right in what I was doing." "Part of me relished the feelings of power I had."

Both types of reactions were usually rationalized by the conditioners. The rationalization that they had been instructed to do this by an authority was common. This was true, of course, yet people recognized that this thought had a certain emotional intensity and feeling of falseness to it that made them suspicious that this was being used in a nonrealistic way. Other rationalizations were even less realistic, such as thinking that the conditionee had probably been bad and so deserved to be punished!

As with the conditionees, the conditioners also found they tended to lose full contact with reality. Aside from specific rationalizations for their actions, they tended to get involved with fantasies instead of paying attention to the actual reactions of their conditionees. They also found themselves remembering times they had been punished as children, and feeling like children. The conditioners' simulations of current reality started becoming distorted.

Given the purpose of showing that conditioning was an important factor in my students' lives, the demonstration was a great success. All the students in the class felt that they now understood what conditioning was about, and realized that it was quite relevant not just to human life in general, but to their own lives in particular. Later class discussions showed the students had developed much more sensitivity to possible ways they had been conditioned in the course of their personal development.

I found this demonstration disturbing, just as my students did. It was worth the distress in terms of its educational value, though. If you don't know you've been conditioned, you have little chance of ever doing anything about it, so a little suffering is a small price to pay for an insight of such great value. I often tell students in workshops about this demonstration, but seldom do it.

The demonstration of conditioning was complete, but it would not have been right to stop there. We then had an extinction session: I repeatedly clapped the rulers together with no slaps or scoldings administered, until the fear reactions had died out in all the conditionees. While it was not standard conditioning procedure, I then broke both the metal rulers and threw them on the floor, where everybody, conditionees and conditioners alike, stamped on them! Conditioners and conditionees then hugged each other, and, except for the lesson, the conditioning was dead.

The analogue of conditioning in our crane/sorter is simple programming. We program its brain that when event/stimulus A occurs, response B is to follow, regardless of whether there is any natural connection between A and B. We can do whatever we want, and we can always do it in a single trial. Human conditioning might take many trials, but it sometimes occurs in a single trial, especially if the situation arouses intense emotions. Conditioning a human being is like programming a computer. As more and more of our experiences and actions involve patterns of conditioned responses, we become more and more automated.

How much of a role has conditioning played in your life? How much of what seems a natural reaction was not part of your essential self, but the result of forced pairings of events by people and conditions in your life?

9

Hypnosis

> *trance* 1. A state of partly suspended animation or of inability to function; a daze; a stupor. 2. A state of profound abstraction of mind or spirit as in religious contemplation; ecstasy. 3. A sleeplike state such as that of deep hypnosis.
> —*Webster's New Collegiate Dictionary* (1973)

The word *trance* usually has negative connotations for us. If someone acts stupidly, we are liable to say he is in a trance. A trance need not be merely passive stupidity, but can include an active, organized pursuit of the wrong things. When we feel someone is in a trance, we tell him to wake up, to use his natural abilities to the full.

Trance is no longer common as a scientific word, partly because it carries negative connotations, partly because it has never been clearly enough defined.[1] A scientific technical word should be clearly descriptive of what phenomena are, without confusing what they are with what we feel about them. It is the negative connotations that concern us here.

In spite of the positive uses of hypnosis in medicine and psychotherapy and as an aid to learning, and in spite of decades of work by responsible professionals to educate the public to have a more positive view of hypnosis, in common usage hypnosis is still usually referred to as a trance. Hypnosis has negative connotations: a hypnotized person is thought to lack animation, to be partly asleep, to be in the power of the superior mind and will of the hypnotist, to be controlled and manipulated.

Is there, perhaps, a deeper reason for the negative image of hypnosis, of trance, to persist?

Gurdjieff was, among many other things, an accomplished hypnotist.

His knowledge included Eastern versions of hypnosis and its application that are still little known in the West today. He knew that *hypnosis, in various forms, is a major part of everyday life for almost all people,* rather than being an exotic and unusual phenomenon. When hypnosis is carried out in a formal way, with a designated "subject" and "hypnotist," with a formal procedure for inducing, testing, using, and terminating it, we recognize its great power. When hypnoticlike procedures and states are interwoven with many life activities, they are not so obvious, yet can be just as powerful. We will look at hypnosis in detail, for it can alert us to less obvious things that are part of our everyday lives.

Hypnosis fascinated me from my early teenage years and was the major focus of the first decade of my research career. My master's thesis and doctoral dissertation were studies of new uses for hypnosis in actively controlling both the process and the content of nocturnal dreaming. I spent two years in intense postdoctoral study of hypnosis at Stanford University and carried out research studies for several years thereafter. I am supposed to be an expert on hypnosis, yet in spite of years of study I still find it quite incredible.

SETTING AND PRELIMINARIES

Let us look at a modern hypnotic procedure, the administration of the Stanford Hypnotic Susceptibility Scale, Form C. This is a standardized psychological test procedure widely used in research for determining how hypnotizable a subject is.

There is nothing obviously theatrical or mysterious about administering the scale. The hypnotist does not wear a cloak or "gesture hypnotically," there is no "Look into my eyes!" rigmarole. It is standardized to the point where, after initially getting acquainted, the procedure is read word for word from printed instructions. Responses are evaluated in a standardized way: "Does the subject's arm move less than x inches in y seconds?," for example.

The setting is low key. Typically the subject, often a college student seeking extra credit, reports to a psychological laboratory that is basically just a quiet room with a comfortable chair. The subject usually has not met the hypnotist before and knows nothing about him except that he is, presumably, competent to practice hypnosis. After a few minutes of casual conversation and filling out of forms, the usual getting-acquainted ritual, the hypnotist asks the subject to sit comfortably. He reassures the subject that there is nothing dangerous or threatening about what is going to happen, that it won't be embarrassing, and that being hypnotized is actually a rather normal sort of occurrence.

BEGINNING THE INDUCTION

The formal induction of hypnosis begins by asking the subject to look steadily at a small, shiny spot on the wall (such as a chrome-plated thumbtack) while listening to the hypnotist. The point of fixation is called the target.

A number of suggestions to guide the subject's thoughts and perceptions are then repeated over and over. "Suggestions" means just what it ordinarily means, verbal statements to lead the subject's thoughts. An example would be "Think how it would feel to be very relaxed and sleepy." There are small variations in wording in the printed instructions, rather than simple repetition, and the hypnotist will usually speak without long pauses, to keep the subject's mind occupied with the suggestions.

The hypnotist suggests that the subject keep looking steadily at the target, that he can be hypnotized if he looks at the target and follows the hypnotist's instructions, if he concentrates on what the hypnotist says. The hypnotist suggests that the subject's very presence there indicates that he is willing to be hypnotized. The subject should just let himself go, just let things happen.

The hypnotist continues to suggest that if the subject's mind wanders from following the hypnotist's voice, he should gently bring it back to following it. Interspersed with these suggestions are further reassurances that hypnosis is normal, that it's like things the subject has already experienced, such as being so absorbed in a conversation while driving that you don't notice the scenery going by. He is further reassured that his experience will be interesting.

While this is going on, the subject has been gazing steadily at the target. Most people don't think about it, but gazing steadily at anything fatigues the eye such that the image starts to undergo unusual changes. Parts of it may fade or brighten, colors may change, shadows may appear or disappear. Early in the induction procedure the hypnotist suggests that these changes will occur: when they do, the subject interprets them as an effect of the procedure, a sign that he is beginning to be hypnotized. In one way, this is a trick: the changes would have occurred without the hypnosis induction. In another way it is an effective and useful way of creating a connection between ideas and experience, between the hypnotist's suggestions and what happens. It seems that the hypnotist's suggestions are working, which reinforces the subject's belief that the hypnotist can indeed hypnotize him. If the suggestions have already started taking effect, the heaviness in the eyes is also a genuine effect.

THE SLEEP PARALLEL

After a few minutes the hypnotist suggests that the subject's eyes are feeling tired (as they likely are anyway from gazing intently), that it would be very pleasant to close his eyes, that he would welcome their closing of themselves. He suggests that the subject is already very relaxed and getting more relaxed. Thinking of relaxation brings on relaxation: his body is getting numb and heavy, his eyelids are heavy, he's breathing freely and deeply and feeling more and more drowsy. (You may notice that even reading these suggestions tends to make you feel sleepy. Resist!) The hypnotist suggests that the subject give up trying to actively control his experience, that he just relax and experience these pleasant feelings of drowsiness and relaxation. He is experiencing pleasant, warm sensations in his body; he's going deeply asleep. Even though he's going to sleep, he can clearly and easily hear the hypnotist, and he will want to do what the hypnotist says.

The analogy with sleep implicitly drawn in the suggestions and the repeated suggestions of sleepy, drowsy feelings are very powerful. Hypnosis does not have to be induced by reference to sleep, but it is the most common way. Sleep is the universal altered state of consciousness, the one we have all experienced, the one we all understand. There is an implicit understanding between hypnotist and subject, of course, that this is not ordinary sleep but hypnotic sleep, a special sleeplike state in which the subject can still hear and respond to the hypnotist.

The sleep suggestions become more and more frequent as the induction goes on, and become more direct. Instead of suggestions that you feel sleepy, the suggestions become statements that you *are* asleep and you are going even deeper asleep all the time. Further suggestions are added that nothing will disturb the pleasant quality of that sleep, that the subject will stay deeply asleep, experiencing whatever the hypnotist suggests, until the hypnotist tells the subject to wake up. The subject is told he can even move or talk or open his eyes in response to the hypnotist's suggestions without waking.

This standardized induction procedure takes between twelve and fifteen minutes, depending on how rapidly the hypnotist reads the script. Following this induction, a standard set of instructions is followed to test how responsive the subject is, how deeply hypnotized he is.

HYPNOTIZABILITY

People's responses to this induction procedure vary a good deal. At one extreme, a subject might suddenly sit up and say, "When is something going to happen? I'm bored." More typically, the subject will gaze with a fixed look; his eyelids will begin to droop and finally close, looking as if they are closing by themselves rather than as a result of the subject's volition. Typical subjects will tell you later that this was indeed the case.

The twelve standard suggestibility tests of the Stanford Hypnotic Susceptibility Scale that follow the induction are designed to test how well the subject behaves like a classically hypnotized person. The first tests are fairly easy in that many people pass them; the later tests get more difficult. If you count up the number of tests passed as your measure of hypnotizability, you almost get a normal, bell-shaped distribution. The majority of people are moderately suggestible or hypnotizable; a few are not hypnotizable at all, and a few are very hypnotizable. The "almost" qualification comes from the fact that there are considerably more subjects scoring at the high extreme than at the low extreme. This has been interpreted to mean that there is a normal distribution of hypnotic susceptibility that almost everyone fits into, but there are also a small number of people who have some special hypnotic talent, so they swell the numbers who pass all the tests. To put it in rough numbers, about 5 percent of people show almost no response to this (and similar) hypnotic procedures; they are unhypnotizable. Most people show moderate responses; they are lightly to moderately hypnotized. About 10 percent are very responsive, and some of these people can be hypnotized to extremely deep degrees.

Contrary to popular stereotypes, a person's degree of hypnotizability does not show any strong correlations with obvious personality characteristics. A deeply hypnotizable person is not necessarily smarter or dumber than average, more or less gullible, male or female, extroverted or introverted, healthy or neurotic. The idea that a superior hypnotist uses his will to master a dumb, subservient, or gullible person doesn't fit reality very well.

We will now examine the effects that can be experienced in the hypnotic state. For convenience I will describe them as they are experienced by the more talented hypnotic subjects, rather than those who don't respond very well to the induction.

THE EFFECTS OF HYPNOSIS

The first formal test of the effectiveness of the induction is whether the subject's eyes close by themselves by a certain point in the induction. If they don't, the hypnotist requests the subject to close them deliberately.

The subject is then asked to hold his arm straight out horizontally and imagine that it is becoming very heavy. The arm will feel heavy to the subject, too heavy to hold up, and start lowering, eventually coming to rest in his lap.

Now the subject holds his arms out horizontally about a foot apart. The suggestion is that there is a force developing between his hands, pushing them apart. Subjects often experience this as being like magnetic repulsion. Without their conscious volition, their hands repel each other and move apart.

A perceptual suggestion is then given, namely that a mosquito has gotten into the room. This annoying mosquito lands on the subject's head. Slap! Responsive subjects kill the mosquito before it can bite them. They later report hearing its buzz and feeling it landing.

The hypnotist further modifies perception by suggesting that the subject tastes a sweet or sour taste. The subject's mouth may pucker up, and the taste experience may be quite strong.

The above suggestions may be experienced to some degree, even strongly, by a fair number of people. The following are more difficult but are experienced with complete realism (sometimes "realer" than real) by talented subjects.

The subject is again asked to hold his arm out. Now he is told his arm is becoming rigid, by itself, so rigid that if he tried he wouldn't be able to bend it. Eventually he is challenged to try to bend his arm. In spite of great effort, the arm does not bend; he has lost his normal muscular control over it.

Now we leave altered perceptions of body and reality and go within.

The subject is told he will have a dream, a vivid dream, and then is given a period of silence. Asked to recount his experience afterward, he will often report a vivid dream. When subjects are asked to compare the reality of these dreams with their nocturnal dreams, they report that these dreams are sometimes just as real, sometimes even more intense. The content of the dream can also be affected by suggestion, as in suggesting that the dream will represent what it is like to be hypnotized.

Age regression is one of the more dramatic hypnotic phenomena. The subject is told he is going back in time, that he is no longer his adult self but much younger. A specific time to regress to, such as a birthday party at a certain age, is typically suggested. The degree of effect varies, but the most responsive subjects experience themselves as children again. Their manner of speaking and writing can change, and they feel as if they are reexperiencing an earlier part of their life rather than remembering it.

A particularly dramatic test is anosmia, the inability to smell. In spite of the number of times I have administered it and seen it passed, it continues to amaze me. After I have suggested to the subject that he cannot smell anything, a bottle of household ammonia is held under his nose and he is asked to take a good sniff. Talented, deeply hypnotized subjects take a deep sniff, show no reaction, and deny that they smelled anything. The smell of ammonia is not only extremely strong but painful in our ordinary state of consciousness. Although it is not further tested in Form C, other standardized hypnosis procedures administer a variety of painful stimuli after suggestions that the subject cannot feel pain. This ability to reduce or eliminate pain is one of the most puzzling (and useful) aspects of hypnosis.

We have seen external sensations reinterpreted or eliminated, and external perceptions replaced with a dream. They can also be replaced with hallucinated perceptions, perceptions for which there is no physical basis at all. In the next test the subject is told that the research laboratory's secretary forgot to ask him some preliminary questions, but will now ask them over the intercom in the lab. Responsive subjects hear the questions and reply to them!

An extreme modification of perception is now tested, a negative hallucination. The subject is told that when he opens his eyes he will see two boxes on the table in front of him. Actually there are three boxes, but the highly responsive subject will see only two. Maintaining the hypnotic state with eyes open is also a mark of a highly talented subject.

Finally, the hypnotist suggests that when the subject awakens from the hypnosis he will not remember anything about what happened. When the hypnotist gives a certain cue, however, his memories of what happened will return. The subject is now dehypnotized and questioned about what went on. A responsive subject will report coming in to be hypnotized, sitting down and relaxing, and then feeling that he must have fallen asleep, as he can't recall anything else. On cue, the full memories return.

Another common hypnotic effect that is routinely tested, although not in this particular susceptibility scale, is posthypnotic suggestion. While the subject is in the hypnotic state, it is suggested that sometime after he awakens from the hypnotic state, the hypnotist will give him some sort of cue, such as mentioning that the day is pretty warm. Whenever the subject hears this cue, he will do some specified thing, such as opening the door and looking into the hall. The hypnotist also suggests that the subject will have no memory of being given this posthypnotic suggestion.

After the hypnotist has dehypnotized the subject, and the latter is presumably in his ordinary state of consciousness, the hypnotist will occasionally give the cue, usually casually working it into ordinary conversation. The responsive subject will carry out the suggested action, without remembering that he is responding to a posthypnotic suggestion.

For the example of opening the hall door and looking out, after this has happened several times, most people would think this was a strange thing to do. The talented subject will provide a rationalization for his odd behavior, often without even being asked. "I thought I heard a funny noise outside," or "It's stuffy in here; I'm letting a little air in." Posthypnotic suggestions are striking demonstrations of how we can be totally unaware of the reasons for our behavior.

In spite of its great power, hypnosis does not give the hypnotist total control over the subject. If the hypnotist suggests that the subject do something quite dangerous or antisocial, for instance, such as shoot someone, the subject will usually ignore the suggestion or awaken from the hypnotic state, sometimes feeling very upset. This is usually interpreted to mean that hypnotic suggestions will work well as long as they do not conflict with our deeper convictions.

There is a more disturbing interpretation, which will become clearer after you read the next chapter on consensus trance. When someone is hypnotized, the hypnotist can give a posthypnotic suggestion that the subject will not be able to be hypnotized by any other hypnotist than the original one. Until this suggestion wears off, which may take hours in some cases or months in others, the subject will not respond to a hypnotic induction by someone else, but will remain hypnotizable by the original hypnotist. This suggestion could be modified so that the subject would be hypnotizable by others, but unable to respond to certain kinds of suggestions. When we examine the construction of ordinary consciousness and its trancelike qualities, we will see that resistance to an antisocial suggestion in hypnosis may partially represent moral virtue, but may also simply show that the original hypnotist, the culture, has left posthypnoticlike suggestions operative that block later change.

DISBELIEF IN THE REALITY OF HYPNOSIS

If a part of your mind is rather incredulous, it is quite understandable—especially if I add that there are more dramatic hypnotic phenomena than those included in Form C: we have two forms of the Stanford Hypnotic Susceptibility Scales for testing really talented subjects!

I have hypnotized people with these standardized tests and seen these phenomena dozens and dozens of times. I must accept their reality because of my repeated experience. Or must I?

After all, they smack of magic. There were no drugs, no operations on the brain, no powerful emotions to push people to extremes of functioning. Two strangers sat in a rather ordinary room. The one called the hypnotist did nothing but talk to the one called the subject. And yet the subject's reality changed in drastic, impossible-seeming ways. Isn't that magic, when the magician's spell (words) changes reality?

EXPLANATIONS OF HYPNOSIS

In trying to understand and explain hypnosis, most theorists roughly fall into two general classes, the credulous and the skeptical. The credulous theorists generally take the subject's behavior and reports at close to face value: when the subject doesn't react to the sniff of ammonia and reports that he smelled nothing, it is because he smelled nothing. Skeptical theorists see the phenomena of hypnosis as inherently unlikely or impossible, and so view the subject as involved in some sort of pretense: he smelled the ammonia and it was painful, but he acted *as if* he didn't smell it and lied about his experience.

Experiential Theories of Hypnosis

I think the designation of the first class of theorists as "credulous" must have been coined by a skeptical theorist, since *credulous* has a connotation of naiveté. I shall substitute the term *experiential*, to indicate in a more neutral manner that these theorists accept the behavior and reports of the hypnotized subject as reasonably accurate indicators of their experiences.

The experiential theorists run into problems when they try to further explain the experience of the hypnotized subjects. *Why* can their experience be so profoundly altered? A major line of speculation has been that hypnosis involves profound physiological changes in the nervous system, comparable to sleep or drug-induced states. Unfortunately for this theory, these changes have not been found. While brain waves are a crude measure, the brain waves of hypnotized subjects are pretty much the same as those of people in ordinary states. Other physiological changes in the body turn out to be associated with the relaxation that is normally part of hypnosis. You can eliminate the relaxation and associated physiological changes with suggestion, though, yet the person can still remain deeply hypnotized.

We will probably find some sorts of physiological changes in hypnosis when our instrumentation becomes sufficiently advanced and sensitive. There are already hints of changes in the evoked potentials of the brain in conjunction with negative hallucinations, for example, but there are no gross changes to explain what hypnosis is at this time. Even more important, we are still unable to explain how such profound changes can be brought about just by talking to someone.

Skeptical Theories of Hypnosis

The skeptical theorists assume that the behaviors associated with hypnosis are actually "normal," that is, within our ordinary capacity. They are just rare and unusual. When we see a lot of them together in the context designated hypnosis, we mistakenly think there is something special about them. Further, these theorists usually reason that the overt compliance with the suggestions is largely a matter of play-acting. The subject is not in some sort of mysterious hypnotic "state," but is in a normal state acting the part of a hypnotized subject.

Skeptical theories have been with us since hypnosis was introduced to our culture by Anton Mesmer as "animal magnetism." For example, a British physician stationed in India, James Esdaile, discovered that hypnosis could be used to anesthetize many patients for surgery. Chemical anesthesia had not been discovered yet. Ninety-five percent of patients who had surgery died from it, as well as suffering terribly. Esdaile reported that not only did his Indian patients feel no pain, but 95 percent survived the operation.

The British medical journals refused to publish his papers. When he returned to Britain, he put on a demonstration for his colleagues of the British College of Physicians and Surgeons. After hypnotizing a man with a gangrenous leg, he amputated it in front of them while the man lay there calmly smiling. The conclusion of his skeptical colleagues? Esdaile was fooling them. He had hired a hardened rogue for a gold piece to lie there and pretend that he was feeling no pain.

They must have had very hard rogues in those days.

THREE DIMENSIONS OF HYPNOSIS

I believe the reality is that there is a wide variety of reactions to hypnotic induction, such that both the experiential and the skeptical positions are partly true, depending on what particular person at what particular time they are talking about.

Ronald Shor, a prominent investigator of hypnosis, talked of three dimensions of hypnotic depth,[2] three different kinds of alterations of psychological functioning that could occur singly or in combination as a result of the induction. These dimensions were role-playing involvement, trance, and archaic regression. Variations in our mental functioning also occur along these dimensions in everyday life.

Role-Playing Involvement

The concept of role playing is something we all understand. An actor plays Hamlet on the stage, but he knows he is not Hamlet, only himself playing Hamlet. We play various roles in life that are clearly artificial; they are not us. When told that the research laboratory secretary needs to ask him some questions over the intercom, for example, the subject who is playing the role of a deeply hypnotized subject figures out the kinds of questions that are likely to be asked in that situation and speaks some reasonable answers aloud. What may start as deliberate role playing can change, though. The concept of role-playing involvement refers to the fact that we can start to become identified with a role we are playing, instead of just deliberately playing it. Our heart is in it; we forget that it is just a role. It can take over, and the role plays us.

A few people can simply play the role of a hypnotized subject in response to the induction, but for most the role will start to become automatic, unconscious to various degrees. At its extreme, the subject deeply caught up in a role involvement will show all the external behavior of a deeply hypnotized subject. Indeed, it doesn't occur to him that he has any choice; he automatically complies with the expectations he has about how a hypnotized subject behaves; he forgets that he is playing a role. If questioned about his internal experiences later, though, he is likely to report that he experienced nothing out of the ordinary. His arm did not *feel* heavy, but there seemed no other reasonable thing to do than to lower his arm as if it felt heavy. Role-playing involvement is a form of identification, a powerful process we will examine in Chapters 11 and 12.

Trance

The trance dimension refers to a fading of the intellectual framework by which we automatically evaluate our experiences. Shor called this framework the *generalized reality orientation*. I have renamed it the *consensus reality orientation* (CRO), to take away that quality of obvious truthfulness that "general" implies and to remind us that our orientation to reality is very much a product of our particular culture's consensus of what is real and what is important. We shall deal with these cultural factors at length in later chapters.

Ordinarily, when someone says something to you, it is immediately and automatically evaluated in relation to the accumulated knowledge that forms part of the CRO. If a salesperson, for example, says, "This is the best product on the market," you immediately and automatically evaluate it in terms of your CRO knowledge that salespeople exaggerate, even lie, about the things they have a stake in selling. You take in the statement, but you add the qualification to it that it has questionable truth value.

As the CRO fades in response to the hypnotic induction, the hypnotist's statements stop being automatically evaluated. At the beginning of the induction, for example, the hypnotist might suggest, "It would be so pleasant to drift off to sleep." With a fully functioning CRO you might think about that statement: "Do I really want to go to sleep now? Is sleep really that pleasant? Might I miss something if I go to sleep? He's suggested I'm already sleepy, but do I really feel sleepy?" With the automatic processing of the CRO fading as you become more hypnotized, the statement becomes a simple, unevaluated statement of fact: it *would* be so pleasant to drift off to sleep. Your experiences become "dissociated," no longer automatically or consciously associated with relevant information, a point we shall examine at length later.

The trance dimension, then, is one in which experiences occur in isolation, without automatic or conscious evaluation with respect to your general CRO knowledge. Either there is no evaluation at all or the evaluation is done only with respect to a specialized set of knowledge peculiar to the trance state. A subject who is deeply hypnotized on the trance dimension experiences all the classic phenomena: they are perfectly real to him, and his externally responding as if he is experiencing what is suggested is indeed a straightforward reflection of his internal experiences.

Archaic Regression

The archaic regression dimension of hypnosis evolves from the experiences we all had as children in relating to our parents. We were small, ignorant, and almost powerless, with little self-understanding or internal control. Our parents were giants, possessed of knowledge, control, and power far beyond our understanding. Compared to us, they were godlike. We developed an automatized perception of them as godlike, as understanding us, as expecting unquestioning obedience. In turn they rewarded us by caring for our physical needs and loving us. Our expectations were apparently validated.

Underneath the surface of our sophisticated adult selves, this set of automatic attitudes still exists and can operate without our knowledge. Freud spoke of it as *transference*: we transfer this childlike cognitive/emotional attitude onto some people in our world, often with confusing and unhappy results. Suppose your boss asks you to perform some task for him, and in doing it part of your mind makes him into your father. All your expectations of how your father ought to relate to you start to color your relationship with your boss. Since he doesn't know he's supposed to love you and understand your deepest feelings without your needing to express them overtly, his behavior, by ignoring these needs, seems to reject you. You begin to think that he doesn't like you. Misunderstanding can pile on top of misunderstanding.

One response to the induction of hypnosis is to unknowingly transfer the attitudes you had toward one or the other (or both) of your parents onto the hypnotist. The hypnotist now has the sort of magical qualities your parent had when you were a child. Of course the things he suggests become true. It would be *bad* if you didn't obey and experience the things the hypnotist/parent says. This can make for occasional intense emotional episodes around the hypnotic procedure, as well as overt external compliance with the hypnotist's suggestions. Internally the suggestions may be experienced with great reality.

A hypnotized subject can show strong degrees of psychological change along one or more of these dimensions. All of these dimensions of altered psychological functioning affect us far more than we realize in everyday life.

AVERSION TO "TRANCE"

In writing the above descriptions of hypnosis and some of the internal processes underlying it, I have mostly written in a scientifically neutral style, a sort of "here are the facts, I make no judgments about them" approach that is supposed to characterize the objective scientist.[3] Even so, what sort of feeling do you get about the hypnotized subject? Though the subject agreed to be hypnotized in the first place, hasn't he given up his will to someone else and yielded to more "primitive" psychological functioning? The hypnotist now has an extremely large and powerful (but not complete) control over the subject's reality.

I think that part of our aversion to a trance state such as hypnosis arises because at some level we recognize a very unpleasant fact. We are already in a trance. We have spent too much of our life in one or another kind of trance. Our behavior and our internal experiences *are* strongly controlled by others, and we have little hope of change. Hypnosis only stands out as an obvious "trance" because the particular things we do in it are socially unusual.

Modern psychological research has discovered many of the mechanisms whereby our trancelike state is induced and maintained, without discovering the fact that we are in a trance. Gurdjieff recognized our trancelike state, studied it in great detail to see exactly what the factors were that kept us in this waking trance, and provided hope of waking up and methods for waking up. If an outsider, a hypnotist, can have such great effects on us, what would be possible if we could take control of our own minds? An outside hypnotist is also limited in that he is probably just as entranced as we are. Suppose we were our own controllers and were awake? The nature of waking trance and our possibilities for waking up are what this book is about.

IO

Consensus Trance

The Sleep of Everyday Life

trance 1. A state of partly suspended animation or of inability to function; a daze; a stupor. 2. A state of profound abstraction of mind or spirit as in religious contemplation; ecstasy. 3. A sleeplike state such as that of deep hypnosis.
—*Webster's New Collegiate Dictionary* (1973)

In this chapter we examine our everyday, "normal" state of consciousness, but we will look at it in the way we examined the phenomena of hypnosis. What is the setting in which everyday consciousness develops? What are the induction procedures for creating it? What are the phenomena that the "hypnotist" can bring about? Normal consciousness will be referred to as *consensus trance;* the hypnotist will be personified as the culture. The "subject," the person subjected to this process, is you.

This may seem somewhat artificial at first, but we will come to see that consensus trance is a much more pervasive, powerful, and artificial state than ordinary hypnosis, and it is all too trancelike. Consensus trance involves a loss of much of our essential vitality. It is (all too much) a state of partly suspended animation and inability to function, a daze, a stupor. It is also a state of profound abstraction, a great retreat from immediate sensory/instinctual reality to abstractions about reality. As to the definition of trance as a state of ecstasy, consensus trance has its rewards, but it is questionable to call it "ecstasy."

Remember that the emphasis of the second part of this book is diagnostic of the psychopathology of everyday human life: what is lacking in human life that makes us so unhappy? Love, courage, compassion, creativity, and other positive aspects will concern us later. Here I will be emphasizing the negative side of culture and consensus trance induction. Nevertheless, we need culture. It gives us enormous benefits and is the matrix out of which our possible future evolution must arise. Keep in mind, also, that the consensus trance induction process is imperfect. We all have our own personal history that has uniquely shaped our own everyday consciousness. Just as people vary in their hypnotizability, we vary in how deep our consensus trance is. Thus the picture given below is too stereotyped, too simplified . . . yet all too accurate.

CULTURE

Anthropologists have defined a culture as a group of people who share basic beliefs about the world and practices for coping with it. They interact with each other in a way that ensures the survival of the group, as well as a reinforcement and perpetuation of their basic beliefs. We speak of Chinese people and know that we are looking at quite different beliefs about the world than when we speak of Eskimos or Anglo-Americans.

Cultural Relativity

Anthropology has made a unique contribution to our understanding. By studying its detailed documentation of the differences, as well as the similarities, between many cultures, we have a better chance to realize individually the relativity of many (if not most) of our cultural beliefs. Societies of intelligent people, people who have passed the basic test of surviving as a culture, have quite different beliefs about many of the things we hold to be obvious or sacred. Much that we hold to be obvious about the world, much that we consider sacred truths, could and should be called into question.

As an example, I often present my students with this hypothetical situation: "Your brother has just been murdered. You know who the murderer is. How many of you would call the police?" Usually every hand goes up. If I then ask how many people would feel shamed and disgraced for calling the police, I get puzzled frowns. What am I talking about?

From the viewpoint of quite a few cultures, the class has just revealed itself to be composed of the dregs of human society, shameful people who should be shunned. When a blood relative has been murdered, that is *family*. Personally avenging one's family is a matter of personal honor! Do these people plan to do the honorable thing and personally avenge the murder? No, they will let the matter be handled by a group of *strangers*, strangers (the police) who do it for *money*! How degraded can humanity get! It's no wonder that you can't trust foreigners and that the world is such a terrible place!

ENCULTURATION

When we are born, we are a mass of potentials, possibilities waiting to be developed. We are not born into an environment that is completely neutral about our potentials, though, nor into one that will try to develop all of our potentials. We are born with the potential to take personal vengeance on someone who murders a family member, and feel proud that we have done the decent and honorable thing. We are born with a potential to feel fine about letting the police handle it. It's unlikely that both of these potentials will be developed.

Each of us is born into a culture, a group of people with a shared belief system, a consensus about how things are and how they ought to be. As soon as we are born, the culture, primarily through the agency of the parents, begins to pick and choose among our potentials. Some are considered good and are actively encouraged. Consider the following example that was obviously proper in our culture for a long time but now has become questionable: "You're a good girl for telling the teacher about that kid who hit your little brother! I'm proud of you!" Other potentials are considered bad, and their flowering is actively inhibited and punished. "You were a bad girl to hit that boy who hit your brother! You shouldn't do things like that! Nice little girls don't do things like that! How can I love you when you do things like that? Go to your room!"

"Normalcy" and Membership in Your Culture

Becoming "normal," becoming a full-fledged member of your culture, involves a selective shaping, a development of approved ("natural," "godly," "polite," "civil") potentials, an inhibition of disapproved ("evil," "criminal," "delinquent," "disrespectful") ones. While it might be theoretically possible to role-play only in accordance with social norms, without internalizing them, this is difficult for most people. From a culture's point of view, it is far better if your everyday mind, the habitual, automatized way you think and feel, is shaped to reflect the culture's consensus beliefs and values. Then you will automatically experience the right perceptions and interpretations, and so it will be "natural" to act in the culturally appropriate way, even when there are no agents of social coercion around. When you automatically think, behave, and feel "normally," when the internal workings of your mind automatically echo most of the values and beliefs of your culture, you have achieved cultural consensus trance. This interlocking set of beliefs includes a belief that we don't have a "belief system." Foreigners have strange "beliefs," but we know what's right!

Cultures almost never encourage their members to question them. Physical survival has been too precarious for too many people for most of our history, so there is a deep, if implicit, feeling that our culture has kept us alive in a rough world; don't ask questions, don't rock the boat. Cultures try to be closed systems.

Yet many intelligent people have come to a realization of the relativity of some of their cultural values through personal experience. In the past those who traveled a lot, and who had the openness to see that not everyone else was a "savage" or "foreigner," could learn this. Our time is unique in that the enormous amount of anthropological material available on cultural relativity makes this realization much more readily available, even without travel. The kind of self-observation Gurdjieff taught, which we will discuss in detail later, can also help in transcending the limitations of our culture.

ESSENCE

Gurdjieff characterized a newborn baby as pure *essence*. Essence is your genuine, deepest self, your desires, tastes, likes and dislikes, potentials, inherent in you before the consensus trance induction process has begun to change it. Essence is who we really were when we came into this world.

Obviously we have limited repertoires as a newborn. Our characteristics include such things as being a good or a fitful sleeper, being generally content or irritable, liking certain tastes and not others. Essence also includes, in all those who become normal, the ability to learn a language and absorb a culture. But we are not a *tabula rasa*, a blank slate, on which culture can write as it pleases with no consequences to us. We also have our unique genetic and spiritual endowment, which will begin to manifest more as we grow, so we might dislike athletics and like walking in the woods, for example, or find the taste of carrots disgusting and like the smell of sweat, or enjoy poetry but find math boring, or search for the inner light in spite of being ridiculed by others.

Consensus trance induction is a process of shaping the behavior and the consciousness of the baby, the subject, to be "normal," to ensure that there is a high level of standardization of behavior and consciousness in all people so they fit social norms. To be American, you must speak good English, you must have reasonably polite manners of the kind peculiar to your culture, you must look both ways before crossing the street, you must respect your parents and teachers, respect the American flag, you must etc., etc., etc.—add your favorite five thousand beliefs and attitudes here.

We cultural hypnotists do not think of what we do as consensus trance induction, of course. Most of us would be horrified at the idea of inducing a trance that involves lessening animation, reducing reality contact, and that resembles stupor. We sincerely think of what we do with children as "education," as teaching them skills that they must have to live a happy life. We are helping the children, not entrancing them! And this is, of course, true in many ways. A child *must* learn to look both ways before crossing the street, for example, or he may be killed. Just as an ordinary hypnotist utilized truths (your vision is getting blurry and you see changing colors around the target) to induce the formal hypnotic trance, the cultural hypnotist utilizes many truths in inducing consensus trance.

What happens to essence, the basic and essential you, in the induction of consensus trance?

Suppression of Essence

If you are very lucky, and most of the characteristics of your essence are ones that happen to be valued in your culture, the induction of consensus trance is very smooth and free of conflict. Your adult life will probably be "normal" and successful. If your essence is short-tempered and aggressive, for example, and you happen to be born in a culture that

admires warriors who are tough and proud, you may have to deal with realistic consequences of living in that kind of world, but there's no
agonizing over whether you are normal. Suppose your essence is short-
tempered and aggressive, but you happen to be born a woman in a culture
where women are supposed to be docile and subservient. You may get
into a lot of trouble when your temper comes out.

What would be even worse in this latter example, this aspect of your
essence would probably be invalidated and punished until its external
manifestations were suppressed. As an adult you would act docilely and
subserviently, and try to feel that way inside. You would tell yourself
that you are a good person, a normal person. Others would tell you you
are normal, and would accept you as a friend, reinforcing your docile behavior and reinforcing your internal feeling of goodness. But inside,
something, a part of your essence, has been squashed. If it has been
squashed very thoroughly, so you don't even feel that quick temper, you
may only have a vague feeling that something isn't right, that even
though you should be happy, you don't feel very happy. Some of your animation, your essential energy, has been lost to the maintenance of
consensus trance.

If the suppression hasn't been quite that thorough, so you know that
lots of things make you angry but you can't or won't express the anger,
then you can worry. "Am I normal? I'm not supposed to feel things like
this, normal women don't get upset by these situations." Some of your
essential energy has been lost by being tied up in knots, some goes into
"neurotic" worrying about not being normal. Again, you have lost
some animation.

Now we can begin our comparison of consensus trance induction
with the induction of formal hypnotic trance.

SETTING AND PRELIMINARIES FOR CULTURAL HYPNOSIS

Recall the setting of our model hypnotic procedure. The Stanford
Hypnotic Susceptibility Scale was administered in a relatively ordinary
setting, a quiet room, a comfortable chair. The thought of being hypnotized adds a little glamour to the setting and procedure, but the usual
scientific setting is low key and plays glamour down. The hypnotist may
be somewhat older or of higher prestige than the subject, an "expert,"

but the hypnotic relationship is basically a relationship between two normal, competent, and consenting adults.

Constraints on Ordinary Hypnotic Induction

Although they may not be explicitly discussed, there are clear constraints on the hypnosis. For example:

a. It is time-limited, usually an hour or two.
b. The subject does not expect to be bullied, threatened, or harmed in any real way by the hypnotist.
c. If the hypnosis does not work very well, the hypnotist will not blame the subject.
d. The hypnosis may work well, producing a deep "trance," but the subject expects that the effects will only be temporary, and he will not be basically changed by his experience.

Basically, formal hypnotic induction is a voluntary and limited relationship between consenting adults, undertaken for scientific or educational reasons. The power given to the hypnotist by the subject is limited by time and the other deep ethical constraints mentioned above. A profound change in experience may occur for a while, but no basic or long-term changes in his personality or his reality are expected by the subject.

Consensus trance induction starts in conditions that give far more power and influence to the cultural hypnotists than is ever given in in ordinary hypnosis induction.

Involuntary Nature of Consensus Trance Induction

First, consensus trance induction does not begin as a voluntary and limited relationship between two consenting and knowledgeable adults. It begins with birth.[1] A newborn comes into the world with an immature body and nervous system, totally dependent upon its parents for its very survival, as well as its happiness. There is a sort of natural consent to learn, yet the power relationship puts a strong forced quality on that consent.

While the child will slowly acquire consciousness and capabilities to fill his own needs, the power relationship will remain *very* unbalanced for many years. Indeed, the power balance is much more like one we imagined and developed in myths, the power balance between gods and mere mortals, than like that between adults. The parents and other agents of the culture, the hypnotists, are relatively omniscient and omnipotent compared to the subject. Thus the setting for consensus trance induction involves much more power on the hypnotists' side than the usual hypnosis induction.

Unlimited Time for Consensus Trance Induction

Second, consensus trance induction is not limited to an hour's session. It involves *years* of repeated inductions and reinforcement of the effects of previous inductions. Given the way children experience time, the cultural hypnotists have forever to work on their subjects. Further, consensus trance is intended to last for a lifetime: there are no cultural hypnotists waiting to give you a suggestion to wake up.

This book is a suggestion to wake up. I am very glad that the power of the culture is not so strong that this suggestion cannot be given.

Use of Physical Force

Third, ordinary hypnotists cannot use force to persuade their subjects to cooperate in the process of being hypnotized. Indeed, it would be counterproductive in the usual setting. Cultural hypnotists, on the contrary, can use physical threats as needed, and actualize them with slaps, spankings, beatings, revocation of privileges, or confiscation of toys, when necessary. The fear of punishment and pain on the subject's part makes him very attentive to the desires of the cultural hypnotists and quick to act in the desired way. Since *the easiest way to act in the culturally approved way is to feel that way inside,* the fear of punishment helps structure internal mental and emotional processes in culturally approved ways.

Use of Emotional Force

Cultural hypnotists are not limited to physical threats and punishment. Since the parents are the major source of love and self-esteem for the subject, they may threaten to withold love and approval from the subject, or actually withold it until compliance is achieved. "I can't love such a dirty little boy!" Manipulating the natural love children have for parents is another variation of this: "You wouldn't do that if you loved Mommy!" Many psychologists have felt that this conditional use of love (I'll love you if . . .), coupled with invalidation of the child's own perceptions and feelings, has a far deeper impact than simple physical punishment. Since love and affection are so real and so vital, they are exceptionally powerful manipulators. The fact that there is so much real love in most parent-child relationships adds to the confusion that assists in consensus trance induction: when is behavior manipulative and when is it just love?

Love and Validation as Rewards for Conformity

Fourth, cultural hypnotists can offer love and personal validation as a reward for compliant behavior. "What a sweet thought you had. You're a good girl. I love you!" "All A's! You're so smart!" The ordinary hypnotist can offer approval ("You're doing fine"), but it seldom has the potency that love and approval from his parents had on a child.[2]

The personal validation aspect of consensus trance induction is very important. We all have a "social instinct," a desire to be accepted by others, to have friends, to have a place in our social world, to be respected, to be "normal." At early ages this acceptance and validation are mediated almost exclusively by parents: they define what being normal means. As the child establishes social relationships with other adults and children (who also act as agents of the culture), he learns more about how he must act to be accepted. As these approved habits of acting become established and rewarded, they further structure the habitual patterns of mental functioning. Fear of rejection is a powerful motivator. All of us probably have some memories of childhood agonies about whether we were "normal."

Guilt

Fifth, the subject, the child, is clearly at fault for failing to act in the culturally desired way. "Good girls do their homework!" By not doing your homework, you are a bad girl. Nobody likes being thought bad, so pleasing the cultural hypnotist is much more important than pleasing an ordinary hypnotist. We are invalidated in so many ways and told we are bad so often that a general sense of unworthiness and guilt can easily be built up. New condemnations or invalidations tap into this accumulated guilt, giving the new incident a power beyond that it inherently has. This in turn further adds to the underlying feelings of inadequacy and guilt. Origin myths of original sin make the matter worse.

Dissociation

Another factor that gives the consensus trance induction process great power is that the mental state of a young child is similar to the mental state of a deeply hypnotized subject in important ways. This increases the power of the "suggestions" made by the cultural hypnotists.

In a deep hypnotic state, for example, the consensus reality orientation (CRO) has faded into the background. When a particular experience is suggested, the suggestion and resulting experiences occur in relative isolation from other mental processes. When the hypnotist suggests your arm is heavy, a host of previous knowledge about normal arm processes and social situations does not immediately spring to mind an take energy away from the suggestion.

In our ordinary state there is an enormous amount of automatic association of previous knowledge to incoming stimuli. When something happens, this automatic association of all sorts of relevant knowledge helps you decide how to deal with the situation. A man begins talking to you as you walk down the street, for example. You notice the strangeness of his clothes, the odd way he pronounces words, a funny look in his eyes. Without seeming to think about it deliberately, you "instantly recognize" the man as a "crazy person." Your accumulated, culturally approved knowledge tells you to not get involved with crazy people, so you take no notice of him and walk on. Without these immediate associations that enabled you to recognize the situation as threatening or unpleasant, you might have gotten "involved" with this "crazy man," and who knows what might have happened then?

This kind of association is so automatic that we do not usually notice it, and it takes a look at *dis*sociation to make us realize the pervasiveness and importance of *as*sociation. The child's mental state is similar to that of the deeply hypnotized subject whose CRO has faded into relative inactivity. He does not have very much other information to come automatically to mind, nor is the association process so automatized that it always brings a wider context to ongoing events, so the cultural hypnotist's suggestions operate in a dissociated, nonassociated state that increases their power.

Much of our early enculturation and conditioning occurs before we have acquired much language. I suspect that language vastly increases our ability to associate information, so this lack of language further contributes to the dissociated quality of the child's mind. When we try, as adults, as predominantly verbal thinkers, to understand our enculturation and conditioning, it is difficult to recall because it is not stored in verbal form. This further increases the power of early enculturation.

Instinctive Trust in Parents

A subject in a deep hypnotic state, especially if it is deep along the archaic regression dimension, has developed considerable trust in the hypnotist. Indeed this trust has a magical quality to it, for some amazing things have happened just because the hypnotist said they would happen. Children have a similar deep trust in their parents. As we noted earlier, the parent often seems omniscient and omnipotent to the child, so this deep trust has magical qualities, and further opens the subject/child to further suggestions.

Expectations of Permanency

Finally, and most important, consensus trance is expected to be *permanent* rather than merely an interesting experience that is strictly time limited. The mental, emotional, and physical habits of a lifetime are laid down while we are especially vulnerable and suggestible as children. Many of these habits are not just learned but conditioned; that is, they have that compulsive quality that conditioning has. Because they are automatized habits, they do not need the support of a specially defined situation, such as formal hypnosis usually requires; they operate in almost all circumstances. You no longer have to work at maintaining consensus trance: it is automatic.

We can imagine an individual who could see that the things taught him as so important are merely the quaint notions of the particular tribe he was born into, not necessarily universal truths, but most of us cannot see that about the content of the consensus trance that was induced in us. In too many ways we *are* that trance.

INDUCTION OF CONSENSUS TRANCE

We begin the induction of consensus trance, then, with far more power, knowledge, resources, and sophistication on the part of the cultural hypnotist than the ordinary hypnotist can ever hope to have. The cultural hypnotist also possesses the "power of innocence": he is unconscious of the consensus trance he himself is in and simply sees himself as acting "naturally." The child, the subject, knows little and is genuinely dependent on the cultural hypnotists for survival, love, happiness, and validation. It is no wonder that the process induces a lifelong trance.

Cultural trance induction consists of several major groups of suggestions. Each group is repeated over and over, in a variety of forms. Punishment is given for failure to comply, as well as suggestions that you will be able to comply if you really try, if you are good. Love, pleasure, and validation are given as rewards for compliance.

Standards for "Goodness"

One major group of suggestions is concerned with developing potentials that the local culture considers good. "You can get along with the (respectable) neighbor's boy." "You can learn math; you should even try to enjoy it; you need it to get ahead in life." "Be nice to your uncle; he really does like you even if you don't think so." There are immediate rewards for developing potentials the culture values. The culture implicitly and explicitly promises that everything a person could want, all happiness, is attainable by developing these potentials, by becoming normal. Our most obvious example is the American Dream: anyone can become a millionaire with hard work.

Suppressing Deviant Thought and Behavior

A second major group of suggestions is focused on suppressing first the behavioral manifestation and then the internal experiencing of thoughts and feelings that the culture considers bad. "You must not get into shouting matches with your teacher!" "It's impolite (bad) to shout at people," for example.[3] "Normal people talk rationally about their differences, they don't shout." "Your teacher isn't really picking on you, so you have no reason to get mad." "You're a good boy for learning to control your temper; you're so much nicer now." Many consensus trance suggestions are intended to suppress disapproved or unknown types of internal experiences from occurring at all. "You only dreamed you saw a funny man in your room last night, Johnny, no matter how real you think it was." "It was just your imagination." "Nice girls never think about . . ."

Creating a Sense of Duty

A third major group of suggestions is focused on creating a sense of duty to cultural norms. "We are proud to be Americans!" "What do you want to be when you grow up? A doctor?" "It must be fun to want to be a garbage man, but when you get older you might want to be someone really important, like a lawyer or a businessman." The culture gets credit for making life safe, meaningful, and worthwhile. In return you must come to believe and accept its positive values and its prejudices.

Our culture tends to think the universe is a cold, hostile place. Then culture becomes the thing that protects us from this hostile universe, our only hope. We then have a quite natural-seeming duty to protect the culture.

And we are taught, of course, that we are the best. When you are the best, other cultures may be dismissed as quaint at best and inhuman or evil at the worst, especially when their actions might make you question your cultural givens.

Everything Not Permitted Is Forbidden

There is a common saying that mocks authoritarian organizations and cultures: "Everything not permitted is forbidden! Everything permitted is compulsory!" Unfortunately this is true in multitudes of ways in all cultures. Luckily for us, there are possibilities the culture never thought of forbidding because it doesn't know about them, and there are both misfits and truly mature people who keep trying out alternative ways of living and experiencing in spite of the fact that they are forbidden. Essence, also, wants to live and grow, and will try to grow in spite of the constraints of culture. Add to this the fact that our culture is full of inconsistencies and contradictions in this time of rapid change, and there are many "cracks" for the prepared mind to find ways out.

PARALLELS: HYPNOTIC TRANCE PHENOMENA
AND CONSENSUS TRANCE PHENOMENA

Let us look at some parallels between the hypnotic trance phenomena discussed in the previous chapter and phenomena of everyday consciousness, of consensus trance.

Automatized Body Movements

The hypnotic phenomena of eye closure, hand lowering, and hands apart are three examples of automatized body movements. The common denominator of these hypnotic phenomena is that a mental image of bodily movement is created by the hypnotist's suggestions, and the corresponding movements then take place automatically in the subject's body. The key word is *automatically*. The subject does not experience doing these things voluntarily. His eyes close or his hands move involuntarily, as if they had volition of their own, as if the subject were merely a passive spectator.

At first glance these seem exotic phenomena: our bodies don't move by themselves in everyday life, but only when we will them to. Or do they?

Consider the behavioral phenomena of maintaining "personal space." Psychologist Robert Sommer at the University of California at Davis and others have shown that people have a semiconscious or unconscious sense of the space about them and get uncomfortable if others move into that space. People space themselves a certain distance apart for conversation, for instance. If one approaches, the other backs off. This behavior is usually completely unconscious, automatized, not requiring conscious attention. The body just maintains the proper distance without bothering to inform consciousness about it. The cultural hypnotist has, in effect, suggested, "Normal people stay X feet apart (unless the other is an intimate friend or loved one and the situation is defined as an embrace). You want to be normal."

It was probably not suggested so explicitly, of course. Children are natural imitators. We saw the spaces our parents kept (automatically)

from others. We saw their retreats when people got too close. Perhaps we were punished for being too close when we got older. We imitated. Our imitation was probably conscious at first, but it quickly faded from consciousness and became automatized. Now we automatically stand at a "natural" distance from people. It feels "natural," but it's quite artificial, like so many consensus trance actions.

This is a minor example of automatized behavior, as, in most cases, personal space behavior can readily be made conscious by calling people's attention to it and asking them to observe themselves.[4] When a conscious action becomes automatized, though, it may be difficult to make it conscious again, especially if there were unpleasant emotional experiences associated with the action. For example, suppose a boy was called a clingy wimp for frequently hugging and hanging around his father, and was pushed away by his father. There may be an unconscious equation that "Too close = unloved by Daddy."

An interesting situation results when members of different cultures whose definition of "proper" interpersonal distance differs interact. Typically, southern Europeans stand closer to others for conversations than Americans. A southern European talking to an American at a cocktail party may sometimes be seen slowly backing the American across the room. The American may feel pressured: he is trying to establish a "normal" distance. The European may feel rejected: he is also trying to establish a "normal" distance. The circumstances may force the cultural rules about proper distances into consciousness. If the unconscious equation "Too close = unloved by Daddy" is operative, though, the cultural rules about distance may not become conscious: they carry the danger of reminding the American about his fear that his father didn't love him. His mind may supply some convenient rationalization: "Europeans are pushy people. It's this man's personality that offends me."

This personal spacing behavior has characteristics like hypnotic suggestion. The stimulus of someone standing too close or too far activates the nonconscious, conditioned, automatized parts of the mind to correct the distance.

Gurdjieff stated that our movements are quite automatized. We have a fixed number of characteristic movements, gestures, postures, definitions of appropriate personal space, and the like, each keyed to certain situations and subpersonalities that bring them out. We will examine subpersonalities in later chapters.

Attitudes

The mosquito hallucination is an example of hypnotically creating an attitude, a perception of annoyance. The hypnotist suggested that a mosquito was buzzing around, then landing on the subject's neck, ready to bite him, emphasizing that the subject didn't like this mosquito and could slap it. Many hypnotized subjects will slap it in response to feeling annoyed. Some will actually hear the mosquito. We will focus on the suggested annoyance and muscular response, and leave the hallucination itself for later consideration. Our basic phenomenon is this: in response to a cue, someone expresses annoyance and reacts to a "danger" that isn't actually present.

How often does someone read a newspaper article about an unpleasant event that harmed someone else and then become upset? You read about a murder in another town, become frightened, and then worry about whether that could happen to you. Your worry can spoil the evening for you.

It is one of the greatest human talents (operational thinking) to be able to read about danger that happened elsewhere and then realistically think about any parallels in your own life that might put you in danger. You simulate your world on a mental level, change conditions, see what happens then in your internal simulation, and draw conclusions about what to do, all without risking your body in the physical world. You can then take appropriate action to reduce your risk. Perhaps you put better locks on your apartment door, or decide not to walk through a poorly lit street on your way home at night.

But in this case, why the feeling of fright? Especially since this is probably the thousandth time you've read about a murder in the newspaper. You long ago put your life in reasonable order so there were no clear unnecessary risks. Why do you continue to read stories about murders in distant towns anyway, when you know that they frighten you?

In some way the cultural hypnotist has suggested that dangerous and tragic distant events will frighten you. It is like posthypnotic suggestion. Perhaps it came about through simple childish imitation: your aunt read these kinds of stories and became frightened by them; you imitated her. Wasn't she an adult, one of those godlike creatures with superior knowledge? If it frightened her, it ought to frighten you! Did one of the cultural hypnotists, your mother, for example, comfort you whenever you were frightened this way? Now we have another of those unconscious equations:[5] "Feeling frightened = Mommy loves me!" Too, fear was deliberately used to control most of us as children: "If you're bad, the bogeyman will get you!" This can lead to further unconscious equations: "I am frightened, and so being good = Mommy loves me."

This kind of automatized and conditioned reaction distorts and interferes with our genuine capacity for empathy with others. Similarly it is important to experience your own mortality and vulnerability, but in genuine rather than conditioned ways.

Secondary Gain

Psychotherapists have studied a phenomenon known as secondary gain, which arises when a feeling or behavior that is obviously unhappy on the overt level has a hidden, usually unconscious payoff. The hidden payoff often makes the apparently unpleasant or maladaptive experience quite worthwhile. Secondary gains can have very powerful influences on experience and behavior.

Gurdjieff observed that it was easy to make his students carry out frightening, unpleasant, demanding tasks, but almost impossible to make them give up their suffering. I have observed the same thing with my students. Work on something unpleasant in themselves? Yes. Be happy and nice to themselves for five minutes? No way!

The cultural hypnotist has linked many reactions and consequent behaviors to a variety of stimuli. Many of these are linkages that an objective observer would characterize as concern about imaginary dangers. We are annoyed by a lot of mosquitoes that aren't there. Why would the culture want you to be insecure in some ways? Because then you need the culture for protection and so will not be likely to question it or rebel against it in an effective way.

Distorted Perceptions

The mosquito hallucination, the sweet and sour taste effect, and the hallucinated voice are examples of hypnotic suggestions drastically altering the perception of the world, substituting a definite sensation for an absence of sensation. There is no mosquito, nothing was put in the subject's mouth, no one spoke over the intercom. Yet a mosquito was heard and felt, sweet and sour were tasted, a voice asked questions.

Psychologists distinguish between illusions and hallucinations. An illusion is a distorted perception of a real physical stimulus in your environment. A hallucination is a total creation of a perception when nothing is really present. If you walk into a dimly lit room and temporarily mistake a coat on a coat rack for a man lurking in the dark, that's an illusion. If the same nonexistent (as far as the rest of us are concerned) man walks out into the well-lit and empty hall with you, that's a hallucination.[6] We can view illusions and hallucinations as extreme points on the continuum of simulation of the world. In illusion the simulation begins with sensory stimulation, but the simulation is a very poor representation. At the other extreme of hallucination, the simulation process produces a perception, an internal simulation, with no external stimulation involved.

The three hypnotic phenomena described are hallucinations. Hallucination can happen in consensus trance, but it's usually viewed (by other people in consensus trance) as so unusual as to be called crazy. Illusions, on the other hand, happen all the time and are not always recognized as illusions. If they are small distortions of the external world, or when others that you respect, who are also in consensus trance (important, "normal" people), have similar illusions, no one thinks it's an illusion; we all believe we're in touch with reality.

Consider the familiar newspaper story in which a seemingly pleasant, normal young man is suddenly revealed as a mass murderer. All the neighbors are shocked: he was such a nice young man. Was he that good at dissembling? No doubt he must have been fairly good at it, but there must have been numerous times he acted "strange," out of character. Our sensory, perceptual equipment is enormously sensitive when it functions properly. How could the neighbors have failed to detect any of those odd instances?

With hindsight, the neighbors will probably begin to remember odd things the young man said or did. They perceived these things at the time they happened, but they didn't "know" them. Since they didn't fit into expectations, they weren't perceived; that is, they weren't included at all in the simulations of external reality that our minds created. Our culture is a rather friendly one, and we like to perceive people as "nice." A few suspicious types might have noticed these odd things, but the majority went along with the polite, decent way of perceiving. Our perceptions are constructions: we select (or rather our automatic habits select) from the large mass of impressions about us just those that fit comfortably into our expectations.

Many people distort their perceptions in the opposite way, of course. They see sinister implications behind actions that are quite innocent. Their automatized simulations of reality highlight the negative instead of the positive aspects of the situation. Indeed, one of the fundamental types in Gurdjieff's system of false personality types sees such sinister possibilities in others' behavior all the time.[7]

Dreams and Daydreams

In hypnosis, a subject will "dream" on suggestion. Often the hypnotist can specify the dream content. For many subjects the hypnotic dream is experienced as a vivid fantasy; for some it is just as vivid and real in many ways as a nocturnal dream. The reader who wants detailed information can see my review paper on hypnotic dreams.[8]

Our Western culture makes little attempt to affect the content of nocturnal dreams, but it does teach many (but not all) people to treat them as trivia, hardly worth the trouble of recalling, certainly not worth taking seriously. Much more effort has gone into influencing the nature and content of our daydreams and fantasies.

When was the last time, for example, that you daydreamed about journeying through the spirit world? Most of us will have to reply that it was a long time ago, if ever. A few will say "Yesterday," but those few seldom discuss such things in public. They know that "normal" people are not supposed to daydream about such things. Money, sex, power, blood-and-guts adventure, travel in this world, all these things are suitable topics for Westerners to daydream about, but not weird stuff. The contents of our dreams and daydreams usually reflect the norms of consensus reality very well. Indeed, most of the "forbidden" things we dream and daydream about are known to the culture. A clever culture has built-in safety valves, officially forbidden things that are widely used to drain off tension. Being able to dismiss these as merely "daydreams" lowers our fear of using them.

Personality Changes

The age regression effect in hypnosis is closely paralleled in consensus trance by the phenomenon of multiple selves or subpersonalities. To be as you were when you were five years old is to be like a different personality from your current one. In a certain situation we not only act a certain role, we identify with that role, we reanimate that subpersonality. The changes are automatic, triggered by the appropriate situational demands. The phenomenon of multiple selves is so pervasive and important that I devote a later chapter to it.

Nonperception

The hypnotic phenomena of anosmia to ammonia and the three-boxes negative hallucination are extreme examples of nonperception. Something is physically present to your vision, but you don't perceive it. At its simplest, you just don't notice something; your simulation of the world is a little fuzzy. In its most developed form, you not only fail to perceive the blocked object, you positively hallucinate an appropriate approved object so that there's no gap in your perceptual field. A really good hypnotic subject, for example, perceives no gap or "blurry spot" where the third box is. He sees the grain of the tabletop where the third box is, just as he would if there were truly nothing covering that part of the tabletop.

In consensus trance we similarly fail to see all sorts of things the cultural hypnotist has suggested we don't see. An especially dramatic example reported in anthropological texts concerns the South Sea islanders, who had never seen a white man or a ship larger than a big canoe. When Captain Cook sailed into a bay of the island for the first time, the islanders gave not the slightest sign of seeing the ship, even though it was right in front of them. When a small boat set out from the ship to land, it was spotted immediately and the islanders were alarmed, as it seemed to have come from nowhere. The idea of a boat as big as Cook's ship was inconceivable to the islanders. Boats all fell within a certain size range, so they apparently had a negative hallucination of it at first.

It is difficult for us to apply this idea personally. How could something be right in front of our eyes but unperceived? Recall the mass murderer: with hindsight, weren't there a number of little actions that were strange, that could have alerted people to his dangerousness?

Insensitivity to smells, as in anosmia, is an interesting phenomenon. In our culture we believe that while animals have an excellent sense of smell, it is rather atrophied in people. Yet human smell is a very sensitive sense, far more so than we realize. Recent research has shown that humans emit pheromones, chemical compounds that have powerful effects. Women living together in a dormitory, for example, begin to have their menstrual periods synchronized after a few months. Mothers are able to distinguish the clothing of family members from that of strangers by the smell of small amounts of sweat in their dirty clothes.

Many people who have managed to break through this cultural taboo claim they can tell something about people's emotional states by their smell. Some psychiatrists, as a further example, have long claimed that they can diagnose schizophrenia because schizophrenics have a characteristic "funny smell." Insofar as this is true (and my own experience supports it), if we are actually interested in how other people feel ("Hi, how are you?"), why don't we sniff their armpits? Why do we routinely dose our armpits with chemicals that will disguise their smell?

As a culture, we are not particularly interested in the process of consensus trance induction per se. We are very concerned with "education" but have little awareness of how much of what is called education is primarily consensus trance induction. We are interested in producing "dependable, normal" people, culturally entranced subjects who automatically experience and do the right thing when the appropriate external-world situation presents itself. When normal people see A, they "naturally" feel B and do C. This is comparable to giving an ordinarily hypnotized subject a suggestion that when he hears or sees X, he will experience Y and do Z.

THE INDUCTION CONTINUES

Although we have focused on early childhood as the most intensive time of consensus trance induction, we must not think the induction process is finished just because we are adults.

Consensus trance is constantly being reinforced and deepened. Some of this effort is conscious, as in television advertising to sell products or, what is much the same thing nowadays, political activity to sell candidates and programs. Advertising is based on the fact that our associations and conditionings are similar enough that the right messages will manipulate us into wanting the product. The appeal to rational thinking in some advertising is usually also manipulative: certain kinds of people need to believe they are rational, so the advertisers give them material to reinforce this belief, meanwhile manipulating them into buying the product.

Much of the effort aimed at reinforcing consensus trance is not deliberate or conscious; it just happens mechanically. Every time you react in an automatized, conditioned way and get by, or get rewarded, consensus trance is reinforced. Much of our social interaction has this effect. I act normal, you act normal, our habits of being normal get a little stronger. Unpleasant consequences of our normal actions can be a great blessing if we are trying to awaken, but we can't depend on accidentally running into just the right combination of unpleasant circumstances to awaken us. Besides, the culture conditions us not to question things too deeply even when life is going poorly, because it offers us hope that everything will be better later. As we shall touch on later, continual effort is required to neutralize the continuing suggestions to sleep comfortably in consensus trance, as well as the effort needed to understand how this trance developed and to wake up from it.

Each of us is in a profound trance, consensus consciousness, a state of partly suspended animation, of stupor, of inability to function at our maximum level. Automatized and conditioned patterns of perception, thinking, feeling, and behaving dominate our lives. For too much of life, we are like the evolved crane/sorter: we appear to be intelligent and conscious, but it is all automatized programs. Many of these automatized and conditioned patterns may have been adaptive once upon a time, but they don't work well anymore: indeed, they may destroy us. We live in and contribute to mass insanity.

"But," you might well say, "I don't *feel* like I'm in a trance!" Of course not. We think of trance as something unusual, and our ordinary state as usual. We can only realize we are in a trance state by reasoning about it, as we have done in this chapter, and/or by experiencing what it is like to be out of trance, awake. We shall continue examining psychological data about consensus consciousness in the next few chapters, but eventually we'll discuss ways of producing the moments of greater wakefulness that give the concept of consensus trance a direct, experiential reality.

II

Identification

Think of the month and day of your birthday. We'll call it M-day. My birthday is April 29. Now read the following two statements aloud, thinking of your birthday where the second statement says "M-day":

People born on April 29 are wimps.

People born on M-day are wimps.

How do you feel about the two statements?

If you're like most people, the first statement about people born on *my* birthday will just be information—a strong statement, perhaps, but essentially the same sort of information as "The temperature is currently thirty-nine degrees in Fairbanks, Alaska." Just data. The same statement about people (you!) born on *your* birthday is different. "Who says I'm a wimp?"

"Sense of Identity" Subsystem

In analyzing the nature of altered states of consciousness some years ago, including ordinary functioning in our ordinary state, I designated one of the components or subsystems of consciousness as the "Sense of Identity" subsystem.

> The primary function of the Sense of Identity subsystem is to attach a "This is me" quality to certain aspects of experience, to certain information in consciousness, and thus to create the sense of an ego. Presumably semi-permanent structures exist incorporating criteria for what the "This is me" quality should be attached to . . . . Any item of information to which the "This is me" quality is attached acquires considerable extra potency and so may arouse strong emotions and otherwise control attention/awareness energy. If I say to you, "The face of someone you don't know, a Mr. Johnson, is

ugly and revolting," this information probably will not be very important to you. But if I say to you, "*Your* face is ugly and revolting," that's a different story! . . . under some circumstances such a statement might preface more aggressive action, against which you want to defend yourself, but often such a remark prefaces no more than additional words of the same sort; yet you react to those words as if to actual physical attack. Adding the ego quality to information *radically* alters the way that information is treated by the system of consciousness as a whole.[1]

Regardless of the ultimate nature of the structures that underlie it, the process of identification is one of the most important affecting human life. It is a process of defining yourself as only a fraction of what you could be. Let us consider this process, without being too concerned for now with the particular nature or quality of the objects of identification, the things, people, causes, concepts, etc., that the quality "This is *me!*" is attached to.

PERVASIVENESS OF IDENTIFICATION

One reason we need not be too concerned now with the objects of identification is that the process is so powerful and pervasive that I suspect a person can identify with anything. Your name, your body, your possessions, your family, your job, the tools you use on your job, your community, "the cause," country, humanity, the planet, the universe, God, your fingernail, a victim in a newspaper story. . . . The list of things people have identified with is endless.

Once an object is identified with, it gets preferential attention and greatly increased psychological power, compared to objects or ideas that are just things or just information. I shall remind us of this by writing about "I!" or "me!" This increased power may be limited to the power given by the amount of attention readily fixed on the object of identification, but it may well be further increased by linking up, consciously or unconsciously, with basic biological self-preservation emotions. A verbal slight, for example, threatens a part of you that you are currently identified with, but because of some basic insecurities this further activates your body's survival instincts, the adrenaline begins to flow as if an actual physical threat were present, and you now have a large amount of energy devoted to dealing with this threat. A threat to the object of identification is a threat to "me!".

A Practical Illustration

To illustrate identification in workshops, I sometimes put a paper bag in the middle of the floor. There is nothing at all special about the bag—yet. An empty cardboard box does just as well. I then ask the workshop participants to focus their gaze and their attention on the bag and to try to identify with that bag, to think of it as "me!," to love the bag and attend to it the way they attend to themselves. This is no complex hypnotic induction or meditation procedure; I just speak casually about this and repeat the instructions two or three times over a period of a minute. The participants are being asked to exert some voluntary control over the normally involuntary process of identification.

Suddenly I walk out to the bag and stamp on it! Gasps come forth involuntarily. People jump. Their faces show a rapid procession of emotions. Sometimes they complain about my cruelty. Many people report they felt a physical pain in their body when I smashed the bag. Many are as shocked as if I had physically hit them. But they get the point. It is all too easy to give the sense of identity to anything, and thereby give away some of our personal power.

Some things are easier to identify with than others. Your sensations ("*I* itch") and your body are naturals. Your thoughts and feelings ("*I* thought of it first"; "*I* am depressed") are also easy to identify with, for we generally take credit for creating our thoughts, and our feelings clearly happen to us. We especially identify with our name.

Korzybski, the founder of general semantics, constantly warned that the map is not the territory. As a psychologist I agree, but have to add that much of the time people seem to prefer the map to the territory! It is often easier to make the map, the internal simulation of reality, do what you want than it is to deal with the territory, the external world.

Names Will Hurt Me

Remember the old childhood rhyme?

> Sticks and stones will hurt my bones,
> But names will never hurt me!
> Call me this and call me that,
> And call yourself a dirty rat!

As adults we can see that this rhyme was intended as a morale builder, but it is clearly a lie. Most of us do not get injured very often by sticks or stones or other physical attacks, but how often are we injured by the names people call us? By the things people say or fail to say? We identify with a wide variety of concepts and objects, and they usually have names. Then we can be psychologically injured by attacks on the names.

We have all read about "primitive" cultures in which people have secret names. These "primitives" are supposedly so foolish that they think they would lay themselves open to magical attack if unfriendly people knew their secret name. Is it superstition, or more psychological sophistication than we have?

ADVANTAGES OF IDENTIFICATION

We usually have a number of socially defined roles with which we identify, such as parent, educated person, good listener, political activist, or pillar of the community. We also commonly identify with other people: an insult to my spouse is an insult to me, and the like. Identifying with people we think of as role models, heroes and heroines, is also quite common. These "heroes" and "heroines" can be losers in the conventional social sense also: recall our discussion of secondary gains in the previous chapter.

From the point of view of the cultural hypnotist, identification is a very useful process, at least when someone in consensus trance has been conditioned to identify with socially approved roles and values. Such identification is part of the (implicit) definition of normality for a given culture. People who automatically identify with the flag and feel personally insulted when they read about flag burners are going to be people who can be counted on to support the official culture.

The process of identification may also seem useful from a personal point of view. When a student walks up to me and asks me a question, my professor identity is immediately induced, with no conscious effort on my part. I act professorially and give the student an answer or tell her where to find out for herself. She is reinforced in her orderly world view, where professors answer students' questions. I am reinforced in my orderly world view, where I am a professor who knows the answers, and who is respected by students who want to know the answers. It all seems so effortless (although it actually takes a lot of energy). Indeed, it takes deliberate volitional control of attention—what we will discuss in detail later as Gurdjieffian self-remembering—to avoid automatically falling into the professor self in this situation if I don't want to do it.

As another example of the apparent usefulness of identification, suppose I am in the middle of a long and boring task, but one that must be done. I really want to stop doing it and rest or play, do something more exciting. Ideas start coming to my mind of other, more interesting things that I think I ought to do instead. My desk should be cleaned off, there are phone calls to be made, and I ought to make some backup copies of my computer diskettes. These ideas (whether they are true or not) function as rationalizations to avoid continuing my necessary but boring job. It is a lot of effort to force myself to go on. But wait! I just remembered that I am a reliable and dependable man! I have an identity as a reliable and dependable person, an identity I can be proud of. By finishing the task, I will be rewarded by feeling proud, for reliable people can be justifiably proud of themselves. Now the anticipation of my (internal) reward helps me get on with the job.

If we look at this example further, we can see that it could be a matter of changing identifications, rather than going from an unidentified state to an identified one. Tasks are not boring or exciting, they are what they are. People get bored or excited. Yet what is an exciting or neutral task for one person may be boring to another. Was my initial boredom a function of having unknowingly identified with one self-concept that was bored by this task out of many possible self-concepts?

Identification, then, seems like a useful process for automatically (and efficiently?) mobilizing attention and energy for useful ends. Actually it can be a very costly process.

THE COSTS OF IDENTIFICATION

There are costs of identification, psychologically speaking, consequences that we may not like.

A Static Process in a Changing World

The first major cost of identification comes from the fact that identification has a "static" quality to it. We identify with things that our minds implicitly believe ought to be permanent (bodies, cars, possessions, and past events, for example). Logically, consciously, we know better, but we seldom think logically and fully consciously about the things we have identified with. Even mental concepts that we identify with usually have a solid, "thingy" quality to them: what you said a minute ago has become permanent; your decisions are supposed to be right forever. The understandings you have about the world should be absolute truths. You should feel good permanently.

The difficulty inherent in identifying with anything in the physical world, or in our own minds, is that reality keeps changing. Many philosophies and spiritual traditions have pointed out that reality is subject to endless change. Thus, when you identify with something, that thing is going to change, not remain what it was when you identified with it. You will eventually be disappointed because the reality of the object of identification is no longer the same. How often have we heard the lament "He/She isn't the wonderful person I married. He/She has *changed*!" Or you will have to force yourself to give up your identification with the changed object of identification. Ordinarily the identification process does not like deliberate change even though its involuntary workings involve many rapid changes all the time.

The body that is "me!" gets ill, ages, and eventually dies. My car breaks down. My possessions break, wear out, may get stolen. I may try to hold on to my memory of past events, but memory may fade and others may question whether that event really happened. A memory isn't as satisfying as a reality anyway. The apparently brilliant insight I had last year starts to fade: was it ever true in the first place? A student in class raises her hand. "On page 157 of your *States of Consciousness* book you said . . ." I'm not sure I think that's a very adequate statement now, but I must defend it, musn't I? By identifying with things, we set ourselves up for eventual loss. The insecurity stemming from the common cultural belief that the universe is hostile, that we are flawed and fragile, makes identification, as an apparent shield against change, even more tempting.

Who Chose Your Identifications?

A second major cost of identification comes from the fact that most of the things and roles you automatically identify with were not your choices in the first place. As part of the enculturation process, the induction of consensus trance, you were cajoled and conditioned to identify with many roles, ideas, people, causes, and values that may have had little or no interest for your essence or that were even contrary to it. Indeed, some of the people we identified with had many maladaptive and psychopathological qualities, and by identifying with them we took in some of their shortcomings. This is especially true of our parents.

People typically discover aspects of these involuntary identifications late in life. Too often we hear things like "I drove myself to get through law school and practiced law for twenty years before I realized one day that I was never really interested in law. My parents just always expected me to follow in my father's footsteps. Something in me has always hated the stress involved, and I've got an ulcer and high blood pressure. I've wasted most of my life doing something I dislike!"

Remember that identification gives attention and energy to things. We don't have unlimited amounts of energy and attention available, so if we give them to some objects of identification, we have to take them away from others. Identification with things that we were conditioned to identify with, regardless of our essence preferences, is a major aspect of life, of what we call our personality. The fact that we automatically identify with so many things that were not our choices is one of the reasons Gurdjieff called personality "false personality."

Automatization of Identification

A third major cost of identification is that the process is too automated. If your various well-developed identities were like a wardrobe, if you *consciously* chose what costumes, what identities, were the most suitable for a given occasion, *given all you know*, identities would be useful tools. What usually happens, though, is that situation K always evokes identity K automatically.

If the situation is really more complex than identity K can handle, identity K (which is "you" for the time being) may perform badly. All the rest of your identities, and whatever real you is behind them, inherit the consequences of what identity K did in that situation. Gurdjieff expressed it as the fact that any one of your many identities can sign a check or a charge slip: all the rest of you is obligated to pay, whether you/they like it or not. How often have we asked ourselves, "Why did I ever promise to do such-and-such?" The person who asks may well not be the person who promised.

The final cost of identification stems from the fact that the ready, automatic availability of conditioned identities can hide from you the fact that you don't know your real identity, your essence, your deeper self behind these surface manifestations. Are you really your name? Your roles? Your feelings? Your intellectual mind? Your body?

You are far more than anything you identify with.

In the next chapter we will consider the results of habitual identification—identity states.

12

Identity States

The unity of consciousness is illusory. Man does more than one thing at a time—all the time—and the conscious representation of these actions is never complete . . . as an active agent, he is always making decisions and formulating or implementing plans, and he likes to believe that he exerts control over what he is doing; often, however, he may be deceived about the causes of his behavior. . . . The unity of consciousness is an illusion, resulting in part from the filling in of the gaps of memory through recognition and recall.

In a larger context, the problem of willing raises the question of the unity of the personality. Is strength of will a pervasive quality that endures through time and gives some unity to the characterization of the individual, or is it something fragmented and influenced by the constraints of the immediate situation? A general answer can be given: personality is much less unified than we would like to believe, and volition is subject to dissociations just as are perceptual processes.

Which of these quotations do you think is from a leading establishment psychologist, and which from a spiritual master?

In the previous chapter we examined the pervasiveness of the process of identification, the way the "This is me!" quality can be attached to almost anything. Although we can identify with many things, there are habitual, automatized patterns of identification, related sets of objects of identification that form recognizable "identity states." We shall examine these identity states, or subselves, in this chapter.

OUR MULTIPLE SELVES

We take ourselves to be one. My name, Charles Tart, signifies a unified organism—presumably. The process of identification makes us automatically say "I!" to almost everything that passes through our consciousness. There are times, though, when we recognize temporary but rather drastic changes in ourselves, so we describe ourselves as if we were someone else: "I wasn't myself." We often put it in the form "I'm sorry, but I wasn't myself!"

Identity Change in Altered States

There is an old maxim in psychiatry that the pathological, because it is an exaggeration of the normal, makes the normal visible. It stands out enough to be seen. The sorts of drastic alterations we collectively refer to as altered states of consciousness are obvious instances of some changes in the pattern of our identity. Examples would be when a person is strongly intoxicated with alcohol or some other mind-altering drug, or when we are dreaming. Sometimes, under conditions of great stress, we can also see that our sense of "I!," our sense of just who we are, can change quite drastically. These drastic alterations of consciousness allow changes in the process and objects of identification to be seen that would otherwise blend into the normal background and be taken for granted, unnoticed. The idea that these gross changes are unusual differences in kind from our ordinary, unitive consciousness, however, perpetuates a great illusion.

The Body as a Source of Identity

We do have an underlying unity in that we each have the same physical body, day in and day out. We have a unity in that very large numbers of factual memories are reliably available to us almost all the time. These memories are all organized with respect to the sensory perceptions of a single body, so it is easy to conclude that they belong to a single self. Too, people call us (or, more precisely, our body) by the same name all the time and have fixed expectations as to how we will act.

This is not much of a basis from which to argue for the unity of our consciousness, though. All those facts about your life could presumably be stored in a single computer, which would then have all of them reliably available in a single "body." The computer would be called by the same name all the time, and people would have fixed expectations about what the computer would do. Our seventh-generation crane/sorter had evolved to this level. Would we want to attribute consciousness, much less unitary consciousness, to the computer?

The Illusion of Unity

In the previous chapter we spoke of the pervasiveness of the process of identification. Anything can be given the "I!" quality. This can happen with great strength and almost instantaneously. Gurdjieff put it this way:

> One of man's important mistakes, . . . one which must be remembered, is his illusion in regard to his I. . . . His I changes as quickly as his thoughts, feelings, and moods, and he makes a profound mistake in considering himself always one and the same person; in reality he is *always a different person*, not the one he was a moment ago.

> *Man has no permanent and unchangeable I.* Every thought, every mood, every desire, every sensation, says "I." And in each case it seems to be taken for granted that this I belongs to the *Whole*, to the whole man. . . . [1]

When Gurdjieff made statements like this in the early part of this century, they seemed contradictory to everything we knew, and certainly insulting to what we wanted to believe about ourselves. I asked which of the two quotations that began this chapter, emphasizing our lack of unity, was from a spiritual master. The answer is neither. Both statements were made by Ernest R. Hilgard, Emeritus Professor of Psychology at Stanford University.[2] He is one of the United States' foremost psychologists, is a highly respected leader of the psychological establishment, and is not considered a proponent of "fringe" ideas. I was fortunate in doing a postdoctoral fellowship in his laboratory.

To understand the unity or lack of it in our personality, in our selves, we must examine much more than factual memory data associated with a single body. We must include likes and dislikes, values, emotional experiences, hopes and fears, intentions, unconscious processes (healthy and unhealthy), and many more subtle psychological processes. When we consider all of our psychological functioning, honest self-observation, as well as observation of others, shows us that we are not one but many. A comprehensive mental "photograph" taken at one moment in time may show a totally different person from that taken at another time. Indeed, if you took away the common body and mass of factual memories, the common name given to you and fixed expectations about you of others, it would sometimes seem ridiculous to believe that these two personalities had *anything* in common.

It is easy to see this for extreme cases. Suppose you observed yourself at a time you were extremely threatened and angry, for instance, or at a time when you were very secure and loving, or at a time you were totally engrossed in some interesting but demanding work. You would look like different people. Gurdjieff emphasized that these drastic differences among our different selves are not exceptional but are extremely pervasive. "I!" can be a different person from moment to moment.

Let me now define an identity state in the same way a state of consciousness was defined in Chapter 1.

An identity state, for a given individual (individual differences are very important), is a unique *configuration* or *system* of psychological structures or subsystems. The parts or aspects of the mind we can distinguish for analytical purposes (such as memories, values, and skills) are arranged in a certain kind of pattern or system to which the sense of "I!" is given. The pattern or system is the state of identity. The nature of the pattern and the elements that make up the pattern determine what you can and can't do in that state. In an identity state that is highly capable and confident, for example, you can take chances that you would not dream of taking in some other identity state.

An identity state is a dynamic process. Aspects of it are constantly changing in their particulars even while the overall pattern remains recognizably the same. The particular content of my last few thoughts, for example, has been different from thought to thought, but they are all obviously occurring as parts of a pattern I call my writer. I sometimes think of a state as being like a juggler throwing several balls around and around in a circle: the balls are always moving, but the pattern they form stays circular.

The pattern of an identity state is fairly stable until some event or events, external or internal, occur which are an important stimulus for some other identity state. Emotions are common triggers of changes in identity states. The usual range of identity states that we function in, ordinarily called personality, was called "false personality" (which will be discussed in Chapter 15) by Gurdjieff because the identity states were forced on us in the process of enculturation rather than being the choice of our essence or our higher consciousness. The collection of usual identity states exists primarily within the overall pattern we call ordinary consciousness (consensus trance).

The Duration of "I!"

Sometimes a particular "I!" may last for minutes, or even hours, but, Gurdjieff insists, that is no credit to us; it is a mechanical result of persisting circumstances that activate that particular "I!" What happened to the "I!" that made the resolution to be fully conscious of the seconds in the exercise that began the Introduction? Without external reinforcement, was it replaced by another "I!" in moments, another "I!" that had no interest in resolutions about remaining conscious while watching a second hand? The processes of identification discussed in the previous chapter makes us say "I!" to every identity state that comes along, but that does not give us any kind of permanent, self-determining I. The manifestation of various "I!"s in consensus trance is directly analogous to posthypnotic suggestions in ordinary hypnosis: when the suggested/ conditioned stimulus appears, the linked behavior, the conditioned response, the particular "I!" appears.

Identity States

We will designate these various "I!"s by a term I introduced while studying states of consciousness: *identity state*.[3] An identity state is a temporary constellation of psychological factors that has recognizable overall qualities that allow you (if you have become skilled at self-observation along the lines discussed later) or outside observers to recognize it as a distinct entity. Recognition by others is expressed in common expressions like "John is drunk again" or "Carol is in one of her moods" or "Billy is looking for trouble today." An identity state, like any state of consciousness, is a construction. Selected characteristics (memories, objects of identification, propensity for certain moods, associated fantasies, certain skills, etc.) temporarily link together to function as a recognizable whole, a whole that has a distinct "flavor." This identity state then determines how you simulate the world around you, and thus how you perceive yourself and your world.

A person caught in an identity state usually does not know he is in some particular state, does not know that that state does not represent the whole of himself: that is the horror of consensus trance. All of your consciousness is identified with the state; nothing remains outside of the state to alert you to what is happening. If you knew immediately, as it was beginning to happen, that a certain identity state of known characteristics was being activated in you, you would be much better off. You could *choose* whether to facilitate or hinder the induction of that identity state. If you were already in it, you could decide whether you wanted to stay in that state or not. "Here comes state D, and I'm in situation X. Is state D useful for attaining my goals in situation X?" This ability to choose an identity state would be like one of the aspects of enlightenment we discussed in Chapter 1, the ability to choose a state (altered or ordinary) of consciousness that is most appropriate for the situation you are in. An identity state, like an altered state of consciousness, would be seen as a *tool,* and you would pick a tool appropriate to your task.

If you knew from past experience, for example, that that particular state always got you in trouble in the circumstances you were in, you might learn how to deactivate that state. Or you might be able to use the state deliberately, in light of your larger goals and knowledge, without identifying with it. But ordinarily we don't know. We automatically say "I!" to practically all of our identity states, often with costly consequences to the rest of our identities and to our true self.

COMPLICATIONS CAUSED BY IDENTITY STATES

The most obvious difficulties resulting from having multiple selves occur in cases of multiple personality. Multiple personalities often have complete amnesia for the experiences and actions of their other selves. Each self may experience long gaps in memory and suddenly awaken to find itself in an involved situation with a perfect stranger. Bodily reactions to illness or drugs may change from one personality to the next. Crabtree's *Multiple Man* (1985) and Keyes' *The Minds of Billy Milligan* (1981) are excellent accounts of multiple personalities. We will stay with the unrecognized multiplicity of ordinary people like you and me, however.

To look at some of the complications that can be caused by our multitudinous identity states, I will create an example based on some life experiences of mine.

Objectively, the situation is this. There is a small creek running through my yard. I had been doing some work in the creek bed, repairing a small bridge that crosses the creek. I left a small ladder in the creek bed, and an unexpectedly heavy overnight rain flooded the creek bed and washed the ladder away. I would like my ladder back, which means I must follow the creek downstream through other people's backyards until I either find the ladder or decide it is irretrievably lost.

How will I walk down the creek bed? Who will walk down it?

State 1: The Explorer

I have three readily available identity states. State 1 has its roots in my childhood. We can call it the Explorer. The Explorer likes to hike around and discover things. This particular identity incorporated important aspects of my essence, as I was always curious about almost everything. The Explorer also believes he has a *right* to walk around outside and resents the way people put up fences and other barriers that impede him.

State 2: The Good Neighbor

State 2 can be called the Good Neighbor. It was developed later in life. When I am in this identity state, I think of myself as a property owner, an owner who values his privacy and the exclusive control of his property. The Good Neighbor is also a friendly person who likes to stay on good terms with his neighbors.

State 3: The Trespasser

State 3, like the Explorer, has roots in my early childhood. We'll call it the Trespasser. His world is full of interesting places that are, unfortunately, owned by powerful, unfriendly grownups, grownups who like to shout at boys who trespass on their property, try to hurt them, and get them in trouble with their parents. The Trespasser's world is rather absolute in its rules.

The physical me walks down the creek, looking for his ladder. In the backyard of a person I am not acquainted with, a man looks out of an open window and shouts, "What are you doing there?" We won't consider yet the possible identity states this man might be in and how they affect the way he shouts; just take his shouting as a simplified description of what actually happens.

How will I react to the shout? What my internal reaction is, how I will respond, and what happens after that are very much a function of what identity state I am in at the moment the man shouts at me.

Suppose the Explorer is dominant at that moment. My perceptions will emphasize the fact that the man shouted at me, an obviously hostile act. Since I am not doing any harm by walking through his yard, it is unjust of him to be angry at me. Reinforcing my feeling that I'm the victim of injustice, I will recall that creek beds are public property, so the man has no *right* to question my presence in the creek bed: it's not as if I were on his property. This "recall" may well be a fabrication rather than an actual memory, but it will probably seem a real memory to me in this identity state, as it fills a need to protect myself. Further, since I'm enjoying seeing some new territory, he's trying to interfere with my pleasure.

The discomfort his shout sets off in me quickly becomes anger: I have to defend myself (myself being identity state 1, the Explorer, but it is my whole "self" at the moment). I am liable to shout back something like "Who are you?" or "What's it to you?" or "Who are you to ask?" A strong response is obviously required to protect myself.

Suppose state 2, the Good Neighbor, is dominant at the critical moment. I am startled by the shout but immediately realize that the man is probably the owner of the property. That is, he is a property owner *like me*. He has every right to be concerned with who I am and what I am doing in his yard, just as I would be were our roles reversed. As a Good Neighbor it is immediately important to me to establish a bond with my fellow, show him that I respect his rights (as I expect him to respect mine), and alleviate his anxiety as to who I am and why I am there.

My response will be friendly, on the order of "Hi, I'm Charley Tart. I'm your neighbor—I live just up the creek a little ways. Sorry to be in your yard, but I'm looking for a ladder of mine that was washed down the creek by the rain last night. That was some rain, wasn't it? Have you seen a small wooden ladder? Do you mind if I just walk on down the creek looking for it?" My identity state is reinforced by this: I'm acting the way a good neighbor would act. Indeed, since I am internally identified with these feelings, it's not an *act*; it is the "real me" (at least for that moment).

Things will be quite different if the Trespasser is my dominant indentity state at the critical moment. I will be shouted at just as I was when I was a kid, at the mercy of powerful, unpleasant adults. I will perceive the man as a powerful adult and myself as someone with little power *who is in the wrong and deserves to be shouted at*. I *am* guilty of trespassing! My perception may actually be distorted, so he looks bigger to me than he really is and my body feels smaller than it really is.

The Trespasser is existing as an adult, though, so I won't just try to run away, I'll respond. I may say something like "I'm sorry, I didn't mean to bother you, I'm a neighbor from up the stream and I'm looking for a ladder that washed down the stream in last night's rain." The Trespasser immediately tries to placate the adult authority by implicitly admitting guilt and expressing remorse, even while apparently using adult words and explanations.

The Other's Identity State

What happens next depends a lot on the identity state of the man who shouted. If he's in some state that makes him unsure about himself, and I'm the Explorer, my counterattack may reinforce his unsure state and get him into explaining that he lives there (a much weaker role than property owner) and wondered what was happening (a less demanding stance). Then I can generously explain that I'm looking for my ladder, but the important psychological event was that I defended *my* (the Explorer's) integrity.

If he's unsure of himself and I'm the Good Neighbor, he can slip into a similar Good Neighbor identity state and we'll rapidly smooth things out, perhaps strike up an acquaintance. If I'm the Trespasser, he might sense my guilt, and that would increase the chances that he would go into some Adult Authority Figure identity state and make me feel even more frightened.

If the man who shouted at me is in an identity state in which he sees himself as a secure property owner, though, his reaction to the Explorer could be quite hostile and he could order me off. His reaction to my Good Neighbor identity state might be friendly.

His identity state at the moment he sees me might also be one triggered off earlier by something totally irrelevant to the present situation, such as a fight with his wife. His shouting at me may be quite angry, but have little to do with me or the real situation that I'm on his property at the moment. I won't know this, of course, and will interpret his reaction based on my assumption that he's dealing with the reality of my presence. Et cetera, et cetera. A wide variety of actions and reactions between the two of us could happen. The variety and unpredictability could be much greater if something either of us did while in our initial identity states in the situation then triggered a transition to another identity state for either or both of us. The objective reality of the situation was fairly simple: the psychology gets very complicated.

SELF-REMEMBERING FOR THE CONTROL OF IDENTITY STATES

Although we will not fully deal with it until Chapter 18, let me introduce the idea of self-remembering here. Basically, self-remembering involves, among other things, the creation of an aspect of consciousness that does not become identified with the particular contents of your consciousness at any given time, and which can keep track of the totality of you. It is a partial to full awakening from consensus trance. Suppose I were remembering myself as I walked down the creek.

In a state of self-remembering I would know that I was indeed trespassing, but I would also realize that in objective terms this trespassing was a very trivial matter. I would remember that my goal is to find my ladder, that walking down the creek is the only effective way of doing it, and I would have an essential confidence that I can probably handle any complications that arise. The totality of my knowledge is more available to me as needed when I am self-remembering.

Because I am far from perfect at self-remembering, the three identity states would probably be activated by the circumstances as I walked along: the situation of walking onto others' property associatively calls them up, activating old conditioning. I would observe them come up as I self-remembered, but try not to identify with any of them. Insofar as I am imperfect at self-remembering and have little control of my identification processes, I might become identified with one of these identity states anyway, but my continual effort to self-remember and my observation of my internal processes would probably result in any of the three identity states fading out, losing potency, fairly quickly.

The man's shout would be a particularly strong stimulus for one or the other of those identity states taking hold of me, given my personal history. Presuming I managed to continue self-remembering and not get into an identity state, though, I would quickly assess the situation in a relatively objective fashion. I am on what is presumably this man's property.

Given our feelings about property rights in this culture, the man is probably feeling threatened, and consequently angry. He probably has other psychological processes also going on, resulting from things extraneous to the current situation.

Given this, what can I perceive about the exact qualities of his shout, the expression on his face, his posture? What may give me further cues about his state? I want to deal with the situation was as much accurate information about it as possible. I also want to deal with it in light of remembering my primary goals relevant to the situation I find myself in. These would include finding my ladder, continuing to self-remember, trying not to identify with any identity states, using all life situations as teaching situations that I may learn things from, and treating others in a friendly and considerate way. I will probably then *consciously* decide to use the learned skills usually associated with my Good Neighbor identity state to act the role of good neighbor. My external behavior may now seem almost identical to that which would occur if I were in the Good Neighbor identity state, *but I am not identified.* My internal state is quite different. This keeps me alert to changes in the situation that may occur, so I can adapt to it and pursue my aims as effectively as possible.

SELECTION OF IDENTITY STATES

The succession of identity states within a person is not a random process. The combined workings of three major factors determine which identity state is active at any given time.

Situational Factors

The first major factor is the physical/social situation you find yourself in. There are generally accepted social rules about what sort of behavior is appropriate in what sort of situation. Public crying is appropriate at a funeral, not at the office. Reading a book is perfectly normal at the library, a strange thing to do at a football game. Dancing shows you are "with it" at a party, but is quite inappropriate in most churches. As children we learned that identifying with the appropriate role was the easiest-seeming way to behave properly, so the situation we are in, *as we perceive it,* tends automatically to call up the appropriate identity and corresponding appropriate behavior. As we have discussed, the question of how accurate our perception is, our simulation of the situation, is another matter. We "fit in," we feel "natural," in the situation when we are in the appropriate identity state.

Perceived Expectations

The second major factor is the set of communicated/perceived expectations of the other people in the particular situation. These may or may not be the same as the cues you get from the physical and conventional social aspects of the situation. You could walk into the office where you work, having put your "office identity" on in the elevator on the way up, but then perceive that people are crying. Inappropriate as that might be for the usual office situation, it would immediately alert you to some drastic change in the usual situation. For a moment you might actually be between identity states. This condition might be perceived as confusing (which it is) or, from another point of view, as a gateway to freedom. You will probably ask, "What's happened?" right away, and get an explanation that a well-liked co-worker was killed in a car accident a few minutes ago. The cues from the people now make it clear that some identity state appropriate for grieving and/or comforting others is called for.

Other people have strong expectations about what your identity should be. They reinforce identity states of yours that meet their expectations, thus stabilizing those states. When the Yaqui man of knowledge Don Juan advises Carlos Castaneda to "erase his personal history," he is giving sound technical advice on a method to reduce the pressures from others so you can discover your inner self. This technical procedure may not work very well for most of us, however.

Personality Structure

The third major factor controlling the induction of identity states is the internal structure of your personality, including the nature of the particular identity states available to you. If you are a "normal" person, as a child you were taught appropriate behavior (and learned the corresponding internal identity state) for most of the ordinary situations you were expected to have to deal with later in life. Thus when you walk into a situation you will automatically scan the physical setting and the behavior of the people in it, know what behavior and identity on your part are appropriate, and automatically slip into that identity state.

Insofar as your upbringing has indeed taught you an appropriate identity state for every situation you meet in life, your life will be apparently easy and automatic. You will seem to be prepared for and at ease in all situations and know the "sensible, civilized" thing to do. Life doesn't always work this way, of course. In the course of enculturation we may not be conditioned to a necessary identity state. This is unfortunate in terms of personal suffering, especially as the culture may have conditioned you to feel guilty when you can't function well. From the point of view of searching for personal freedom, however, the imperfection of the enculturation process is a blessing if we use our suffering to truly examine our situation.

DIFFICULTIES WITH IDENTITY STATES

For one thing, many of us are not fully socialized: we haven't learned all the identity states we could possibly need. There are situations that we know are considered "normal" by others, but we don't fit. We feel awkward and uncomfortable, our behavior is forced and strained, we don't feel adequate to the situation. We may behave in an obviously inappropriate way, or we may behave appropriately but feel phony, artificial. We don't have the appropriate identity state and the skills that go with it to slip into.

Second, we may have internal conflicts that prevent us from developing or using a socially appropriate identity state for some situations. Suppose you habitually identify with an image of yourself as a serious, sober, God-fearing, sin-conscious fundamentalist Christian, one who knows that the Devil is constantly trying to seduce us to his evil ways by offering pleasures of the flesh. What do you do at the socially compulsory office New Year's party? You don't have an identity state in which you can have a few drinks, dance, flirt, gossip, tell dirty jokes, and have a good time. Or worse yet (from your fundamentalist identity's point of view), you do have such an identity state available, and it would be a grievous sin to let it out! If you do slip into that identity state, your normal fundamentalist identity state is going to punish you severely in the morning, and you will be tempted to see your party behavior as some kind of "possession" by evil forces.

Lack of an appropriate identity state or being unable to get out of an inappropriate identity state can be far more serious than just being unable to enjoy life, as in the above example. There are cases, particularly in England, where people have burned to death in their homes, even though they could have escaped. Their bodies were found just inside the unlocked front door. But they were *naked*. Decent people never appear naked in front of anyone but their closest intimate, much less strangers like firefighters or crowds. "Better to hope for rescue, even against all evidence of your senses, than be shamed!" seems to have been the philosophy of whatever identity states last inhabited their bodies. Identity states can kill.

A third class of difficulties arises from the fact that childhood enculturation processes tend to lag far behind current realities when the world is changing. When you have a static society, where people live much as their ancestors did, and there are no outside invaders or situations forcing change on them, then there is much sense in parents bringing up their children to perceive, value, behave, and identify just as they did. Your mind is structured like your parents' minds, like your grandparents', like your great-grandparents', and so on, and since you face the same sort of life situations, the internal states and external behaviors that were adequate for them are adequate (given no change) for you.

When I was sent to Sunday school as a child, I remember being taught that God was a vengeful god, that he visited the sins of the parents onto the children, even down to the fourth generation. This idea was, unfortunately, not as incomprehensible to me as I would have liked: I had seen adults who held grudges for years, so I had models for long-term grudges. Yet it was obviously unfair of God to be like that: how could he punish innocent children for the sins of their great-grandparents? And how could this idea be reconciled with the idea of a loving God? I wasn't that mean, and God was supposed to be infinitely more good than I!

As a psychologist, I now see that the idea of the sins of the parents being visited on the children is an accurate allegory for the unpleasant and unadaptive results that come about when people learn identity states modeled on those of their parents. I doubt that it has any application as a description of God. These states, and their associated skills, values, and views, may have been adaptive for the parents or grandparents or great-grandparents, but often the world has changed and they are no longer very adaptive.

Consider the long-respected role, for instance, of parent of a large family. Having lots of children was a sign of being blessed. Indeed, people had a duty to multiply. Birth control and abortion were sins. Degenerate and sinful pleasure seekers might endorse them, but not decent folk. When the world was largely empty, feeling satisfaction in the identity of the father or mother of many children was quite adaptive. But what about today, when many impoverished countries increase their population faster than their economy, condemning people to death by starvation and malnutrition, and the survivors to even worse poverty?

To be truly awake in Gurdjieff's sense, to be able to use all your abilities and intelligence to realistically assess situations you are in and act as adaptively as possible in light of your genuine, unique values, requires that you not be caught in any identity state, particularly one that interferes with your perception of reality. Something must be developed in consciousness that remains outside the identifications and mechanical actions and experiences of the moment. Life is not smooth when our culture has not given us identity states to fit any and every situation. The awkwardness we then feel and the suffering that can follow, on the other hand, can be a key stimulus to and opportunity for personal growth beyond identity states.

I expect you will not find the above arguments about your multiplicity completely convincing. Isn't this "me!" thinking about them now?

We have been thoroughly conditioned to believe in and defend the unity of consciousness. Trying to see why you resist the idea of your multiplicity can be very insightful. But, to repeat a warning I have given before, you should not find any of my arguments convincing on a logical basis alone. The map is not the territory. The arguments are only a tool to use analytically on your previous experience, and with the experiences of self-observation and self-remembering you can have using the techniques described in later chapters. Then their usefulness will be apparent.

13

Defense Mechanisms

There are numerous disparities and contradictions in the structure of our personalities. A part of us may want constant attention in order to feel secure, for example, while another part is threatened by attention and wants to be left alone. A part may want to work hard and become famous; another part doesn't like work and sleeps late. In some ways we love our mother, in other ways we hate her. Life also provides frustrations: you want something, but you can't have it. The consequent feelings of frustration can cause great suffering, especially if they connect with various aspects of our personality. There are realistic ways of dealing with contradictions and suffering, and unrealistic ways. We shall focus on the latter in this chapter.

We can suffer greatly when we become aware of a single major contradiction in ourselves. What would happen if we became aware of many or all of them? Gurdjieff stated that if a person were suddenly to become conscious of all the contradictory parts of himself, he would probably go mad. Such sudden and complete self-knowledge is very unlikely to happen, fortunately. The fragmented parts of ourselves are not just randomly scattered about, as it were; they are part of an active arrangement of false personality, an arrangement that maintains its organization in spite of change and stress. When we split off parts of ourselves, active mechanisms keep them in their places. Gurdjieff called these mechanisms *buffers*.

The mechanical analogy for psychological buffers was that of buffers on railroad cars. When these cars are coupled together, one is run into another at a speed of several miles per hour in order to lock the couplings together. Imagine what the uncushioned shock and jolt would be like for the passengers as these massive steel cars hit each other. A buffer is a shock absorber: it absorbs much of the sudden energy of the initial jolt and then releases it much more slowly, much less perceptibly. Psychological buffers smooth out the sudden shock that occurs when we switch from one subpersonality to another, making it small enough so that we are not likely to be aware of the change.

This kind of psychological buffering can work within a particular identity state, and shifting between identity states can also act as a buffer, as we shall discuss below.

Notice that with this analogy there is still something there that we *could* notice if we wanted to or trained ourselves to, but ordinarily the change is small enough that it doesn't force itself on our attention. The sudden shock is buffered out. This possibility of noticing the contradictions in ourselves is utilized in Gurdjieff's method of self-observation, discussed in Chapter 17.

PSYCHOLOGICAL DEFENSE MECHANISMS

Gurdjieff did not write very specifically about the nature of buffers. Perhaps he did not think it necessary. If you became very good at self-observation, you would neutralize the buffers, so why take time to study them?

Modern psychology and psychiatry, on the other hand, have learned a great deal about specific kinds of buffers. The general psychological term for these is *defense mechanisms*. I believe this knowledge greatly enriches Gurdjieff's concept of buffers. Understanding these defense mechanisms is very important if we are to transcend them. Conceptual knowledge of them is also important because it looks as if some kinds of buffers might be very resistant to the technique of self-observation: for those defenses, other techniques might be more effective for understanding the structure of personality than unassisted self-observation.

Psychoanalytic theory, which has looked at defense mechanisms in the greatest detail, indicates that we use them when we have some instinctual impulse whose expression is socially prohibited (unrestrained sexuality, for example). The internalized prohibitions of our culture are commonly referred to as the superego. A strong superego can flood us with anxiety and fear for even thinking about a prohibited action, much less doing it. A defense mechanism, by making us unaware of a prohibited impulse prevents a superego attack. Defense mechanisms also buffer our awareness from disappointments and threats in life. While most obvious in people labeled neurotic or psychotic, defense mechanisms are extensively and unwittingly used by normal people. We could not maintain our consensus trance without their buffering effect.

Some people may use one or two of these for almost all their defense needs. That is, they have a chief form of defense that is central in the structure of their false personality.[1] But we all use many of these defenses on occasion. We will look at them primarily in relation to the goal of waking up from consensus trance. I have not attempted to cover all defense mechanisms or all their subleties, but more information about them can be found in any abnormal-psychology text.

There is a major flaw in modern psychological knowledge of defense mechanisms, however. The model of man underlying them is quite negative. Man is seen as an animal, instinctively caring only for his own survival and pleasure, and enjoying hurting and dominating others. Enculturation is then seen as necessary to control this animal nature. We cannot be allowed to grab whatever we need whenever we want it, rape when we are in the mood, kill whoever gets in our way. The restrictions, conditionings, and automatizations in enculturation, the conditioning of a superego to inhibit our baser nature, seem absolutely necessary. Thus defense mechanisms are usually seen as operative in inhibiting our animal nature. It is only when they are too effective, taking away more of our happiness than is really necessary for our compromise with civilized life, that they are viewed as neurotic. It is fine and necessary for a person to be overcome with guilt and anxiety if he thinks about robbing a bank or raping a child, but neurotic if he becomes anxious at the thought of riding an elevator or talking to strangers at a meeting.

I exaggerate the position of Western psychology to make my point. There are now and always have been significant movements in psychology (Jungian, humanistic, and transpersonal psychologies, to mention just three) that see a positive side to our essential nature. But this negative view of man is entwined all through our psychology and our culture.

To partially balance this view, I shall try to show how various defense mechanisms can block the development and manifestation of the deeper and more positive sides of our nature. I firmly believe that we are basically good as well as flawed and twisted. Our task is to understand and correct the distortions, pull the weeds from our gardens, so we can get on with cultivating the goodness.

LYING

All buffers and defense mechanisms are forms of lying. They misrepresent the truth, both to ourselves and to others. Gurdjieff put great emphasis on understanding lying. Although most people believe they never lie or do so only infrequently, Gurdjieff was insistent that *most people lie most of the time.* That they do not know they are lying makes their situation even worse.

Conscious lying can be an effective defense against pressure from others. The person who swears he didn't do it may escape punishment from external sources. Success in bringing off the lie depends on other people's sensitivity to lying and the evidence that might support or undermine the lie. It may sometimes involve the liar's ability to identify with the lie as it's told, so it seems like truth to him as he tells it, giving him an air of conviction that can take in his listeners.

Having few or no superego prohibitions against lying also increases the likelihood of success in taking in others. If you try to lie when you are experiencing guilt and anxiety about it, you will often show signs of distress that alert your listeners to your lying. Since much social cohesiveness and stability come from people not lying about things considered especially important, a lot of the enculturation process is devoted to constructing a strong superego that will punish a person with guilt when he lies. When a strong superego hasn't been created— "strong" meaning that the person will tell the truth about the things *we* think it's important to be truthful about—our culture calls the person a psychopath or sociopath. In common usage this means a morally deficient person, although psychiatrists and psychologists try to avoid making this value judgment in using the term *sociopath* scientifically.

When you know you are deliberately lying, your simulation of the world is probably still adequate. When you identify with the lying and experience the lie as the truth, your simulation has become very distorted.

Sometimes we lie to avoid our more essential and higher natures. We may tell ourselves and others that "Everybody does it; it doesn't mean anything" when something in us knows quite well we have not lived up to our higher self. This kind of lying may be used to avoid some command of the superego, of course, but I know, as Gurdjieff insisted, that there is some sort of innate, higher aspect of ourselves that knows a deeper morality, and we try to avoid living up to that.

The Morality of Lying

Gurdjieff was not particularly concerned about the morality of everyday lying, for he recognized the cultural relativity and hypocrisy of most of our beliefs about morality. *Unconscious, habitual, automated lying is the real problem.* People in consensus trance are like machines, they must do what they have been conditioned to do. Machines are not good or bad, Pavlov's dogs are not moral or immoral for salivating when the bell rings. When a person has developed a genuine capacity to choose whether to lie or not, then questions of morality become relevant. Before that development, questions of morality are a diversion from the real problem, namely our lack of genuine consciousness and will.[2]

SUPPRESSION

Suppression is a conscious defense mechanism. In suppression you are aware of an unacceptable desire or urge, but deliberately keep it from manifesting. The unacceptability may result from superego prohibitions and/or social conventions.

As an example, suppose you are in an important business meeting and you have a very annoying itch on your scalp. Social norms in our culture are that it is crude and undignified to scratch in public, especially the kind of prolonged, powerful scratch it would take to satisfy this itch. In spite of the great desire to scratch, you keep yourself from doing it and from even visibly expressing any discomfort. This can mean actively watching yourself—your hand might just come up and start scratching "all by itself" the moment your attention wanders—and actively opposing your desire, putting your energies into the more important desire to appear polite and dignified. That's suppression, used realistically in this instance. When you are alone, you can scratch to your heart's content . . . perhaps.

If you were brought up to believe that scratching in front of others is what's bad, you can do it when you're alone. If, unfortunately, you were brought up to believe that scratching itches is bad per se, you can't ever scratch, at least not without feeling guilty. Suppression is then used to avoid an attack from the superego.

Suppression is often used to thwart our better selves. "I should protect that kid who is being cruelly teased. But the gang will turn on me too if I do that. They'll say I'm just a dumb kid too, and I want them to think I'm as grownup as they are. I won't say anything."

Consciousness as world simulator is functioning quite well in suppression. Both the outside world and your own position are represented realistically. Your operational thinking, simulation of the consequences, is realistic ("I won't make a good impression on the people if I scratch"), and so your behavior is adaptive. The simulation of the world and your position in it is realistic, but you deliberately control the attention and energy available to parts of the simulation so that the urge to scratch is starved.

Suppression is often healthy, at least at a surface level, for you know what you are doing. At a deeper level, you may not really understand the reasons why you think you must suppress a desire or feeling. They may have been conditioned in you as part of consensus trance, so suppression may be a manifestation of other pathology.

REACTION FORMATION

Reaction formation and the defense mechanisms discussed from now on are stronger manifestations of waking sleep because they involve blocks and distortions of our ordinary consciousness, quite aside from preventing our awakening and development of higher consciousness. Lying that is identified with, so that it is simulated as the truth, is also a very serious distortion.

Reaction formation is a leaping to the opposite in order to deny an unacceptable desire or feeling. The initiating desire or feeling is not directly experienced: the machinery of false personality automatically steps in and an opposite feeling or desire is strongly experienced instead. The reaction is formed almost instantly, without any feeling of effort.

Suppose you were deeply religious as a child, but your expectations weren't met. A loved friend may have died, for example, in spite of your fervent prayers. You turn bitter and denounce all your religious feelings. Now in adult life, when something religious is mentioned, you automatically ridicule it. This is reaction formation.

As another example, suppose you learn that a rival, let's call him John, has just received a major promotion that you believe should have gone to you. Your deep-level response is envy and anger and wanting somehow to attack John, but, for whatever reasons, envy and anger are completely unacceptable to you. As a result of reaction formation operating almost instantly, you don't feel any anger or desire to attack. Instead you feel a burst of "Christian charity" and enthusiastically tell your friends how wonderful it is that John has been rewarded for his efforts. As another example, suppose you find life very disappointing, but your conditioning makes you feel like a sinner if you question God's providence. Reaction formation blocks you from directly feeling the disappointment; instead you spend a lot of time telling people how wonderful and just God's providence is. Whenever you are unrealistically overenthusiastic about something, it is useful to question whether this is a reaction formation defense to hide some other feeling.

Reaction formation is the mechanism of the "sour grapes" reaction. You can't get something, so you start seeing its negative aspects: "I didn't really want that crummy thing anyway!" This is a mild form of reaction formation, in that the initial desire was clearly in consciousness before the reaction formed.

In looking at consciousness from the world simulator model in previous chapters, we noted that an effective and healthy simulation is one that accurately mirrors the outside world and our own essential or deeper feelings and values. The more accurately the outside physical world is simulated, the more useful simulations of various courses of action (operational thinking) will be. Reaction formation is a major distortion of the world simulation process, for what we perceive about our reaction to an event is opposite to our more basic initial reaction. Our simulations about further courses of actions and their consequences, and our subsequent behavior, will then be flawed.

As you become skilled at self-observation, especially in noticing the more subtle, quiet aspects of your feelings, you may be able to notice the feelings that reaction formation is hiding and explore them more deeply. This defense can also be explored by systematically asking yourself whether you have any feelings whatsoever that are opposite to or being held down by your strongly held convictions. As with all the defense mechanisms, assistance from a skilled therapist or growth facilitator is especially useful and can enable you to see aspects of your functioning that may be difficult to discover on your own.

REPRESSION

Repression is a total blocking from awareness of an unacceptable feeling or desire. It is a splitting of your mind into a conscious part with no awareness of the unacceptable, and an unconscious part where there may be a strong reaction. The unacceptable is forcibly kept out of awareness, with no conscious realization that anything is being repressed. It's as if there were material stored in our memories with special signs on it: "Warning! It would be so devastating to know or experience this material that it must be *always* be kept from consciousness!"

Some material that is now repressed was initially conscious. Repression served to take the pain away. It is also possible for repression to operate almost instantly on freshly perceived material, repressing it right away, leaving no memory at all of it in consciousness, as in perceptual defense.

Evidence for Repression

At first glance the concept of repression might seem inherently contradictory. How do you really know someone feels something or desires something when he insists that he has absolutely no conscious experience of feeling or desiring it? The idea of repression could become just another form of name calling in arguments. "You hate me! What do you mean you don't feel any hate? You're just repressing your feelings!" Repression is a defense mechanism often used against powerful feelings and desires, though, so it can have indirect effects that allow an outside observer to infer that repression is taking place.

Suppose a patient starts therapy. In initial interviews the therapist will want to get some idea about the patient's feelings about various issues liable to be important. The therapist asks, "How do you get along with your mother?" The patient says, "Just fine, I love her very much," but the therapist notes that his face turns pale as he says this, his fists clench, and his posture becomes rigid. Exploring more, the therapist asks, "Any problems at all with her, even little ones?" "No!" the patient replies in an angry tone of voice. Further questioning may show that the patient has no awareness of the angry, strongly emotional quality of his nonverbal behavior and, to the best of his conscious knowledge, believes that his feelings toward his mother are all positive. We infer repression: negative feelings toward his mother are so strong and so unacceptable that they are completely blocked from awareness.

Repression is still an inference in this example, a theory, not direct knowledge to either the therapist or the patient. If, in the course of psychotherapy, the patient does eventually experience strong negative feelings toward his mother, we will believe our inference about these repressed feelings was quite accurate.

Repression of our essence was instituted in the enculturation process and for many people is now very thorough. As a vital child, you could not have walked by a strange animal on the sidewalk without stopping to look and wonder. As an adult, chances are you don't even feel the urge to look. You're too important; you have to get to work. The widespread repression of most of our native curiosity, so that you are only allowed to be curious about things the culture defines as important, is one of the most horrible things about enculturation.

Consciousness as world simulator thoroughly rebuilds reality in repression. As soon as a perception, thought, or feeling triggers a line of thought or feeling that might release repressed desires and feelings, an active blocking occurs such that the stimulation does not bring the repressed material into the ongoing simulation of reality at all. If we think of simulations of the world and our experience as being like actors who walk onto the stage of our mind and play their parts, then in repression an unacceptable actor is simply not allowed on stage. A sensitive observer sometimes notes some turmoil backstage at this point, though. The indirect effects of repression can give it away.

Self-Observation and Repression

It may be particularly hard for you to bring up information and feelings about repressed material, even if you are practicing the systematic type of self-observation that will be discussed in Chapter 17. By definition, there is a powerful reason why the material is being blocked from consciousness, and the desire to know yourself through self-observation may not be sufficient to overcome this block. You may become sensitive to "peculiar" reactions at times, the indirect effects of repression, like our patient's angry tone of voice that was so much at variance with his statement that he loved his mother; but it may take outside intervention, from a therapist or teacher, to help you uncover repressed material.

IDENTIFICATION

We looked at many aspects of identification in Chapters 11 and 12, so here we need only look at its function as a defense mechanism.

If I tell you that some Nazi concentration camp guards were sadistic killers, that they enjoyed torture and murder, that they got a semisexual thrill from others' pain, this is an unpleasant thing to think about, and probably you would dismiss it quickly and not get too upset about it. If I say that *you* get a sexual thrill out of causing others pain and would enjoy torturing and killing if you could get away with it, that's a different matter!

The acceptability and unacceptability of *my* feelings and desires is a much more important matter than the acceptability and unacceptability of someone else's. If a feeling or desire is triggered in you that is unacceptable, if you identify with some other aspect of yourself or another subself that doesn't have such feelings and desires, then you distance yourself from it, you disown it. It was a passing fancy, a minor aberration perhaps, but it wasn't *me*, you don't have to think about it or deal with it any longer.

We have discussed ways in which identification keeps us from searching for our essential self in Chapters 11 and 12.

Subselves and Compartmentalization

The transitions between subselves can thus form an effective defense against fully experiencing or having to deal with the unacceptable. Indeed, by staying in an acceptable set of subselves, identifying only with them all the time, we greatly reduce the possibility of unacceptable feelings and desires being aroused at all. Suppose I have a subself that enjoys being cruel to animals, but "I" (in the sense of my essence or deeper self) or my usual subselves are revolted by this cruel subself and its feelings. By concentrating on being in acceptable subselves, I can use up all of my attention and energy so that it's less likely that the cruel subself will ever be activated, even when "appropriate" circumstances come along. I can never be certain that the undesirable subself will not be activated, though, so a constant (even if not always conscious) thread of uncertainty and defensiveness is introduced into my life.

Identification is a quality created in the world simulation process. The quality "This is me!" originally stems from straightforward sensory connections: I see my hand in front of my face, it is connected to my arm, it responds to my will, a touch on my hand by someone else feels quite different than when that person touches the furniture, and so on. The "This is me!" quality is then applied to some mental processes, some simulations, so when a certain experience is retrieved from memory, it comes already tagged with the "This is me! Priority treatment!" quality.

Self-observation can make us aware of our subselves and the functions they serve. Practice allows the observation of a certain "flavor" to consciousness that indicates that the sense of identity subsystem is adding the "I!" quality to the contents of consciousness. The increased self-acceptance that should come from self-observation and self-remembering should then make this kind of fragmentation less necessary and make identification a voluntary process, a tool we can use if we wish, rather than an automatic defense mechanism.

INTROJECTION

Introjection is a more primitive form of identification. An object, concept, or person seems to be inside you, a part of you, even while still seeming foreign or separate in some way. Being a part of you, it has special power.

Suppose you are in a situation when a guest has been making a series of negative remarks. She doesn't like your curtains, your furniture needs repair, you don't have enough of the "right" books on your shelves, your cooking isn't like the wonderful food she had elsewhere, and so forth. You are getting angry, you want to retaliate and ask her to leave. But in your development you introjected an image, a simulation, of your mother. She feels as if she were "inside" you in some sense, and she is telling you that you must always be polite to guests because nice people never offend a guest in their home. So you don't act on your inner feelings and you stay polite, even though you are suffering inside. This is introjection. Your mother is indeed inside you in the form of an active simulation of her.

The simulation of the person introjected inside you can also inhibit your desires to be generous, caring, and sensitive.

Psychoanalysts believe that if something has been introjected for some time, then it will be identified with. In our example, if you become identified with the simulation of your mother, it will be *your* attitude that you must always be polite to guests. It won't seem like something foreign inside you that exerts pressure on you; it has become you. In practice the terms *identification* and *introjection* are often not clearly differentiated by therapists, but we can sometimes see the difference in the process in ourselves.

The conflict experienced with introjection makes the process quite accessible to self-observation, although the dynamic reasons that provide the power behind introjection may not be accessible without more effort.

In isolation or dissociation, unacceptable desires and feelings are attenuated by splitting yourself into unconnected parts. Compartmentalization is another name for this defense. If feeling A is threatening or unacceptable because you also believe in B, then keep A and B in separate compartments in your mind so you do not experience them simultaneously: thus no conflict. Don't put mental energy into *as*sociating them, and they will stay *dis*sociated. Isolation can also involve a splitting of what normally is a unified experience into parts that dissociate its emotional charge.

The defensive effect is similar to using identification, where conflicting desires or feelings can be kept in separate identities, separate subselves, and so not meet. Isolation doesn't require the energy of adding the strong "This is me!" quality to the isolated desires or feelings, though, or organizing them, *as*sociating them into subselves.

Isolation can keep insights and vital experiences from helping you to grow. I have known people who have had deep spiritual experiences, and have yet used isolation to buffer this positive shock, so nothing in their life changes.

Isolation defenses can be inferred when you notice someone (including yourself) holding two strong and contradictory opinions, usually at different moments or in different contexts, without feeling conflict or anxiety about this inconsistency or conflict. If you point out this inconsistency to him, he seems to evade looking at the inconsistency, preserving the isolation. The simulation aspect of consciousness is deficient at creating connections, associations between different stored experiences.

Self-observation, especially the disciplined type discussed in Chapter 17, can provide knowledge about isolated aspects of mental functioning, but without a deliberate effort to compare and contrast observations, the observations themselves may be stored in an isolated fashion, so they have little impetus toward producing change. One major type of false personality pattern centers on this kind of isolation defense.[3] This type is very good at self-observation, does it habitually, yet is little affected by what is observed. Having a therapist or teacher who confronts you with contradictory aspects of yourself that you have kept isolated can be very useful.

PROJECTION

Projection is the opposite of identification. When an unacceptable feeling or desire comes up, instead of being labeled "This is me!" the world simulation process labels it "This is what someone else feels or wants." Since projective defense occurs about unacceptable, bad feelings and desires, other people are seen as bad.

Suppose you have been brought up to believe that anger is a bad emotion: good people don't get angry; they are understanding and patient. Not only were you punished as a child when you got angry, but on many occasions your feelings were invalidated: "You don't really feel angry. That's not nice anyway. You're just tired." Such invalidation of children's feelings is very common. Now you're in a store where a clerk who is waiting on you is very slow and inefficient. He has to keep looking up information and brings you the wrong products to look at. In reality this clerk doesn't know his job very well yet, although he is doing his best. You're in a hurry, though, and the delays and mistakes make you angry. But since being angry is unacceptable to you, you start to believe that the clerk must not like you, is angry at you, and is deliberately annoying you! The clerk is bad and angry, while you are innocent, good, and too patient. Once this initial projection has taken place it will further affect your perception/simulation of the world so that you become even more aware of everything the clerk does wrong, a distorted perception that will seem to validate your initial projection.

Projection can also be used to project the goodness in yourself onto others, so as not to threaten a poor self-image and whatever secondary gains arise from it. Salvation is always looked for outside. "Someone will come along who will set things right." "Things will change for the better." When you project too much of your own goodness outside, you become susceptible to unhealthy manipulation by others. I have found self-observation and self-remembering along Gurdjieff's lines to lead to a curious thing in this respect. You see all your flaws very clearly, and your self-importance drops. At the same time, most of this self-importance was imaginary anyway, and having dropped it, you now find a genuine inner strength. This strength seems adequate to handle almost anything, yet it's not the sort of thing you would make any fuss about. There may be some real suffering at times over real problems, but the unnecessary sufferings start to drop away.

One of the functions of world simulation is not only to represent an experience per se, but to locate it in space, in time, and on the me/not-me dimension. In projection the external aspects of the experience are initially simulated well, but there is a total reversal on the me/not-me location of your own feelings. This is a serious and all too common distortion of reality perception. How many unpleasant people have we met who claim that they usually find other people quite unpleasant?

Projections can sometimes be observed by noting their flavor, by becoming mentally fast enough in self-observation to notice the fleeting moment when, for example, *you* felt angry before you began perceiving another as angry. It is also very helpful to check your projections by asking other people what they are actually feeling. This doesn't always work, of course, as others can be dishonest, but with people you can realistically put some trust in and who are also committed to growth, it can be very useful. Watch out for the tendency to assume that anyone who doesn't confirm your perception (projection) of him is lying!

RATIONALIZATION

Rationalization is a defense that allows some response to situations that trigger unacceptable feelings and desires, but which obscures and dilutes their unacceptableness by substituting a plausible and acceptable rationale for the unacceptable motivations.

Suppose you were troubled by feelings of inadequacy as a child, and you hated to feel that way. You discovered that giving advice to others who were troubled by problems made you forget your feelings of inadequacy, indeed made you feel important and competent. Now when you meet someone who appears troubled, it starts to empathically trigger your own feelings of inadequacy, but these feelings are immediately papered over, rationalized, by a laudable desire to help the other person. You can now help them and feel good about it: you believe you're operating from the best of motives. Your rationalization of why you want to give advice has buffered you from your true, unacceptable feelings of inadequacy. Indeed, we have a natural essence desire to help others, so there is a good deal of truth mixed in with this rationalization. The more truth there is mixed in with defensiveness, the better rationalization can function. Much of what passes for rational thought is actually rationalization.

Suppose you have gotten insight into the fact that you compulsively help others who are suffering in order to cover up your own feelings of inadequacy. "Well," you say, "no more advice giving! I have my own psychological problems, so I can't give decent advice; it's just a sham." Perhaps. This may also be a rationalization defense against responding to your natural empathy and concern for others.

Self-observation is very useful for spotting rationalization and putting you in touch with the original feelings. Developing sensitivity to your emotional feelings is crucial here, as it is the rejected feelings that drive the mechanism of rationalization. There is a moment before rationalization obscures these feelings, so if you're practicing self-observation, you'll see that feeling and the desire to rationalize it away.

In rationalization, the world simulation process constructs a good simulation of the external situation but a poor representation of your position in the matter.

SUBLIMATION

The psychoanalytic concept of sublimation is that you take the instinctual desire/energy that was originally attached to an unacceptable object and focus this energy on an approved object. Freud theorized, for instance, that a boy's sexual instincts originally focus on his mother. Incest is taboo, so there can be no gratification there. When the boy matures and later marries, however, he may pick a woman who is like his mother in important ways. His unconscious mind equates his wife and his mother, so sexual intercourse with his wife partly gratifies the original desire for sexual relations with his mother, without the conflicts that conscious awareness of this desire would bring. A person who believed that sex was inherently sinful might live a celibate life and try to sublimate his sexual energy into good works. A physically aggressive person, knowing that direct violence would get him in trouble, might become a very sharp bargainer in business transactions.

Without necessarily accepting all of this theory, we can see sublimation as substitute gratification, getting something that is satisfying enough to your desires to relieve at least some of the pressure. At one extreme this can be a conscious process, knowing you're making a compromise as required by reality. At the other extreme you may not know what you're doing and may use rationalization or other defense mechanisms to support your sublimation.

You may also sublimate spiritual energies into mundane activities. I have met several people, for instance, who had long histories of medical problems, such as years of migraine headaches. The best medical attention did nothing to cure them. Finally they became involved in psychic and spiritual activities, and the medical problems disappeared. They realized afterward that they had a natural gift for psychic and/or spiritual work but had not developed it because it wasn't approved of in the culture. They had tried to take that kind of energy and use it all in everyday activities. This partially succeeded, but only partially, and the medical problems were the result of sublimation's not being that effective.

Developing the ability to detect sublimations grows from a general development of the ability to self-observe and self-remember, discussed later in Chapters 17 and 18. These processes lead to increasing awareness of and growth of your essence, so what you really care about becomes clearer.

DENIAL

Denial opposes force with force. When an unacceptable desire or feeling comes up, your mind marshals a strong counterforce which says "No! I do *not* want that, I do *not* feel that way!" There is a strong, violent quality to this direct style of defense. The strength of it, the apparent willfullness involved, makes the user feel alive and determined.

Denial is different from suppression, which acknowledges the validity of the desire or experience but denies it expression, for (usually) realistic reasons, without your being fooled about what it is you would like. It is different from reaction formation because of the apparent willfulness involved. You feel you are choosing (whether you really have a choice or not) to reject something, whereas in reaction formation your going to the opposite extreme is automatized and seems like your natural reaction. The conflict isn't sensed. The attack on religion we used as an example of defense against religious feelings in our discussion of reaction formation could also occur with denial. Here there would be conscious experience of the strength of the rejection and attack.

Denial can be detected in operation by especially observing your strong reactions of rejection, looking for the flavor underneath of something else.

NARCOTICIZATION/DISTRACTION

Narcoticization/distraction is an active fragmentation of attention, a dispersion of energies, a distraction from the unacceptable. For practical purposes (ignoring the effects of training) we have a relatively fixed amount of mental attention available. The simulation process can only handle so many things at once. An unacceptable desire or feeling only becomes really disturbing when it captures a lot of our available attention. If that attention keeps jumping from one thing to the next, it is hard to capture.

Suppose you are in conversation with someone who mentions that *Consumer Reports* has tested the model of expensive car you just bought and found it poorly made, trouble-prone, and a bad buy. Most of us have considerable identification with our cars, as well as being affected by the reality that they are a major investment, so it's upsetting to have our judgment questioned this way. But as you begin to react to the negative implications about your judgment, that reminds you that the car is due for servicing tomorrow, which reminds you about the movie you are planning to see tomorrow night, and then you notice that your friend's hairstyle is quite attractive and you say something about that, which reminds you of a picnic you once took together, so now you notice that you're hungry, and so on. Narcoticization dulls you to the threatening aspects of your reality, not by taking away your mental energy per se to make things dull but by moving it around so much that you are distracted from events that might upset you.

The world simulator is not lazy here. If anything, it's working overtime creating an interesting world, but the process is giving equal energy and attention to everything, thus failing to emphasize what's essential.

When narcoticization is the dominant style of false personality, you lead a very busy life, but somehow the really important things are neglected in spite of all that activity. The busyness can further lead to being tired much of the time, and the tiredness dulls you so that you cannot see what is missing in your life. Narcoticization can be a primary defense against real growth. Going from one teacher to another, doing several different spiritual practices at once, all keep you too busy to hear your essential self.

Questioning excessive busyness, looking for the quiet feeling being hidden by all the activity, can reveal that the narcoticization defense is operating.

REGRESSION

Regression is generally seen as a last-ditch defense, used when more "adult" defense mechanisms haven't been adequate. A person regresses to the personality and psychological structures he had at an earlier age, when things presumably worked out more satisfactorily. The regression may not be as obvious as in hypnotic age regression, where the subject claims to be younger and acts very convincingly as if he were, but instead involves a shift in emotional attitudes to an earlier age. The regression may last for only a few moments or for much longer periods.

I developed a useful technique for observing these regressions some years ago. "Flash answers," instant verbal responses to questions, with no time to formulate or think about (censor) them, can be very revealing if you have made a commitment to learning and speaking the truth. Make this commitment with a friend or your spouse, and tell him or her to unexpectedly ask you the question, "How old are you?" during moments when you are emotional. Answer *immediately* when asked, with the first number that pops into your mind, no matter how you judge the answer.

The answers are usually surprisingly young. When done by both people in an argument, it is surprising how many arguments disappear in laughter when both parties recognize that they are operating from an emotional age of three or four. It must be done in an atmosphere of mutual trust and basic respect, however, not as a way for the other person to win arguments by forcing you to admit that you're being childish. This flash answer technique can be used in many other ways to learn about yourself.

I suspect partial and brief regressions are much more common than is recognized. Regressions demonstrate the arbitrariness of our false personality. All the elements of our younger selves are available: by adding the sense of "This is me!" to them, we resurrect a younger self.

Consensus trance is a difficult state. Too much of our essence, our deep feelings, desires, and talents, was invalidated and twisted in the course of conditioning us to conform to the consensus about what was normal. Thus consensus trance is full of tensions and strains. Defense mechanisms are strain relievers, buffers, to allow adequate (by social standards) functioning of the culture as a whole.

Yet the cost to the individual is very high. The light is very dim, if not out. There is a quality of tension and hurry to life that alienates us from ourselves and from other people. Interacting with and greatly amplifying this self-alienation, the distortions of our perception of external reality, especially other people, and of our own feelings that occur because of our automatizations and defense mechanisms lead to frequent maladaptive actions.

The consequences of these actions create enormous amounts of what I call stupid suffering. This stupid suffering is absolutely unnecessary and diverts energy that could be used to solve real problems. Much of the suffering in our world is stupid, unnecessary suffering, the miscreation of entranced people. The common belief in our culture that a fair amount of suffering is inevitable and normal acts as a further costly defense mechanism, which prevents us from questioning ourselves and our culture. Secondary gains further hinder our natural desire to intelligence and happiness. Stupid suffering may be common, but it is certainly not "normal" in the sense of healthy. It is a terrible waste!

If we could wake up, what could we not do?

14

Balance and Imbalance in Three-Brained Beings

In previous chapters we have examined many ways in which we are entranced, in which our perceptions are distorted and our intelligence is lessened, in which we create unnecessary suffering and lose too much of our vital life energies. We shall look at a further characteristic of consensus trance that involves the nature of intelligence.

Gurdjieff constantly emphasized an idea that at first glance seems very strange: we are three-brained beings. Yet this idea is central in the development of modern growth psychologies.

When we think of the brain, we think of that physical organ in our head whose function is to *think*, to simulate reality. Thinking is a logical process, and we obviously have one thinking brain, so what could a three-brained being be?

"Brain" does indeed mean an organ or process that "thinks," but let us consider what "thinking" means in a general sense. Thinking usually starts with perception: you take in information so you have something to think about. (As we have seen, perception is not a simple act once you consider that ways we have been enculturated to perceive in culturally relevant ways, but we'll leave it simple for now.) Then thinking starts working over these input data: you look for patterns in it, compare it with other information in your memory, and apply logic to it. That is, you create a simulation of the current situation and simulations of possible outcomes based on various alternatives open to you, and see which outcome is most desirable. Some of the simulation is in images; much is usually in words. This finally results in some sort of conclusion being reached.

Our mistake is in limiting our idea of thinking to the intellectual kind, especially the verbal kind. There are actually many kinds of thinking, of simulation. Because the word *thinking* has such strong connotations of intellectual, especially verbal activity, I shall use *evaluation* from now on as a more general term. Gurdjieff's concept of man as a three-brained being, then, specifies that there are three major types of evaluation: intellectual, as we ordinarily conceive of it, emotional, and body/instinctive.[1]

Emotional evaluation? Instinctual evaluation? Aren't emotions something more "primitive" than logical, intellectual thought, something that often interferes with logical thought? Aren't instincts even more "primitive"?

Yes, in an evolutionary sense: lower animals are pretty much one- or two-brained beings compared to us, not possessing the intellectual brain we have to any comparable degree. And yes, in a practical sense: many people's emotional brains and body/instinctive brains are indeed in a primitive state compared to their intellectual brains. But Gurdjieff claimed that both emotional evaluation and body/instinctive evaluation *could* be developed and educated to as high a level, in their special ways, as intellectual thought. Indeed, some people have highly developed emotional brains, but usually their intellectual and body/instinctive brains are greatly underdeveloped. Some people have highly developed body/instinctive brains but are poorly developed in intellectual and emotional evaluation. This lack of *balanced* development of all three types of evaluation processes is a major cause of human suffering.

THE PARABLE OF THE HORSE, CARRIAGE, AND DRIVER

There is an Eastern parable of the horse, carriage, and driver that richly illustrates our nature as three-brained beings and the problems resulting from poor development of each and from imbalance.

A horse, carriage, and driver together comprise a transportation and support system for taking a potential passenger, the Master, where he or she wants to go. The carriage provides the physical support for conveying the Master comfortably and safely, the horse provides the motive power, and the driver provides the practical knowledge for guiding the whole system to the Master's destination. The horse, carriage, and driver should be ready to go whenever the Master appears and wishes to go somewhere. Typically, though, the system does not function well.

The driver frequently lets the carriage sit out in the rain and snow when it should be garaged, so many parts are rusty or rotting. Maintenance has been poor, parts need replacement, and hazards to safe travel are present. Lack of proper usage has created further deterioration. The carriage has a built-in self-lubrication system, for example, so that the bumps of the road pump the lubricants about, but since it has sat still for long periods, many joints are frozen and corroded. Its appearance has become shabby and unattractive. The kind of "feel" for the road, important for safe and efficient driving, that would come from a well-balanced and well-maintained carriage is distorted by its poor condition.

The horse spends a lot of time harnessed to the carriage, out in the hot sun or rain and snow, when it should be in the stable. The driver doesn't pay enough attention to the horse's diet, so its food is of poor quality and it suffers from nutritional deficiency diseases. Sometimes it is neglected and not fed at all for long periods and starves; at other times it gets too much rich food. Sometimes it is groomed and cared for lovingly; at other times the driver abuses and whips the horse for no apparent reason. As a result the horse is unpredictable and neurotic, sometimes pulling the carriage too powerfully and rashly, at other times refusing to go, sometimes obeying the commands of the driver, sometimes trying to bite him.

The driver should be nearby, ready to leap to the box at the Master's appearance, prepared to guide the horse and carriage to the destination the Master commands, and is also responsible for the maintenance of the horse and carriage. Typically, though, the driver has wandered off to a tavern and gotten drunk with a bunch of other drivers. They are partying one moment and fighting the next, getting sentimental, and swapping exaggerations and lies about wonderful (but largely imaginary) journeys they have taken, or about the powerful Masters they like to imagine they are serving or will serve. Actual experience and fantasy are not distinguished very well.

In the midst of this perpetual drunken revel, the driver usually does not hear the Master's call to come to the carriage, harness the horse, and take the Master to his destination. On those occasions when the call is heard, the drunken condition of the driver is more likely to get the carriage stuck or lost or crash it than to safely and swiftly convey the Master to his destination.

Is it any wonder that the Master seldom even tries to use the horse, carriage, and driver? Or that the driver, in his moments of partial sobriety, feels that some sort of important mission in his life is not being fulfilled? That the horse is full of resentment and fitful alternations of anger and despair?

There are frequent partial exceptions to the above state of affairs. Sometimes the driver is fairly sober and intelligent, but in spite of his intentions to obey, the Master can't get very far with his neurotic, half-starved horse and broken-down carriage. Sometimes there is a magnificent, well-fed, powerful, and obedient horse hitched to the carriage, but with the defective brakes on the carriage locked half the time and the driver drunk, the journey may be exciting but end up nowhere. Sometimes the carriage is of magnificent appearance and comfort, and meticulously maintained, but with the drunken driver and half-starved horse it provides only a plush ride to nowhere.

The carriage is our physical body. The horse is our emotions. The driver is our intellectual mind. The Master is what we could become if we provided for the development of our higher nature.

Body

Our physical bodies are often badly neglected in modern times. Most of us in our culture can easily get enough to eat, yet we often eat poorly balanced diets, or diets that try to slim us into the current anorexic fashion, rather than listen to our bodies' essential needs. The external appearance of our bodies, their fashionability, too often gets far more attention than their basic soundness, until illness temporarily gets our attention. Proper evaluation by the body/instinctive brain should alert us to the early beginning of illness.

Our bodies were designed to move and to do physical work. Not only is skillful physical effort rewarding in itself, but it operates the carriage's self-lubrication system. But the height of "success" for most people in our culture is sitting behind a desk all day and doing no physical work whatsoever. Physical laborers usually have the lowest prestige in our culture. The current popularity of jogging and other physical fitness sports is some improvement: let us hope that it lasts.

Depression is very common today. If a middle-aged, sedentary person goes to a psychotherapist complaining of depression, an interesting argument could be made that he should immediately be referred to a physical fitness program instead of being given psychotherapy. After all, the patient is neglecting his body in the most fundamental way, and medical knowledge tells us there is a high probability that he will consequently be sick and will probably die years sooner than he otherwise might. He *should* be depressed! Talking about his feelings will not exercise his body! If he still has complaints after getting into good physical condition, then psychotherapy might be worthwhile.

We do have some people who have developed their body/instinctive intelligence, though usually in a very specialized way: athletes. In order to *win*, selected aspects of strength, coordination, and body/instinctive intelligence have been pushed to high levels. A skilled athlete is not only strong, but skilled. The athlete senses what his body is telling him, the messages of his body/instinctive brain, in order to learn to perform better. Often this specialized development exacts a high price in terms of neglect of other areas of life.

Sometimes this specialized athletic development grows into an overall concern with "feeling" what the body has to say in general, to using it fully and intelligently in many areas of life. There are also disciplines that deliberately train for general sensitivity and development. The Oriental martial arts known as "internal" arts, like T'ai Chi or Aikido, are good examples of this, emphasizing intelligent sensing with the body and intelligent flow of movement rather than brute strength.

Developing the body/instinctive brain also leads to the development of a special kind of will power, one that does not depend on the push of strong emotional desire to win or brutish stubbornness, but on steadiness, skillfulness, and clarity of intent. To those of us whose body/instinctive brains are poorly developed, the feats of skill in internal martial arts like Aikido often seem miraculous.

Body/instinctive development, aside from specialized athletic training, is not simply neglected in our culture; it is often badly distorted. A sense of shame about the body is often inculcated in infancy or childhood: "You are a dirty child! Shame! Look what you've done!" Psychoanalytic findings suggest that this can begin at the earliest stages of life if parents reject the natural body functions of infants. Explicit cultural teachings may reinforce this rejection of the body, as in some Christian ideas that the body and its functions are inherently sinful. A general neglect and rejection of the body/instinctive function can persist into adulthood, so not only have we not developed this kind of evaluation to higher levels, but we reject the information it is already providing.

My experience is that the body/instinctive brain evaluates reality and expresses many of its conclusions in the form of sensations and feelings in the body. If you don't pay attention to your body because it is rejected, or if you automatically misinterpret all body sensations as sinful, you can't get the message of the body/instinctive brain.

Emotions

Our emotional brain provides the power, the motivation, the force to move us and the joy of being alive. It evaluates events all the time: I like this, I dislike that. This is appealing, that is repellent. This is worthwhile, that is boring or wrong. This makes me afraid, that makes me want to help.

When we go to school we are required to take innumerable courses designed to develop our intellectual intelligence, and even a few physical education courses to develop specialized aspects of our body/instinctive intelligence. But there is an almost total lack of education of our emotional brains. Some of us were fortunate enough to be born with exceptional emotional talent and sensitivity, or our lives forced us to develop and refine our emotional sensitivities. For most of us, though, our emotional brain remains largely at the level of an untrained idiot.

Emotional sensitivity per se may not be a blessing, of course, if you are surrounded by suffering and dissimulating people. Since this situation is all too common, many of us worked hard to inhibit the natural emotional sensitivity we had so as not to be overwhelmed. This was fine for that time, but it now cripples our lives. As we have seen in the chapters on enculturation and defense mechanisms, though, our emotional functioning can be so seriously distorted that we usually end not just as emotional idiots but as neurotic emotional idiots. We need to learn not just emotional sensitivity, but also how to handle the inevitable negative feelings of others, and of our own, that we will then perceive.

In terms of our parable, we were frequently starved for love and other emotional attention when we needed it, at other times given lots of it for no apparent reason. Often we had to change ourselves, deny our essence, to buy love, even while being told it was being freely given. Our feelings, our natural emotional intelligence, were often invalidated—"You don't really feel like that!"—by parents and other authorities. Innumerable times we were told what we *should* feel along with invalidation of what we *did* feel.

The quality of emotion and emotional attention given us was often very poor, so we developed emotional deficiency diseases, analogous to physical nutritional deficiency diseases. Like the half-starved, diseased, erratically treated horse, we crave feelings and we fear them; we get carried away by powerful feelings sometimes and can't get up any motivation to act at other times. We want love and attention and kindness, and we fear it. Sometimes we bite the hand that feeds us. Certainly we give the carriage and driver, our body and intellectual mind, an unreliable and often frightening ride through life.

Is it any wonder that so many of us have a profound distrust of emotions?

Intellect

In our parable, the driver was drunk, a good description for the intoxication with ideas that results from the overdevelopment and unbalanced dominance of the intellectual brain. As we discussed in Chapter 5 on operational thinking, we can visualize, simulate, logically predict, and imagine "what would happen if . . . ," and it is one of our greatest talents. When such extrapolation and simulation are not modulated by the evaluations of the emotional and body/instinctive brains, however, the intellectual brain gets carried away with its own simulations, its fantasies. A clever simulation is rewarding in and of itself, and one clever thought leads to another, so we really do get drunk on them.

Operational thinking requires the use of some kind of logic, some set of rules as to what is allowed and what is not. A major problem with intellectual functioning in our society, though, is the use of "logic" in the singular—our implicit belief that there is only one, correct, logical way of thinking. Philosophically we now understand that there are many systems of logic, and each one is *arbitrary.*

A system of logic is created by making some assumptions. *You can assume anything you want to* in creating a logic. To use a logic we are all familiar with, geometry, consider the idea that parallel lines stay the same distance apart no matter how far you extend them. This is one of the "axioms," basic assumptions, of ordinary, Euclidean geometry, the kind of geometry taught in high school. But it's obviously true, isn't it?

True is a very powerful word, with its absolute qualities. It's too powerful. What we actually know is that this Euclidean assumption produces very practical results in a lot of ordinary physical-world situations. This is its truth value. There is also a geometry, though, that

assumes that as parallel lines are extended to infinity, they get infinitesi-
mally closer and closer, until they meet at infinity. There is a third
geometry that assumes parallel lines slowly diverge as they are infinitely
extended until they are infinitely far apart! These different geometries
are very useful to mathematicians and of practical value in space navigation. Are these other two geometries "true"? Yes, just as true as
Euclidean geometry, if you apply them appropriately.

Which of the three is "really" true? In what reality are you asking
about their truth? In mental space? In curved Einsteinian space near a
huge gravity source like a sun? In your backyard? In ordinary physical
reality, who could actually extend any parallel lines to infinity to find
out, anyway? The basic point is that our intellectual functioning is limited and warped as long as we believe there is only one true logic. What is
an error, is misleading in one logic, one set of assumptions, may be a correct and useful thing to do in another.

To actually know a system of logic and use it correctly are among the
greatest human talents. To further know when that system of logic is inappropriate and when *not* to use it is even greater. Then you can
consider using a more appropriate system of logic. This includes not
only other intellectual logics, but the logics of the emotional brain and
the body/instinctive brain, and the logics of the various altered states of
consciousness that we discussed in Chapter 1.

Further, it is important to realize that the ideas we get drunk on are
often contaminated moonshine: the actual thinking we use is often applied in a sloppy and incorrect way with respect to the rules and
assumptions of the logic system we believe we are using, which puts our
simulations of reality, our ideas about what is, even further out of touch
with reality. Rationalization also frequently replaces real logic.

BODY/INSTINCTIVE, EMOTIONAL, AND INTELLECTUAL MAN

Any given person is liable to have one of the three brains developed
fairly strongly while the other two are weak and/or badly distorted in
their functioning. It is useful to characterize such a person by his
dominant mode of evaluation, even though all three modes function to
some extent.

Gurdjieff called anyone dominated by his body/instinctive functioning Man Number 1, anyone dominated by his emotional functioning
Man Number 2, and anyone dominated by his intellectual functioning

Man Number 3. An evolved person who had all three modes functioning well and interacting harmoniously was called Man Number 4.

I find that this particular terminology leads to some confusion, though, for our habitual understanding of numbers implies that Man Number 3 is more evolved than Man Number 2 or Number 1, and that Man Number 2 is more evolved than Man Number 1. In fact, any of the three types is just as unevolved as any other, Man Number 3 having no general advantage. To avoid this misleading implication we shall speak of Body/Instinctive Man, Emotional Man, and Intellectual Man. Man Number 4, Balanced Man, is definitely evolved beyond the other three types.

WHEN ONE BRAIN DOES ANOTHER'S WORK

In addition to the unbalanced level of development of the three brains, another problem Gurdjieff pointed out occurs when one brain inappropriately does the work of another.

An emotional problem may be evaluated and handled by the intellectual brain, for example. Instead of *emotionally* perceiving, comparing, and evaluating the problem, you *intellectually* think about it. Since intellect cannot fully grasp emotional knowledge, the problem cannot be adequately evaluated. Indeed, your understanding may be badly distorted because intellectual thoughts about feelings may misrepresent them and/ or because unconscious defense mechanisms have deliberately distorted the intellectual representation of the emotion.

As an example, my wife, who is a nurse specializing in neonatology, once told me about a premature infant who had died on her shift. The death had saddened her deeply. I felt a little sadness, said a sympathetic word, and put the matter out of my mind. A minute later I noticed that I had suddenly developed a headache. The news of the infant's death had actually touched me deeply, had been fully received and evaluated by my emotional brain, but my intellectual brain, preoccupied with its plans for the day, had handled the news intellectually instead of allowing my emotional brain to work properly. The resulting interference by the head with the appropriate heartache resulted in a headache.

Further, an intellectual response to a feeling communication from another may be taken as a personal rejection. As one who has always been overly intellectual, for example, I have often had others become angry at me for being "shallow," for not having and sharing an emotional response to their emotional communication.

Handling an intellectual problem with the emotional brain, on the other hand, can be just as disastrous. Finding the solution may require rigorous and prolonged intellectual logic. Having an emotional reaction of "I don't like it! Don't bother me!" that inhibits further thought is of no help. Rationalization, one of our main defense mechanisms, is a common example of emotion interfering with thought. It interferes because the emotion is not recognized as an emotion that should be evaluated by the emotional brain, but is mistaken for an intellectual thought.

Body/instinctive problems can also be wrongly handled by other brains. As an Intellectual Man this was difficult for me to understand, and did not become clear until I began studying the Japanese self-defense art of Aikido in 1971. My instructor, Alan Grow, held a black belt in Aikido, an honor that must be earned by many years of practice and demonstrated accomplishment. Alan did not speak much about Aikido: he taught by doing and demonstrating, with his body. I didn't grasp this at all at first. Indeed, I found that within two weeks I could give a marvelous *verbal* description of the nature and philosophy of Aikido, the principles behind its techniques, and its relationship to other systems of spiritual development. But I kept noticing something: Alan could throw me across the room with what seemed a flick of his wrist, whereas I could hardly walk across the mat by myself without wobbling!

In spite of this constant reminder that Aikido was not words, I spent two years trying to learn Aikido the way I had succeeded in most other areas of life, with words and thoughts. "Left foot here, right foot there, move forward and to the side as the punch comes in, remember the principle of getting off the line, keep my back straight, feel consciousness centered in my belly, visualize energy flowing out in front of me, right hand up and around, visualize the energy of the strike and blend with it," et cetera et cetera.

It didn't work very well. Finally I discovered a way of sitting still and watching the demonstration of a technique "with my body," with few or no words. I began learning from a whole new perspective. My body/instinctive brain was now handling my body, and was far better at it than my intellectual brain.

The body/instinctive brain can also wrongly handle the work of other brains. A person who acts out his ideas and feelings with no regard for the consequences—hitting others whenever he gets angry, for example—gets in trouble. Psychosomatic illness is another example: what should have been evaluated and handled on a feeling level gets displaced to a body level.

Note that it is not always inappropriate for one brain to do the work of another, at least if you know what you are doing. In my wife's nursing work, for example, she often must inhibit a full emotional-brain evaluation and reaction to a patient because the effective response that will save the patient's life requires highly developed intellectual, technological skills that would be impaired by emotions. The key is knowing what you're doing so you are doing it deliberately, rather than having the interactions of the three brains run on automated habit and unconscious processes, and in the developing skilled and balanced use of all three brains. In terms of the parable, the next higher stage of evolution comes when the Master begins to use the horse, carriage, and driver for the purposes of Masters.

THE FOUR WAYS

Specializing in the development of any one of these brains can lead to extraordinary growth. Gurdjieff spoke of spiritual paths that specialized in working primarily with one type of man as "ways." Development on any of these ways is generally, but not always, preferable to no development at all. Focusing your efforts on a way that is intended for a different type of man than you are could be very inefficient, of course.

The First Way is the way of the body, typified by the fakir in Indian culture, and perhaps sometimes approached in championship athletic training in our culture. The term *fakir* is often used loosely to indicate any kind of beggar or traveling holy man, but Gurdjieff used it more precisely for those who have developed extraordinary control over the body. He described a fakir he had seen in India, for example, who had stood outside of a temple on his toes and fingertips for decades.[2] His body was permanently stiffened in that position, so that his disciples had to carry him to the river to wash him as if he were an inanimate object. A terrible fate, it seems, and Gurdjieff would probably agree, but think of the incredible will and discipline it took for that man to keep practicing and practicing, ignoring pain, the weather, onlookers, his hopes and fears, and to *will* himself to maintain that posture.

Any way by itself may produce marvelous but useless results. The fakir develops incredible will, but to what end? We get a monomaniacal development, extraordinary results at a price of extraordinary narrowing. Gurdjieff claimed, though, that if such a fakir were helped by someone on one of the other ways, he might be able to end the fanatic devotion to body control and apply that will power to developing his other brains.

The Second Way is that of the monk, the emotional, religious way. Fervent prayer, faith, devotion, deep longing, and ecstatic devotion are the keys. Emotional functioning must be extremely strong, though generally quite specialized. Proper emotions must be strengthened, unwanted ones struggled with until they are suppressed. The emotional will developed through this struggle can be quite extraordinary.

Although fakirs generally learn from individual fakirs they become attached to, the way of the monk is usually pursued in organized schools, monastaries full of people devoted to religion. Emotional *intensity* is developed to a very high degree, hopefully along with emotional intelligence. The intense emotions become a driving force, the horse of our parable, that can make extraordinary results possible, including, according to Gurdjieff, the development of psychic abilities.[3]

As with the First Way, the results can also be very unbalanced and useless, producing what Gurdjieff termed a "stupid saint," someone who manifests "miracles" that are not really helpful. Imagine, for example, a "saint" who cures a couple's infertility by prayer, in a country where most people already suffer and starve because of overpopulation.

The Third Way is the way of the yogi, the development of intellect and insight into the human condition through the cultivation of altered states of consciousness. As we have seen, the state-specific knowledge available only in some altered states of consciousness is essential for full human development, so the ability to enter and intelligently function in various altered states is essential. The yogi can know essential and vital things about life that must forever remain "secrets" to those who cannot enter those states.

In the extreme, this way can produce a "weak yogi," someone who knows what must be done but doesn't have the motivation and/or the will to actually accomplish much. Being an professor, I am always particularly struck (and a little frightened) by this concept, as I am surrounded by colleagues who have marvelous insights (even if they access only consensus consciousness) into life but make a mess of it anyway for lack of body/instinctive and emotional development. On too many days I also see in myself how much my (abstract) knowledge of what should be done for full awakening and development far outstrips my motivation or ability to do it. The yogi may have some advantage compared to the fakir or monk, though, in that at least his broad insights enable him to know what he is lacking on the emotional and body/instinctive dimensions. As he may not develop his intellectual brain to the fullest, but may stop with lesser accomplishments, however, he may remain a weak yogi.

Note that Gurdjieff uses *fakir, monk,* and *yogi* in specialized ways, so these remarks should not necessarily be generalized to all systems associated with these words.

The Fourth Way of spiritual development, which Gurdjieff represented, combines the other three ways, aiming at developing all three brains in a relatively equal and harmonious fashion. This is obviously desirable in and of itself, as well as setting the stage for the development of an entirely different kind of center for the self, the center that we call the Master in the parable. Various characteristics of Fourth Way work will be discussed in the remainder of this book, and some have been mentioned already, although not specifically identified as such. One of the primary tasks of self-observation, discussed in Chapter 17, is the personal observation of the different "flavors" of the three brains and of the wrong work of one brain for another.

15

False Personality and Essence

This chapter will be a brief summing up of the problems of consensus trance that we have looked at in this section. We will be looking in more detail at the concepts of personality, false personality, and essence.

In the Introduction to this book I spoke of the loss of our vital energies as the loss of the light that we once saw, but now can see no more, using the first two verses of Wordsworth's "Intimations of Immortality." Let us return to that theme with the first two verses of Stephen Spender's "I Think Continually of Those Who Were Truly Great."

> I think continually of those who were truly great.
> Who, from the womb, remembered the soul's history
> Through corridors of light where the hours are suns,
> Endless and singing. Whose lovely ambition
> Was that their lips, still touched with fire,
> Should tell of the Spirit, clothed from head to foot in song.
> And who hoarded from the Spring branches
> The desires falling across their bodies like blossoms.
>
> What is precious, is never to forget
> The essential delight of the blood drawn from ageless springs
> Breaking through rocks in worlds before our earth.
> Never to deny its pleasure in the morning simple light
> Nor its grave evening demand for love.
> Never to allow gradually the traffic to smother
> With noise and fog, the flowering of the Spirit.[1]

PERSONALITY

The study of personality is one of the major areas of specialization in modern psychology—I specialized in it in my graduate training—and a fascinating subject for almost everyone. Do I have a good personality or a bad one? Should I take a course in improving my personality?

By personality we usually mean an enduring and persisting set of attitudes, traits, motivations, beliefs, and response patterns that characterize an individual and distinguish him or her from others. The term *personality* is usually equivalent to *self* in everyday usage. "John is aggressive" and "John has an aggressive personality" are used interchangeably. From the inside, your personality is usually considered your ultimate identity: "I *am* a person who is against crime in the streets, is sympathetic, is motivated to succeed in business, believes in the Constitution, and responds coolly in emergencies," for example.

We value, defend, and cling to our personality, even when it has characteristics that cause suffering. The characteristics of our personality do set us up for suffering. If your personality is "moral," for example, then you can feel deeply hurt if someone accuses you of being "sinful" or "hypocritical." Personality traits that obviously create suffering, such as feeling fearful in situations that don't bother most people, are seen as qualities to correct by replacing them with a more valued trait of personality, not as phenomena that question the whole idea of personality. Indeed, we value "strong" personalities, people with very powerful or flamboyant characteristics. On radio and TV, the guest on a show is referred to as a "personality." Wouldn't it be wonderful if you could be a personality?

Modern psychology has recognized that for some people the overall structure of their personality is so pathological that they would be better off if it could somehow be destroyed and replaced with a "normal" personality. By and large, though, psychologists do not question the desirability of personality per se.

ESSENCE VERSUS FALSE PERSONALITY

The great spiritual traditions, on the other hand, have frequently condemned personality. Each of us is (or could be) something far more basic and important than we are. To the extent that personality consumes our vital energy and/or actively interferes with the discovery, development, and manifestation of our deeper self, it is an enemy of real growth.

Gurdjieff expressed this traditional dichotomy as the conflict between *essence* and *false personality*.

Essence is what is uniquely you. You were born as a unique combination of physical, biological, mental, emotional, and spiritual traits and potentials. Most of this is only potential at birth and may never manifest unless the right circumstances are created by your world, or by you yourself later in life. Some of these potentials are highly desirable in a universal sense: the essential delight of the blood, or the capacity for love. Others may be troublesome if they develop, such as an inability to delay gratification in favor of some later goal, or too quick a temper. Some of these potentials may be very general, the particular form of their eventual manifestation depending on your environment; others might be quite specific. You might, to create a very specific example, have an inherent talent for mathematics and music, find the taste of vanilla disgusting, have an exceptionally high body/instinctive intelligence for the kind of coordination and balance required for gymnastics, be very short-tempered, and have the physical potential to have babies.

As we have discussed at length in examining the enculturation process and the nature of consensus trance, your parents and your culture begin shaping your development from the moment of your birth. Certain manifestations of your essence are rewarded, some are simply neglected, some are denied and punished. This enculturation process is exceptionally powerful because its agents are so capable and knowledgeable and you are so helpless and ignorant by comparison. It is powerful because your physical and emotional well-being are at stake and because you have an inherent social instinct, a desire to belong, to be "normal."

From the inside, growing up is a mixed experience. In some ways it is wonderful to learn new things, to discover the knowledge and power of the culture. In other ways you are badly hurt and invalidated and must deny your essential self. In the course of her personal growth work, for example, my wife recalled a distinct childhood event where she finally gave up her own perceptions, which were constantly being invalidated by adults: she surrendered and decided she would just accept as true what they said was true. We have all gone through this kind of surrender, although more usually in a series of gradual surrenders rather than a single, dramatic giving in.

With each surrender of an aspect of our essential self, energy is taken from essence and channeled into supporting our developing personality. The original meaning of *persona*—a mask used by actors—is apropos here. Slowly we create a more and more comprehensive mask that is a socially approved presentation of ourselves, something that will get us acceptance and approval, something that makes us "normal," like everybody else. As we identify more and more completely with the mask, with personality, as we forget that we are acting a role and become the role, more and more of our natural energy goes into personality, and essence withers. As false personality becomes more powerful, it may itself work to stifle essence and use its energy for its own, self-important ends.

We can sublimate some aspects of our essential nature that are not allowed direct expression to partially salvage them. A few may persist because our culture happens to value them. For many aspects of our essence, their energy is either lost altogether or sublimated into false personality. For too many of us, too much of essence withers.

Gradually, with noise and fog, the traffic of consensus trance has smothered the flowering of the vital spirit.

Recall the essential potentials in the example above: an inherent talent for mathematics and music, finding the taste of vanilla disgusting, an exceptionally high body/instinctive intelligence for the kind of coordination and balance required for gymnastics, being short-tempered, and the physical potential to have babies. Obviously this person should study mathematics and music, be on a gymnastics team, not eat food with vanilla flavoring, try to learn to control her temper, and have babies. But what have a woman's chances been through most of our cultural history of going to college and studying math, or being a gymnast?

This exemplifies why Gurdjieff called personality *false* personality. A culture has its own ideas of the way people should be, and these ideas often take little heed of an individual's unique potentials. For most of our cultural history, the woman in our example would receive little or no education in anything, much less mathematics and music, would certainly not be allowed to use her body joyously in gymnastics, must less be trained in it, and would end up having lots of babies whether she actually liked this particular potential or not. Her quick temper would get her in trouble because it threatened male dominance, quite aside from its generally troublesome qualities. A few people are lucky: many of their essential desires and talents correspond to what is wanted in their culture. For most of us, regardless of sex, much of our essence is denied.

This denial can destroy our lives, for essence is the vital part of us, the truly living spark. It is the light that was found in meadow, grove, and stream, the earth and every common sight. As false personality eventually uses up almost all of our vital energy, the light fades, and life is a mechanical, automated set of habits, lifelessly moving us along with crowds of other lifeless, automatized victims, further reinforcing our depression and emptiness. Gurdjieff put it quite harshly, stating that many of the people you see walking down the street are dead. Essence has had so much of its energy stolen, false personality has become so mechanized and automatized, that there is no real hope for change: these people have become mechanical things, living mechanical lives, destined to die a mechanical death.

FALSE PERSONALITY MUST DIE

We are our false personalities, and yet . . . There is at least some essence still alive, still reachable. If there weren't, you probably would not be trying to grow. There is hope of real change.

This section has been about the nuts and bolts of false personality, the way it developed, the habits and defenses that sustain it. To really change, false personality must die. But not in a harsh, punitive way, not by way of superego attacks—they are part of false personality too. The death of false personality should be a transformation process, a recycling process, a skilled process based on the knowledge gained through extensive self-observation.

If you could just suddenly be your essence, it would be a great relief for a while, but eventually quite tiring. Essence stopped growing in early childhood, and it's difficult to live an adult life as a child. Gurdjieff reportedly demonstrated this by temporarily returning a person to essence, using a combination of unknown drugs and hypnosis.[2] Recall the phenomenon of hypnotic age regression discussed in Chapter 9. In my study of marijuana intoxication, I found one of the most common effects to be that of feeling more childlike and open, an obvious component of the drug's appeal.[3] For permanent results, though, we need to rediscover essence and then nourish it, love and cherish it, as a more enlightened parent would have done. Since we live in false personality, false personality has to use its best resources to do this.

Gradually essence can grow and begin to use the resources, knowledge, and power now automatically used by false personality. Instead of being the usual, say, 2 percent essence and 98 percent false personality, you can get a gradual shift toward more and more essence, more and more vitality and essential joy in life, and less and less false personality. This needs to be accompanied by the development of the higher kind of consciousness we are calling awakening. Then false personality is "dead" as a dominant, automatized center of control, but all its skills and knowledge are available as a tool to be used from a higher level of consciousness. We need the skills and knowledge now bound up in false personality for more vital goals than maintaining consensus trance. Sometimes we also need these skills to correct characteristics of our essence that are negative in our present reality, even if they are truly ours. Such correction of essence must come from a more awakened state that has first revitalized essence, however, not from the mechanical and roughshod suppression and distortion of essence that occur in enculturation.

The idea that false personality must die is misleading when the superego takes it up and uses it as fuel for more mechanical attacks on you. Yet the metaphor of death is quite accurate in another way, for the magnitude of change possible (and required) for full awakening is indeed like a death and rebirth. As so many spiritual traditions have said in one fashion or another, "Except ye become as little children . . ."

The theme of this section has been harsh. This has been necessary. Compared to what we could be, we are disspirited, entranced, mechanical, conditioned, automatized. We have created and we actively maintain a world of unnecessary stupidities and horrors. We have forgotten the soul's history through corridors of light. Our lips are cold instead of touched with fire when we tell of the Spirit. But the light is part of our nature and will not go away.

I do not know what full awakening would be like, as I have not personally experienced it. I do know what deep sleep is like, from far too much personal experience. I know that we can find so much light and joy and intelligence that our deepest sleep, our deepest consensus trance, does indeed seem like an unpleasant dream by comparison.

The final section of this book is about some of the ways you can begin to realize and understand the problems of consensus trance in yourself and, even more important, begin the process of awakening.

Part Three

Practices

16

Toward Awakening

Ideas about awakening, enlightenment, and spiritual growth are absolutely vital to us. They are also dangerous ideas. They are dangerous to the comfort and stability of our ordinary lives. If you have reached a certain level of development which I describe below as that of the "successful and perceptive malcontent," you should welcome this danger. If you haven't reached this level, these ideas will be of value, but also somewhat dangerous, for reasons discussed below.

DEVELOPMENTAL TASKS

Ordinary life is a series of developmental tasks. Starting as an infant, you must learn to crawl and then walk, to talk, to control your bowels and bladder, and so on. You especially must grasp the intricacies of language so that you can express yourself adequately. You must grasp the basic values of your culture and integrate and automatize them into your mental structure sufficiently to do and say the right things without undue strain. You must differentiate yourself from your parents, learn a trade, and support yourself. You must learn how to have friends and have a reasonably satisfying emotional life. Most of us must learn how to relate to a mate and be a parent. It's quite a bit to do, and none of us is perfect at it, but most people make a reasonable success of basic living.

Psychopathology as Failure of Development

A major form of psychopathology understood by Western psychology is that resulting from failures at these developmental tasks.[1] Thus from the developmental failure perspective, the neurotic doesn't know how to make friends or feel comfortable around other people or hold a job as a result of not learning common skills, or of mislearning them in some maladaptive form. Or the neurotic has failed to fully internalize consensus reality, to mold his consciousness so it automatically functions in a way that reflects consensus reality.

The psychotic has failed even more obviously at one or more of these developmental tasks, especially at internalizing consensus reality, or has developed other modes of functioning that severely interfere with ordinary skills, and now lives in an internal world simulation, a *non*consensus reality, so much at variance with the way the rest of us simulate the world that he is obviously badly out of touch with what consensus consciousness calls reality. Successful psychotherapy can then be seen as some combination of finding and eliminating the reasons for failing to grasp or practice common developmental skills, and/or teaching specific skills that were not learned in the course of development.

No one likes to feel he is a failure at ordinary developmental tasks. If you are, though, one way to apparently reduce the pain of it is to rationalize your failings by taking a new view: "I haven't failed. I've seen the wrongness and phoniness of what everyone else pretends is right and I've transcended it!" If you can't feel comfortable talking with people, for example, it's not that you haven't acquired some basic social skills, it's that other people are phony or cruel or uncaring. Naturally you, a superior and sensitive being, are not comfortable around them! If you can't hold a steady job it's not because you lack or won't use certain common skills, it's the fault of the capitalist system that exploits and oppresses the workers!

The fact that there is often much truth in these kinds of defensive views makes them all the more powerful. Of course people are phony and cruel and uncaring to some degree. Of course there is some exploitation and oppression of workers in almost any system. But ordinary people can be genuine and caring to an amazing degree, and jobs can be lost because you won't or can't do them right. Yet most ordinary people can be a reasonable success in getting along in life.

The Danger of Ideas about Awakening

Here is where the danger of ideas about awakening and enlightenment comes in. If you haven't mastered various ordinary developmental tasks yet, these ideas provide glamorous and prestigious rationalizations for avoiding facing your shortcomings and working on correcting them. "I feel uncomfortable around ordinary people because they are asleep, just like Gurdjieff said, so why should a sensitive soul like me, a person on the Path, associate with them?" "I don't stay long in any job because I see the phoniness in mindless enculturation. I am above such common and degraded things as being a steady, mindless worker." At best, these ideas are fuel for pleasant daydreams about your situation, which you are not really intending to change anyway. At worst, they encourage you to let go of the few social skills you do have and contribute to further maladjustment to your culture.

Maslow's Hierarchy of Needs

Abraham Maslow, one of the founders of humanistic psychology, realized that modern psychology was very one-sided with its emphasis on studying psychopathology and then developing models for ordinary people based on projections from this. He studied happy, creative people who enjoyed their life and felt fulfilled. From this study he developed, among other things, the concept of the hierarchy of needs. Lower needs usually have to be adequately filled before needs higher in the hierarchy, like creativity or authenticity, become very important. A starving man, for example, is not too concerned with his social image if sacrificing it will get him food.

From the top down, Maslow's hierarchy of needs is as follows:

SELF-ACTUALIZATION

SELF-ESTEEM

LOVE AND BELONGINGNESS

SAFETY AND SECURITY NEEDS

BASIC PHYSIOLOGICAL NEEDS

"Higher" and "lower" in this scheme carry no moral connotations. There is nothing "bad" about a starving man wanting food.

Self-actualization refers to an inherent need to fulfill yourself, to discover and develop and use all of your potentials and abilities to the fullest. Unfortunately, few people are able to do this. In Maslow's terms, this book is about self-actualization. The more you wake from consensus trance, the more you can actualize your higher self and potentials. Gurdjieff's ideas go far beyond Maslow's, however.

This hierarchy of needs is a dynamic scheme. You do not achieve some higher level of needs and then stay there all the time: even saints get hungry. You can also be concerned with higher needs even when your lower needs are not well taken care of: sometimes the suffering from lack of fulfillment of lower needs can galvanize you to seriously consider higher needs. In general, but with important exceptions, you are just more likely to be distracted by the lower ones, or confuse higher and lower needs, if there is not a reasonable degree of fulfillment of lower needs. Joining a Fourth Way development group, for example, could be counterproductive if what you are really trying to do is fill the need of having friends, one of the problems with group work we will discuss in Chapter 22. With increasing self-actualization, though, you spend more of your time and energy living in the service of higher needs.

THE SUCCESSFUL AND PERCEPTIVE MALCONTENT

The Fourth Way is intended to begin at a level of being that I call the successful and perceptive malcontent.

A successful person is defined for our purposes as someone who has reasonable mastery of the ordinary skills of his culture. He can hold a job, take care of basic survival and ordinary happiness needs, make and keep friends, have a reasonably satisfactory love life, raise a family if he desires, and so on. He can behave adequately by ordinary social standards.

The successful malcontent is not content with the reasonable level of success he has attained in ordinary life, however. Something or many things are wrong. What those things are considered to be is a function of the successful malcontent's perceptiveness and level of development.

If his level of consensus trance is still deep, he may buy the promise that *more* of the rewards the culture offers is what will satisfy him. This is a very frequent belief and one actively encouraged by the culture itself. It keeps people working hard and distracts their attention from deeper questions. We see innumerable examples of, say, someone who is very well off financially nevertheless working himself to death to get more and more wealth, never slowing down to enjoy life.

Rebellion against mainstream culture does not necessarily indicate any lightening of consensus trance. Since the seeds of rebellion are built into the culture itself, the successful malcontent may rebel against what he considers the wrongs of society and may be quite successful (by ordinary standards) in his rebellion. There are many things wrong that need correction, of course, so this is a very attractive path. The categories of "reformer" and "outlaw" and "rebel" are just as well known in our culture as that of "conservative," however, so outward rebellion may not raise any deep questions about the person's own consensus trance. You switch identifications from what is socially defined as "good" to what is socially defined as "bad," but you are still asleep in identification. This is not to say that we shouldn't work against injustice and rebel against the system when that is the most effective way to really help people. But, from the perspective of trying to awaken, to do so without transcending identification and other aspects of consensus trance is still mechanical and may reinforce our sleep instead of helping us awaken. Recall the discussion of lying in Chapter 13. Material goods, fame, power, success, and the like are not obstacles to awakening in themselves: it is our attachment to them, our identification with them, that creates the obstacles.

The successful and *perceptive* (in the important ways focused on in this book) malcontent, like successful malcontents in general, has tasted the rewards society has promised for being normal (respect, consumer goods, security, etc.) and the rewards for rebelling, and has found that while the rewards for either may be pleasant, they are not enough. Something vital is missing. The perceptive malcontent realizes that more material possessions or social respect or the romance of rebellion will not satisfy this need for something vital.

The successful and perceptive malcontent may outwardly appear to lead a very ordinary life, or may rebel externally against some aspects of his culture. But the successful malcontent isn't *forced* to rebel externally as a rationalization because he can't be successful at ordinary things: he can. If he rebels, it is a rebellion from strength, not weakness. He isn't necessarily rich or famous, but he gets by in a reasonable way. If he chooses to live a lifestyle that looks simple or impoverished by cultural standards, that is a genuine choice, not a lack of ability to earn more money. It is important here to distinguish what we really *need* to be reasonably comfortable and secure from the vast inflation of these desires by advertising and other forms of cultural pressure. What may be comfortable and happy by realistic standards may get classified as poor by the standards of a consumer society in which material greed has often replaced spiritual striving.

This is not to say that all aspects of a successful person's life are satisfactory, or that there are never any inner doubts or disappointments, or that they conform to social standards in all ways. If you wait for perfection in all ordinary things before trying to awaken, you will have a long time to wait! Since perfection is impossible at ordinary levels of life anyway, you will wait forever.

EXISTENTIAL NEUROSIS

Psychology began to recognize successful malcontents in the 1950s. Psychotherapists were used to treating ordinary neurotics, people who had not mastered all the ordinary developmental tasks and so weren't happy. They wanted to be "normal," to fit in and enjoy life like normal people. Then a new kind of patient started showing up, the people who were successful by social standards but who still weren't content. A typical complaint might be: "I'm a vice-president of the company I work for and may become president someday. I make good money. I'm respected in my community. I have a happy marriage and good kids. We take two nice vacations every year. Yet my life is empty. Isn't there anything more?"

Therapists called such patients "existential neurotics" to indicate that they were struggling with questions about the ultimate meaning of life rather than how to get along. This terminology, however, showed how much the therapists themselves were still caught in the delusions of our culture. Why was it "neurotic" to find that ordinary life wasn't enough? Now we can recognize that the successful malcontents were unhappy because their spiritual life was empty. Consensus trance really isn't enough for beings who possess the innate ability to wake up. "Existential neurosis" is actually a healthy sign of potential growth.

The analyses and practices presented in this book are for perceptive malcontents. They may well increase your discontent and, in some ways, alienate you from everyday life. At the same time it is vital that these ideas and practices not be used as excuses to rationalize failure at ordinary life tasks, or to be cruel and uncaring toward others, for that will pervert their potential and increase your delusions.

I worry that you, dear reader, may now get overly concerned with questions about whether you are successful enough and perceptive enough to be a "successful and perceptive" malcontent. If you have read this far you are probably perceptive enough, but how many imperfections are you allowed to have? Is a minimum income level required? What about those really crazy thoughts and feelings you sometimes have in spite of "passing for normal," those periods of self-doubt, and the like?

Be reasonable about this. If there are lots of ways you can't function at ordinary levels of accomplishment, you probably should work on those problems before you concentrate too strongly on pursuing these ideas about awakening—although some of the ideas in this book may help you improve ordinary levels of functioning. If you are a malcontent, but not a reasonably successful one, there is a real risk of distorting the purpose of this book to try to gain more of the rewards society offers, forgetting that its real purpose is to transcend society. That is the reason the Fourth Way is intended to start at the level of the successful and perceptive malcontent.

If you aren't sure, try these ideas and practices and see what happens. If they help you to take care of yourself and your loved ones satisfactorily and behave decently toward others with at least ordinary levels of success (without necessarily accepting the ordinary reasons for doing so), then they are worth pursuing. If the level of your consensus trance begins to lighten, so much the better.

SERIOUSNESS AND SECRECY

The various practices presented in this section were (and still are) intended for the serious, committed student. Some of them were originally given only in confidential teacher-student relationships. They were, in more dramatic terms, "secret practices." Why?

There are two major reasons for genuine growth practices to be secret. First, a given practice may be capable of producing such powerful effects that if you are not prepared for them, they could harm you or others. They are dangerous in the hands of the unprepared.

None of the practices I shall present are obviously dangerous, but they are powerful. Some of the insights they can lead to can be upsetting—a danger of any growth technique—but their effects should be beneficial in the long run. The upset potential also depends on your current level of maturity: thus my emphasis above that you should have reasonable mastery of ordinary developmental tasks before undertaking to awaken. If you have many defenses against things in yourself you don't want to acknowledge, the insights gained through self-observation can be upsetting, and you may want to work slowly, at a pace appropriate to you, rather than plunge into very intense work. If you are in a seriously disturbed state, and/or relying on psychotherapeutic care or tranquilizers to get you through ordinary life, I recommend that you not practice these exercises intensely until you have mastered a reasonable level of functioning in consensus reality. Just don't interpret "reasonable" as the level of perfect functioning your superego probably demands of you: I doubt that any real human being will ever reach that level.

The second reason why some of these practices have sometimes been secret has to do with your readiness to respond, the "shock value" they might have in requiring a radical reorientation. Think for a moment: how many techniques for improving yourself have you heard about already?

How many of them did you try at all?

How many of those that you actually tried practicing did you *thoroughly* try?

Most of us have heard of self-improvement practices that we thought we ought to try but never did. And there are others that we fooled with a little and, when we didn't see anything spectacular happening, stopped trying after a few attempts. Psychologically, this has resulted in an implicit (and perhaps explicit) attitude toward growth practices that has cheapened them ("There are so many, a dime a dozen"; "I know about those already; there's nothing interesting in what I already know"), associated growth practices with failure ("I already tried and it didn't work"), and blunted our sensitivity and possible response and commitment to new ones ("This is a tiny addition to the many I already know, which don't work anyway").

The Function of Secrecy

Secrecy is a useful way of handling these problems. If most techniques were secret, you wouldn't have the blunting effect of knowledge of so many you never really tried, or the attitude caused by the residues of many failure experiences from half-heartedly trying some. The presentation of a new growth technique would command far more of your attention than it does now. If, in addition, you had to prove yourself worthy of having a technique revealed to you, not to mention the "glamour" of being sworn to secrecy, even more attention would be given to the technique. It would have more surprise value, be more of an attention-getting shock. The result is that you would give a great deal of energy and attention to practicing the technique, and it would have a much greater chance of affecting you. For most growth practices, the old rule holds: it works if you work.

The last two decades have been a time of drastic change, though. Many of the "secret" techniques of spiritual paths are now available in paperback at your corner bookstore. We must deal with the dulling that comes from knowing so many techniques and the probability that it makes it harder to respond appropriately to new techniques. This is advantageous in some ways: secrecy appealed to parts of our minds that were more interested in power and glamour than in growth, for example, so there is now less feeding of that part of us.

A mature approach to dealing with new growth techniques must start with a full acceptance of the fact that we have been exposed to lots of them and have not practiced them. A superego attack is liable to result, of course: "You *should* have done those things because they were good for you. You're lazy, you're bad." You don't need to give any extra energy to the superego attack; in fact, you can observe it to learn more about yourself, as discussed earlier. The important thing is to accept the reality of your past. Similarly, accept the fact that you probably tried some growth techniques in such a half-hearted fashion that they didn't have much chance to work, so it's not surprising if you didn't get much from them. What was, was. Now the real question: what are you going to do with new growth techniques?

The Need to Focus

You should recognize that, realistically, you are not going to do much, if anything, with most of the growth techniques you are exposed to in the future. For one thing, there isn't enough time to deal with many of them, given the plenitude of them we now have. For another thing, some of them go in contradictory directions as practices, so you can't combine them. It's hard, for example, to practice some kind of enhanced awareness of the here and now while simultaneously trying to savor the transcendent sensations that can be produced by concentrating on repeating a mantra over and over.

Since you only have so much attention and energy to give, you must decide to focus on some particular growth technique that really appeals to you, and do it wholeheartedly for a long enough period of time for it to have a chance to affect you. Naturally you will fool around with a variety of techniques and systems first to get some experiential feel for them before deciding to make such a commitment, but once you have decided that practice X is for you, commit yourself to doing only it for a long time, say several months, and then *do it*.

This is the attitude with which you should approach the techniques in this book. If they appeal to you, play around with them a little to get a feel for them. Indeed, I do not expect you to believe many of the statements I have made about our being asleep, in consensus trance, until you find out for yourself by trying to awaken. This is the kind of experiential feel you need to get for the ideas and techniques. Be aware that you're playing around, not seriously working. Knowing this, it's realistic to expect some results from them, but nothing spectacular.

Suppose little happens. If the practices and the experiences you have with them are not very satisfying, don't just sort of forget about them: consciously tell yourself that they don't appeal to you that much and that you are *deliberately* stopping them. That creates a clean break, a clear ending. You may not have been ready to do them properly. But if you ever decide to come back to them in a more serious way, they haven't lost some of their potential by falling into that large mass of untried and half-heartedly tried practices that are associated with an "Everybody knows that!" attitude and failure.

Conscious Commitment to Practice

If you do find these ideas and practices appealing after some initial experience, I suggest you make a conscious commitment to do them intensely and wholeheartedly for several months. Making the commitment in writing, in a letter to yourself or a friend, is a good way of solidifying your commitment and realizing the seriousness of it. The length of time you commit yourself to serious work should be specified. You may want to consider doing the practices with a friend who is also interested in them, or otherwise associating yourself with others carrying out this kind of practice, such as creating a study group or joining a Fourth Way work group. We will consider these kinds of commitments at length in several later chapters.

A final note for this chapter, before we begin our discussion of self-observation. I have used the word *serious* several times now because a deep desire for awakening is important to make it possible. Our culture has too strong an association between ideas of "serious," "spiritual," "gloomy," and "killjoy," though. We are looking for the light, and while we often must be serious, we must also be able to be lighthearted. Essential joy is not gloom, even though being more aware sometimes makes you aware of and empathic with real suffering. Take yourself and your goal seriously, but always cultivate the capacity to laugh at yourself and your goal, and enjoy that laughter. Gurdjieff was a master at using humor and acting in terribly bad taste in order to shock people out of being overly serious. Sometimes the best possible resolution to some "problem" in the structure of your false personality is to be able to see how funny it is. Humor is absolutely essential on any spiritual path.

Self-Observation

For several decades we have possessed, but not used, a most interesting machine: the automated airliner.

As electronic instruments for navigation developed, it became possible to get more and more precise electronic fixes on exactly where an airliner was, moment by moment. You could know that you were over a certain city, what the distance to your destination was, and so on. Current satellite navigation systems allow you to know your position anywhere in the country to within fifty feet. Added to this were electronic systems that allowed a pilot to land "blind" when fog or other conditions made it impossible to see the runway. Electronic beacons allowed a precise fix: how far you were from each side and each end of the runway, how many feet in the air you were, and the like.

Simultaneously we developed precise ways to electronically operate the controls on a plane, adjusting its altitude or speed, raising or lowering the wheels, etc.

Finally, all these instruments and controls were hooked together. You could feed destination data into the control computer of an airliner and then just sit back and watch, or even get off the plane. At the set starting time the plane would start its engines, taxi to a runway, take off, fly to its destination, compensate for changing winds and weather on the way, land, and taxi to the airport, without a human hand touching a control during the flight. Such systems were tested not just in theory, but also in practice. The first ones had some bugs, of course, requiring pilot intervention en route, but they became very reliable: there was nothing for the human pilot to do.

Would you want to fly on a completely automated airliner?

Since we don't have any scheduled flights on completely automated airliners, in spite of having had the technology for them for some time, it's obvious that most of us don't want to fly in them. We don't trust complete automation when a failure could mean serious injury, probably death. We want a human pilot (and copilot) sitting beside those controls, ready to take over the instant any bug develops in the machinery. No matter how sophisticated the controlling machinery is, even if it's almost always reliable, that's not enough.

OUR MINDS AS AUTOMATIC AIRLINERS

From our discussions in previous chapters of the ways our consciousness becomes automatized and conditioned, you can see the analogy here: our body, mind, and emotions frequently resemble a completely automated airliner. Course and destination have been set by others, automatic mechanisms have been set, and your consciousness is not required for the trip.

Even before we consider the question of whether the programmed destinations are where you really want to go, it is obvious that there ought to be a trained pilot on duty to take over if there is a malfunction, or if unexpected conditions are met. But too many times the pilot isn't on the plane, or is taking a nap, or wasn't trained very well to begin with, or is so involved in a drunken party back in the cabin that he won't pay any attention to messages about being needed in the cockpit. While there hasn't been a crash bad enough to kill you (yet), there have been a lot of bad accidents, far too much unnecessary rough flying, and near misses with other planes that have seriously damaged them and you.

Creating the Pilot

Suppose you have gained enough insight into yourself to realize that you are trapped in a poorly functioning, automated airliner, going to a destination selected by others, surrounded by equally dangerous and misguided automated airliners. Where can you get a pilot?

Fortunately, from some points of view, there are lots of people around who not only claim to be trained pilots, they insist that they want to take over guidance of your airliner so you will have a smooth flight to a wonderful destination! If you will just turn over the little control you do have, and have faith in their vision, even if you can't quite understand it, they promise heaven. And they will be so happy to have saved you! Just join your local Buddhist Neo-Christian New Age Raja Guru Organic Enlightenment Commune, and all will be well.

Attraction to Self-Proclaimed Teachers

It is perfectly natural to be attracted to such would be teachers and saviors. For one thing, there is the childhood transference of the attitudes we had toward parents and other knowing adults, who often really did help us: some wise parent figure should be able to help us. Something inside us emotionally wants to follow a powerful leader. Second, we definitely can get help from others at times, so there is a realistic basis for hope. Third, there are lots of examples of people who have accepted this kind of help from others and who seem happier for it. And if you follow Guruguru Highfalutin Singin, his followers will welcome you and give you lots of social support for your decision.

Gurdjieff, however, argued that our problems result from having had a succession of outside pilots, so getting another new one is not a real solution. At best it can make you "happy," make your automatized psychological machinery run more smoothly and cater to your unrealistic emotional longings for a leader. You may feel better, but you remain in consensus trance, asleep. The content of your dream has changed— you now have "good" dreams instead of "bad" dreams—but this kind of dreaming doesn't help you awaken to reality.

Becoming Your Own Pilot

The Fourth Way that Gurdjieff taught is a matter of first learning how the airliner works, how your psychological machinery operates, and then becoming/creating your own pilot, a genuinely awake and knowledgeable part of your mind, that will fly your plane well and take you to destinations of your own choice. Understanding how your psychological machinery functions is the work of *self-observation*. Creating your own pilot is the work of *self-remembering*. We will discuss self-observation in this chapter and self-remembering in the next: in practice the two kinds of work eventually merge into and potentiate each other.

OBJECTIVE VERSUS SUPEREGO SELF-OBSERVATION

To see what self-observation that leads to awakening is, we must digress a moment to issues of social control, to examine something it is not, but is frequently confused with.

Anthropologists distinguish three general classes of social control mechanisms. The first and most obvious is direct force. A group can physically attack members who are behaving deviantly and injure or kill them. In less extreme form, property or privileges can be taken away. Control rests on interfering with the satisfaction of the lowest level of needs in Maslow's hierarchy, namely survival needs and needs for the avoidance of pain and discomfort.

This type of control is expensive, however. You need to have some members of the culture devote their time to policing others. These enforcers consume food and must be supported at community expense, instead of helping to produce food or other useful items. Physical resources have to be devoted to building police stations, courts, and jails. The more resources you have to devote to this level of control, the fewer resources are available for productive use.

By moving up higher in the hierarchy of needs, to the need for social acceptance, social control mechanisms can be constructed that do not use up so many human and physical resources. You need fewer policemen and jails. One such method is used in what are called "shame cultures." Building on the natural desire to be accepted, the harmony of the group is stressed. Children are enculturated and conditioned to feel especially bad when this harmony is disrupted. If people *knew* that you had done such-and-such a forbidden act, you would be so ashamed, you would disgrace them as well as yourself, and the harmony of the community would be shattered.

Anyone who saw you do the forbidden act would bring down this censure, not just a special class of police. For fear of being shamed, you refrain from doing the forbidden. If you can be sure that no one will know what you've done, though, it is very tempting to do it. It's not so much that the forbidden act is wrong per se, it's the shame that would come from being caught that is wrong. If you do the forbidden and nobody finds out about it, or knows it was you, you need have no bad feelings about it.

Building on the need for self-esteem, what anthropologists call "guilt cultures" go even further. Enculturation fragments the mind into the ego, the conscious part you ordinarily identify with, and the superego, the part that is above or superior to the ego. The superego mechanism contains the moral rules of the culture, an ability to detect when the rules have been transgressed and, most important, the power to punish you emotionally for transgressing. Indeed, a well-developed superego detects when you are just *thinking* about transgressing, "lusting in your heart," and makes you feel bad for even considering it. If you actually do something forbidden, the superego will punish you with guilt even if no one knows it was you. Guilt cultures not only require fewer policemen, they need even less attention devoted to watching other people in the group than in shame cultures.

Most cultures use a mixture of shame and superego control processes for keeping members in line, and there is considerable variation in how effective these mechanisms are in individual cases. Their effectiveness can be further reduced by the operation of various defense mechanisms. Some observers believe that American culture was primarily a guilt culture but is shifting more toward control through shame.

In a sense, then, the superego is a specialized mechanism for self-observation, useful, from the culture's point of view, for keeping individuals in line, for maintaining consensus trance. But it can be lethally deficient for promoting transcendent growth in at least three major respects.

First, as we have discussed earlier, the values the superego upholds are not *your* values: they are values others (your parents, your culture) chose for you and programmed into you with life-and-death intensity. Second, the superego is automated; it is a *psychological machine* and does not require genuinely conscious effort on your part to function. Third, the superego does not stem from an objective commitment to truth, a desire to know *what is really happening in spite of what I want or think I should want to happen*, but from a priori commitments to absolute values that may not apply to reality very well. Recall Chapter 2: "There is no God but Reality. To seek Him elsewhere is the action of the Fall." By ignoring reality, the superego's absolute morality may accomplish the opposite of what it intends.

Superego observation must not be confused with the type of self-observation we need to develop if we wish to awaken from consensus trance. We need to develop a style of observation that puts fidelity to reality above *all* other commitments. The superego can, of course, use the observations obtained from this neutral kind of observation to activate itself and launch an attack, but the attack becomes something to be observed from the more comprehensive kind of self-observation, rather than something to be identified with. Let us now look at some of the factors that can create that type of observation.

THE ABILITY TO OBSERVE YOURSELF

Your ability to observe yourself is a combined function of your desire to observe yourself, opportunities for observation, obstacles to observation, and the availability of special aids to observation.

Desire

If you have little desire to observe yourself and understand how your mind works, you won't see much. Sometimes life will force self-knowledge on you, especially in moments of great stress, suffering, or danger. We have all read of people whose lives changed overnight as a result of insights from some overwhelming crisis experience. That's fine when it happens, but how many more people have you never heard of because they weren't "lucky" enough to have such experiences? And how many more who still refused to see, and suffered, died, or didn't change? It makes sense to be thankful to life when it forces you to learn something about yourself, no matter how difficult it may be at the time, but waiting for such "accidental" forcings is not a reliable method of growth. One of the most high-powered growth experiences a person can have, for example, is the near-death experience, but most people who come that near death just die! There is so much to learn about ourselves, we must begin now.

Opportunity

When we think about opportunities to observe ourselves, we usually think of special times, such as a reflective moment at the end of the day, or what might happen if we could just live off in the woods by ourselves for a few weeks. Our usual implicit assumption is that we're too busy (and therefore too important?) to observe ourselves in the course of our ordinary life. It is precisely this assumption that Gurdjieff questioned.

The Fourth Way, said Gurdjieff, is a way *in life*. You don't need to retreat to a monastery, although temporary, special retreats can sometimes be useful. Indeed, a retreat situation is not generally useful for observing important aspects of your functioning: since you are away from your usual, habitual life, many of the most central aspects of your self are not being activated. Thus ordinary life is actually the best possible situation for observing yourself, as that is where you most fully manifest. Our ordinary life will provide us with just the variety of stimuli needed to activate our full range of functioning, for ordinary life is where that functioning was molded.

Obstacles

Obstacles to observing ourselves are of several types, including lack of motivation, distraction, lack of skill, and active resistance.

Lack of motivation will limit you to the few observations that life crises force on you. Even more, the attitude that comes from lack of motivation will limit you. We have an old saying: he who tastes knows. It's only true in the extreme, where the taste is so strong you are forced to pay attention and learn something about the world or yourself. More accurately: he who tastes has an opportunity to know. Whether he uses that opportunity is a separate question.

Distractions to self-observation abound. There is work to be done at the office, you ought to relax, here's an interesting movie on TV, someone wants to talk to you, how about that party tonight? More fundamentally, our culture does not encourage self-observation, except for the very restricted use of learning to follow the rules. You've been taught how to behave properly, and the rewards come from proper behavior: what's there to observe inside? To go back to our metaphor, the airplane is flying on autopilot and you're back in the cabin having a drunken party with lots of other pilots, who want to swap stories (often imaginary) about sex, money, feats of flying, and power. Your friends don't want you to leave the party, and they don't want to hear stories about planes that have crashed, so enough of this talk of going to the cockpit and checking the autopilot, or trying to figure out how the controls work, or even just looking around. The party is back here!

Social Pressure against Self-Observation

As children much of our early and most basic learning was through imitation. The adults around us almost never provided role models for self-observation, so it was implicitly ruled out at a very deep level.

School seldom, if ever, taught anything about it. Peer culture put its emphasis on external behavior. With our strong social instincts making us want to belong, is it any wonder that we automatically imitate the non-self-observers around us? Even today as adults we can run into considerable pressure if we tell friends that we are now trying to observe ourselves.

Most of us bring a great lack of skill to the practice of self-observation. In many other areas of life we are very skilled: think how much practice you have had at reading or dressing yourself, for example. How much practice have you had at trying to watch yourself *objectively*? Is it any wonder that we often find it very confusing to try to understand ourselves when we have had no practice in observing ourselves in a useful, objective way?

COMMITMENT TO TRUTH

The practice of self-observation begins with a desire and resolution on your part: "I want to know what really *is*, regardless of how I prefer things to be."

This is a resolution that must be constantly reinforced, as it goes against the tide of the automated processes of false personality and easily weakens and is swept under unless you actively *will* to know. Besides requiring will, it requires patience. It is definitely not the case that there are a few things it would be advantageous for you to know and you can find them out in a few weeks of effort. There are enormous numbers of things to know, and the commitment to self-observation should really be a commitment to an attitude to take actively for a lifetime.

It sounds like hard work. In one way, it is. In another way, it is pure pleasure, for it is nourishing one of your most essential qualities: curiosity. I can remember in my childhood that I routinely began every day by waking up with an attitude that was intellectual and emotional and instinctive, an attitude best described as "Wow! Another day! I wonder what interesting things will happen today!" It has taken many years of work on myself to get that attitude back.

It is important that self-observation become associated with our essential curiosity and the inherent joy of that curiosity. Otherwise it can become a hostile action, a sort of paranoid concern that there is always something potentially sinister hidden behind the obvious. That kind of specialized attitude can lead to the same sort of distorted, specialized self-observation as superego self-observation.

PRACTICING SELF-OBSERVATION

In its most general form, the practice of self-observation is simply a matter of paying attention to *everything,* noticing whatever happens, being open-mindedly curious about all that is going on. This everything will almost always be a mixture of perceptions of external events and your internal reactions to them. You should drop all a priori beliefs about what you should be interested in, what is important and not important. Whatever is, is an appropriate focus for observation.

This open-minded attention must be more than just intellectual attention. Remember that we are three-brained beings. Thus the attention we should strive to pay to our world and our selves is an emotional attention and a body attention as well as an intellectual attention. Saying the name of what you are observing to yourself is fine—unless you mistakenly think you are through with the observational process since you've named it. What feelings, if any, does it arouse in you? What effects, if any, does it have on the way you sense your body? Sometimes a given focus of observation only has one or two of these qualities, but we should strive to be open to all of them all of the time.

I cannot stress this point too strongly. Self-observation, indeed all observation, *must* strive at including all of our intelligence—emotional, bodily, and intuitive, as well as intellectual. *Believing that we fully know a thing just because we can give it a verbal name and associate other intellectual knowledge to it is one of the greatest failures of modern culture.* Indeed, we have been so thoroughly conditioned to think that we know something just because we have some words about it that it is a good idea sometimes to practice observation while actually inhibiting naming or thinking about the things you are observing.

To illustrate self-observation in myself at this instant of writing, I just paused to give some thought to what to say next. Glancing down, I notice that when I rest my hands on the edge of the keyboard, my right hand rests almost flat, but my left hand is turned so the index finger is much higher than the little finger, almost a forty-five degree angle. Hmm. That's interesting.

Both hands feel comfortable in these resting positions. Is there something asymmetrical in the muscles or tendons of my body as a whole, being reflected in this hand position? Perhaps I can answer that by paying attention to my body as a whole. Ah, yes, I sense that I'm not sitting symmetrically in my chair. My right buttock has a different pattern of pressure on it; it is a little farther forward on the seat than my left. What would happen if I straightened my body? Yes, both hands now rest flat and feel equally comfortable. An interesting observation on how I'm using my body.

Now the thought arises that I should break off this example, that if it gets too detailed I will lose my readers in detail instead of getting to the main point. The flavor of this thought, as I pay open attention to it, is realistic, but there is a small bit of the emotional flavor I've learned to identify as my superego. A whiff of disapproval. Hmm. What sort of "should" has been activated? Is it unseemly for a professor to mention buttocks? This could be interesting to follow, but my commitment to finishing this book is more important now, so I consciously decide to let the further observation of the thought go and continue with the main point.

The practice of self-observation, then, is the practice of being curious, along with a commitment to do your best to observe and learn whatever is there, regardless of your preferences or fears. I would have preferred to have some profound thought about Man and the Cosmos arise when I decided to illustrate self-observation, and I had a small fear in the back of my mind that nothing would come to mind. Instead I ended up writing about my buttocks! That is perfectly fine. What is, is. Ah, a further observation: my superego does not think this lack of selectivity in favor of the "appropriate" and "good" is fine at all!

Sometimes what you will observe are constant superego disapprovals and attacks. Indeed, the superego would like to take over your newly developing powers of self-observation to search even more deeply for signs of transgression. If that is what is happening, observe it. As you get good at self-observation, you will find that you don't have to identify with or get caught up in every superego attack; they become data, one kind of information among many, rather than overwhelming compulsions.

It is natural for you to want to observe the pleasant things about life more closely but to sleep more deeply when things are unpleasant and you are suffering. Too much of our conditioning has made us believe that we are not strong enough to handle the negative side of things, so it's best to ignore it. Our defenses will help us escape too much awareness of the negative anyway, won't they?

Yes, but at the price of maintaining and deepening consensus trance. Self-observation is to be practiced just as devotedly when you are suffering as when you are happy. Not because you hope that self-observation may eventually diminish your suffering—although it will have that effect—but because you have committed yourself to searching for the truth of whatever is, regardless of your preferences or fears. Indeed, suffering often turns out to be one of your best allies once you have committed yourself to awakening, for it may shock you into seeing aspects of yourself and your world you might never notice otherwise.

I cannot emphasize enough that you should try to observe yourself and your world with complete objectivity. To say this is to risk confusion, however, for part of you will argue, "Who can be really objective? How do I know that I am actually being objective and not just thinking I am?"

The answer will come from practical experience of self-observation rather than intellectual argument. You will discover that you have many ways of obviously (to the eye of systematic self-observation) being very subjective and distorted in your functioning. By paying attention, you can discover and control the mechanisms of distortion and learn to be more objective. This is a continual process. With more practice you will see that past times when you thought you were being relatively objective were actually times when you were quite subjective, but now you can see this because you've become more sensitive to the subtle flavors of subjectivity and distortion. You will never, to my personal knowledge, have an absolute guarantee that you are perfectly objective, but you will certainly have the experience of pronounced movement from deep subjectivity toward much more objectivity. That may be the best we can get. It is certainly a vast improvement over the subjectivity of consensus trance, and quite worth the effort.

Something I have observed in myself and others too many times is that we can create artificial limitations on our abilities by intellectual gymnastics. As one of my graduate students remarked in discussion, the way to learn self-observation is not by "pumping ontological iron," not by endless intellectual discussions of how well you will be able to do it, but by *doing it*.

Sometimes self-observation leads to quite remarkable and life-changing insights. Often it leads to more detailed attention to quite commonplace events. But what does *commonplace* mean other than the fact that you have classified something as repetitive and unimportant, and that classification has become part of the automated functioning of your attention, such that you don't pay any attention to it? You will be surprised how many commonplace things hide the extraordinary if you pay more attention and commit yourself to knowing the truth about them in spite of any preferences or fears you have.

Even the most ordinary things can gain a subtle but special quality when you deliberately observe them, as if some of the light lost in childhood is still there when you deliberately use your attention. It is there, of course, for the light is within you, waiting to be used. So yes, self-observation is work at one level, but there is something inherently rewarding about it. Further, the attitude of being open and curious, and the skill you gain at being able to pay attention, can be far more important than the particular observations you accumulate, for it may make you able to see something quite crucial in some future situation.

Focused Self-Observation

In its most general form self-observation means paying more attention to everything in your world and everything in yourself. It can and sometimes should also be applied in more systematic and focused ways. Be careful that the topic of focus is not always selected in an automatized way, though, or your defense mechanisms may steer you away from observing some area of life that might threaten you. Further, what your superego thinks you ought to study in yourself may not be what you really need to study. Having a teacher assign observational exercises can be very helpful here. An interesting exercise you can do on your own is to open a dictionary at random and devote some focused self-observation to the first topic on the page that is observable.

Observations on the way in which you experience and use your body can be very helpful in developing body/instinctive intelligence. Take a day, for example, to observe how you sit. In what posture do you sit in a certain kind of chair? Do you have more than one posture for that chair? How do you change from one posture to another? How do you feel in each of those postures? Are they comfortable? Are there strains? Are there any "shoulds" associated with the way you sit? If so, do they conflict with comfort? How do you sit in other chairs?

On another day, when you have already made repeated observations of how you sit, try varying the way you sit very slightly. What happens if

you slump a little? Sit a little straighter? Cross your legs when you usually leave them straight? Uncross them when you usually cross them? Are
there any emotional flavors to these activities?

Another day you can observe how you walk. On another you can
systematically observe the physical distances you maintain from others in various situations. On another you can deliberately change
those physical distances and see what happens. The possibilities are
endless and fascinating.

I recommend doing self-observation in simple situations at first, like
sitting or walking. As you get better at it, expand it to more and more
situations, especially interpersonal ones. They are harder at first, as
they are more likely to tap into strong emotions and consequent defenses, but eventually interpersonal situations become the most
rewarding of all to observe.

In these more focused forms of self-observation you must still strive
to observe with all of your being, not just your intellect.

A Note on Meditation

A particularly useful focused form of self-observation is the type of
Buddhist meditation know as vipassana or mindfulness meditation.

Set a time in advance, say twenty minutes, that you will practice.
Using a timer to let you know when the time is up is useful. While sitting
still and upright, with eyes closed, you try to observe *every* thought, feeling, or sensation that comes along. It is important to be totally
nonselective in this. There are no "good" experiences that you should
strive to have and no "bad" experiences that you should try to avoid.
Whatever arises, let each thought, feeling, or sensation arise in its own
way and time. Let it be itself and evolve as it wishes in its own time. Let it
pass away in its own way, in its own time. Do not deliberately hold any
experience to you or prolong it or shorten it or reject it. Do not identify
with it, or forcibly deny that it is you. Just let the stream of thought, feeling, sensation pass in its own way while you pay full attention to it.

This kind of meditation is not a substitute for learning self-
observation in *every* aspect of your life, but it is an excellent form of
specialized attention training. The instructions I give above are very
basic, but enough to get you started. If you find this practice appealing, it
is very worthwhile to find some group that teaches this style of meditation and get further training.

Further discussion of meditation would take us too far from the main thrust of this book, but excellent books discussing techniques and uses of meditation in many spiritual traditions are now available. A technical discussion of their effects in producing altered states of consciousness is available in my book *States of Consciousness*.

Earlier we looked at the question of just how objective you could be at observing yourself. Isn't it a matter of one part of you observing another part of you, one subself, one "I!" looking at another "I!"? Or is it more than many little observers looking at each other? Is there an Observer behind all this activity? A potential Master who eventually understands the horse, carriage, and driver, and begins to use them? I prefer to let these questions be answered by the experience you gain from extensive practice, rather than run logical circles around them.

SELF-OBSERVATION AND SELF-ANALYSIS

Each observation is like taking a photograph of yourself, a candid picture of your actual position in some situation. Occasionally single observations, single photographs, are very revealing. The collections of photographs, the mass of observations you gradually build up about yourself, can be even more important, though, for then you can start making comparisons and analyses, seeing patterns that are not at all obvious from single observations.

It is very important not to confuse self-observation with self-analysis, though. The latter is an intellectual activity that easily gets too abstract and may start to distort the facts. Indeed, some people are caught in endless loops of self-analysis that never lead them anywhere because the activity works mostly with fantasy rather than relatively objective observation of what actually happens.

Self-observation is like data gathering in science, where you strive to observe the facts as objectively as possible. Analysis is like the theory-building part of science, trying to figure out the hidden forces responsible for the facts you see. Analysis is a necessary and rewarding activity: it is always satisfying and sometimes helpful to figure out the "why" of things as well as appreciate the "what."

One of the purposes of self-observation is to eventually figure out the forces and beliefs and attitudes shaping your experiences, as well as to appreciate them. Scientists long ago discovered, however, that analysis is seductive. It feels good to think you understand things, and that feeling can lead you to get sloppy with the adequacy of your analysis, just to keep the feeling. Science has a rule that analysis, theory, must be continuously compared with existing observations and *always* tested against new observations, to make sure the analysis remains really useful.

The same rule must be applied to the analyses you make of your self-observations. Even when you think you now understand, keep on being open to the new, curious about what really is, in spite of any desires you have to retain the clever feeling your understanding gives you. In science there are supposed to be no "final" truths. All theories and understandings are treated as the best explanations we have at the moment, but are always subject to reexamination and revision in the light of subsequent observation. Observations are primary: explanations are secondary. The same rule should apply to our self-observations. Never let an idea you like get in the way to observing what is actually happening in your world and your self.

Self-observation sounds very simple, so simple that you may find a tendency to dismiss it with the idea "I do that anyway." You probably do, but only once in too great a while, and with implicit restrictions on what you apply it to. Try doing it deliberately. All the strings of words in this book are just that, just words, until you use the practice of self-observation to test their reality. If you diligently practice self-observation, you will see much that is painful and much that is joyful, but seeing more of reality will turn out to be highly preferable to living in fantasy. You will begin creating "something" in yourself, a quality, a function, a skill, akin to learning how the controls of your automated airliner work. And you will be pleasantly surprised at how much more there is to life.

18

Self-Remembering

One way of looking at the nature of ordinary consensus consciousness is to see it as fragmented. Because of defense mechanisms and buffers, the conditionings that were created in us in the enculturation process, and the shifting patterns of identification, we are not one. Our knowledge and skills are fragmented, dissociated. In contrast to the idealized picture of an enlightened man or woman drawn in Chapter 1, we do not have all our faculties, our tools, readily available for whatever life task faces us. If we compare our mental state to our body, it's as if parts of our body didn't respond when called on; for example, our hand doesn't pick something up when we want it to or, worse yet, lets go when we want it to grasp. An amputated member like a hand or leg, or a member not under our direct control, does us little good. Parts of our minds are dismembered, lost to us, and we have to re-member ourselves. In terms of our airliner analogy, the pilot must not only observe and study the airliner and its controls until he understands them; he must also get his faculties together, get his crew together, to exercise the needed skills to fly the plan.

Self-remembering is the term for gathering our dissociated faculties into a more unified whole. It involves a deliberate expansion of consciousness such that the whole (ideally) of your being, or at least aspects of that whole, are kept in mind simultaneously with the particulars of consciousness. It is remembering our body and our instincts and our feelings as well as our intellectual knowledge, and so promotes the development and integrated functioning of our three brains. This wider scope of attention prevents us from getting absorbed in and identifying with the particulars of experience and the automated functioning that goes along with such absorption. By creating a *deliberate* center of consciousness that is outside of the usual automated pattern of identifications and conditionings, we create a more awake, less entranced self, the foundation for the Master, with which we can both know ourselves better and function more effectively.

One of the practices Gurdjieff taught for self-remembering actually functions through literally re-membering ourselves, using deliberate attention to the members of our body as a reminder of our greater self, to anchor ourselves against the powerful currents of automated functioning that usually sweep away what little consciousness we have. It can be done at any time in any situation, and ideally should be practiced all the time in all situations, to the best of your ability. The practice is called *sensing, looking, and listening.* Although it is not the whole of self-remembering, I shall use the terms interchangeably in this chapter.

This form of self-remembering usually works more effectively if it is preceded by a more specialized practice in the morning. This practice, the morning exercise, has benefits in and of itself, and leads directly into sensing, looking, and listening.

PREPARATION FOR THE MORNING EXERCISE

This exercise, devised by Gurdjieff, performs many different functions. Among other things, it is a reminder, at the start of your day, that you intend to observe and remember yourself throughout the day. It also begins the processes of self-observation and self-remembering, a sort of priming of the pump. Some of my Awareness Enhancement Training students called it the priming exercise for that reason.

The morning exercise should be carried out before your mind gets seriously involved in anything else. Thus, if you are the type who starts thinking or worrying about things as soon as you wake up, you should start this exercise right after going to the bathroom. If, like some of us, your mind doesn't do anything for a few minutes after waking, you may want to move around a bit and wake up some first: otherwise you may just fall asleep during the exercise. Do not, however, fill your mind with other things first, especially negative things like listening to the news or reading the newspaper.

Sit upright in a reasonably comfortable chair. You don't want to be so comfortable that you'll slump and fall asleep again, nor do you want to be so uncomfortable that you're punishing yourself. Among other things, the morning exercise is a way of liking yourself, of deeming yourself worthy of a few minutes of undivided attention, so treat yourself kindly.

Close your eyes. For the first half minute or minute, just relax and gently pay attention to the fact that you're there. If you usually begin your morning with a short prayer, this is a good time for it. Now you are ready to begin.

THE MORNING EXERCISE

Now focus your attention on your right foot. You are not going to *do* anything with your right foot; you will just pay full attention to whatever sensations there are, at this moment, in your right foot.

It's important to realize that there are no "right" or "wrong" sensations in your right foot. Whatever you feel there at this time is fine, even if it's a lack of sensation or numbness. Actual sensations will vary: your foot might feel warm or cold, it might itch, it might tingle, you might feel the blood pulsing in it, a muscle might feel cramped or relaxed. One sensation might be relatively steady or the sensations might change from moment to moment. Don't reject any sensation or try to hold on to any sensation. As is the case in self-observation practice, what *is* is what's "right." What you are doing is paying open, sensitive attention to whatever is happening in your right foot *now*. Your only act of will is to keep paying attention to whatever you experience in your right foot rather than drifting off and thinking about, say, the work you need to do that day.

Paying full attention to your right foot does *not* mean gritting your teeth and fighting off any other sensation or thought that comes along. If your arm takes that moment to itch, or your stomach to growl, you'll feel it. You are a sentient being. But don't focus on trying to make your arm not itch or your stomach not growl or forcefully suppressing your thoughts about work. That strengthens these distractions. As soon as you realize you've drifted away from paying full attention to your right foot, just gently bring your attention back to sensing it.

These considerations apply to the entire morning exercise.

When you are in touch with your right foot, just keep paying attention to it for about half a minute. Sometimes it will take you a while to feel in contact with it, sometimes, especially as you get more practiced, you will focus in on the stream of sensations there right away. When you have focused in for about half a minute, you are ready for the next step. I emphasize *about* half a minute here: the point is to get in touch with whatever is happening in your right foot, not to count seconds or otherwise "evaluate" the experience.

Shift your attention focus. Now pay attention to whatever sensations there are in the lower half of your right leg. You don't have to hold on to contact with your right foot; just focus on sensing the lower half of your right leg. Pay open attention to the stream of sensations from it for about half a minute.

Now shift your focus and sense whatever is happening in the upper half of your right leg. Sense it for about half a minute.

When you've sensed the upper half of your right leg like this, shift your focus again so you sense whatever is happening in your right hand.

The attention pattern proceeds with half-minute sensing contacts to your right forearm, to your upper right arm, across your body to your upper left arm, and then down to the left forearm, then the left hand, then the upper half of the left leg, then the lower half, and finally the left foot. Don't go on to another part of your body until you've gotten at least some contact with each preceding part.

The time this part of the morning exercise takes will vary from day to day. If it's hard to focus your attention, it might take ten or fifteen minutes, whereas if your attention is under good control it can be done in five or six minutes.

SENSING, LOOKING, AND LISTENING

At this point in the morning exercise you begin a broadening of your attention span that leads you directly into the form of self-remembering that we call sensing, looking, and listening.

Once you have sensed your left foot for half a minute or so, broaden the focus of your attention. Simultaneously sense both feet, both legs (upper and lower halves), both hands, both forearms, both upper arms. Spend half a minute or so sensing the entire pattern of sensations in your arms, hands, legs, and feet all at once. For convenience we'll refer to this as sensing your arms and legs, understanding that the hands and feet are meant as well.

After you have sensed your arms and legs for half a minute or so, broaden the focus of your attention even more. While continuing to sense your arms and legs, actively listen to whatever sounds there are around you. As with the sensations in your arms and legs, there are no "right" or "wrong" sounds to hear or not to hear. While sensing your arms and legs, actively listen to whatever sounds are there to hear. You needn't talk to yourself in your mind about what you're doing (like "That's a dog barking in the distance"), but take a mental attitude of fully, curiously listening to whatever sounds there are while you sense, with the same sort of open curiosity, your arms and legs.

If you drift away into fantasy while sensing and listening, gently bring your mind back to doing it. This is not to say that you should never think about or simulate possibilities in your world while self-remembering: doing that is fine if you continue to self-remember. But when you have resolved to remember your self and you have lost it because of thought or fantasy, bring yourself back to your goal.

This practice of simultaneously listening and sensing your arms and legs can be done by itself as a meditation exercise, but here we only do it for half a minute or so as part of the morning exercise. Now, while continuing to simultaneously listen and sense your arms and legs, broaden the focus of your attention even further. Gently open your eyes and actively look around, so that you are simultaneously sensing, looking, and listening. You are now practicing a form of self-remembering.

Since vision is a dominant sense, most of your attention will go into looking. Hearing is also a very dominant sense, so the second largest portion of your attention will go into listening. Figuratively speaking, about 5 to 10 percent of your attention should go into sensing the sensations in your arms and legs. You should not, of course, ignore other perceptual sensations like taste or smell. I emphasize sight and sound as the exterior senses simply because they are so much more prevalent than others. If a smell wafts your way, actively smell it while sensing your arms and legs. And, as in the systematic practice of self-observation, your looking and listening should be with all of your faculties, your emotional and body/instinctive faculties as well as your intellectual ones.

You are remembering yourself. Continue to sense, look, and listen for the rest of the day. The goal is to become so proficient at it that you can remember yourself for the rest of your life.

DIFFICULTIES IN SENSING, LOOKING, AND LISTENING

When people first try sensing, looking, and listening, they frequently experience a certain kind of subtle clarity, a feeling of being more alive and more present to the reality of the moment. It is a kind of clarity that cannot be appreciated in consensus consciousness and, indeed, cannot really be adequately described in words. I find myself somewhat reluctant to even call it "clarity," for instance, as that word (or any particular word, for that matter) implies it's a steady, unchanging experience. It's not—there are variations—but you will discover that for yourself if you practice this kind of self-remembering.

The first time I practiced remembering myself, as a result of reading Ouspensky's *In Search of the Miraculous*, I saw instantly that this was something important and vital that I needed. *Three months later* I realized that I had stopped remembering myself a few seconds after I had started it! I have since found that my experience is not atypical. After the first moments of sensing, looking, and listening, people forget to keep doing it, in spite of the obvious improved quality of their mental state that they sense while doing it.

The act of sensing, looking, and listening is not easy. It is not that the practice demands a lot of effort: self-remembering requires a rather small amount of volition to deliberately spread your attention to several things at once. The difficulty is in maintaining the continuity of attention and effort that are required. In my experience, *self-remembering cannot become automatic: you must always devote a small amount of deliberate, conscious effort and attention to doing it volitionally.* Some other, beneficial and permanent changes will eventually occur in your mind and may become automatized, but sensing, looking, and listening must be actively pursued or you're not really doing the exercise. Such is the nature of real consciousness, as opposed to the automatized version of it we know as consensus trance. It takes a tiny bit of intentional consciousness to create more intentional consciousness.

Dealing with Superego Attacks

A common reaction to discovering (in consensus consciousness) that you've stopped sensing, looking, and listening is to suffer a superego attack. "I resolved that I was going to do this, and I've failed already. I've failed over and over again. I don't have the most elementary control over my own thought processes. I'm weak! I'm bad!" There may be little or nothing you can do about such superego attacks; after all, they come from a part of your mind that was deliberately constructed so that it would be out of your control. As with superego attacks resulting from the practice of self-observation, you may have to observe it without giving it any more energy than necessary. Indeed, you may learn important things about the structure of your superego from such observation. What is the exact "tone" of the "voice" in your head, for example? Whose voice is it? Lest the superego seem an insurmountable barrier, I should add that these practices can eventually cause it to wither away and be replaced by an innate morality, what Gurdjieff called real conscience.

More important, whether you're experiencing a superego attack or not, as soon as you realize that you've stopped sensing, looking, and listening, *start doing it again.* You will learn to self-remember by doing it, not by forever worrying or thinking about why you're not doing it.

Attention Like a Flabby Muscle

There is a useful analogy here for understanding initial difficulties in self-remembering. Our attention is like a muscle, a muscle that hardly ever gets used because our mental machinery has been automatized so that it easily conveys our attention along its automatic pathways without any real effort on our part. Now you are starting to use that flabby muscle for deliberate attention, but, being unaccustomed to deliberate effort, it tires easily.

If you want to develop your physical muscles, you know that you can't do it by taking thought. You have to push and pull and exercise and move weights, even though it is sweaty, tiring, and sometimes painful. Similarly the only way to strengthen the "attention muscle," so we can do what we wish with it, is to use it, over and over, in all kinds of situations. Then it will gradually get stronger.

AIDS TO SELF-REMEMBERING

There are a number of accessory techniques that can assist you in the process of sensing, looking, and listening. Remember that they are not ends in themselves, but only ways of assisting self-remembering. Eventually they may just become habits or otherwise not help. Then it is time to modify or discontinue them.

Scanning

One of the most common procedures for inducing ordinary hypnosis is to have the subject fix his eyes on some specific spot and keep them there. Since consensus consciousness involves a fair amount of automatized scanning of the environment, which contributes to the stability of that state of consciousness,[1] this fixation of gaze contributes a little toward destabilizing consensus consciousness and liberating some attention from looking at the external world so that the energy of attention becomes available for the hypnotist to use.

When you are practicing sensing, looking, and listening, you will probably find that letting your eyes rest steadily on anything for more than a few seconds is indeed "trance-inducing." Automated habits of perception quickly identify and classify the object you're looking at and effectively dismiss it. You then slide into ordinary daydreaming, forgetting to self-remember.

If you are working very hard at sensing, looking, and listening, or have become quite good at it, you can look fixedly at something and still self-remember, but until then it's definitely easier to self-remember if you combine it with an active visual scanning process. Look *actively, intentionally* at something for a few seconds, then shift your gaze and look actively at something else for a few seconds, and so on. By "look actively," I mean with curiosity, with intellectual, emotional, and bodily/instinctive openness, with a "What is it?" attitude, as opposed to passively letting your eyes rest on something without really giving it any mental attention. This active style of looking is essential to the practice of sensing, looking, and listening.

This kind of deliberate, conscious scanning makes it easier to maintain the quality of higher attention that frequently results from sensing, looking, and listening, and is especially useful to keep you from drifting back into consensus consciousness. Do it in moderation and with common sense. Don't let it develop into a mechanical jerkiness of your eyes or a habitual rhythm: if you're actually paying attention as you self-remember, it is clear that some things call for a brief glance, others a longer one. If something calls for long inspection, you may still find it useful to look actively at it a few seconds, glance at something else, then bring your gaze back. Experience will make the usefulness of scanning clearer.

Scanning is socially difficult when you're conversing with people who equate sincerity with steady gazing into each other's eyes. When you glance away every few seconds, the other person may think you are "shifty" or not interested, or have something to hide. With practice you can make some of your scanning seem like socially appropriate gaze shifts. My experience has been that you can actually pay more real attention to someone, more accurately perceive his state and intentions, when you are scanning and sensing, looking, and listening than when you gaze steadily into his eyes. Steady eye gazing is a powerful promoter of fantasy.

Microgoals

The goal of sensing, looking, and listening continuously, in everything you do, in every moment of your waking day, is a very high one. Because self-remembering is difficult, you are certain to feel as if you are failing if you take the goal in the wrong way or in a strict superego way. After all, you only have to not sense, look, and listen for a moment to fail for that day! The realistic part of you knows that there is no point in dwelling on failure. You are just wasting energy that could go into the practice of self-remembering. But being human, you find it easy to feel as if you've failed and get caught up by that feeling.

If we break the *macro*goal of sensing, looking, and listening every moment of the day into much smaller *micro*goals, we can have many success experiences that will encourage us. I could set the goal, for example, of sensing, looking, and listening from the beginning of this sentence I am typing to its end. There! I have succeeded. Now I can try another microgoal task.

Short tasks with a clear beginning (such as the moment you resolve to self-remember) and a clear end are excellent for this microgoal assistance to learning. Washing the dishes, walking across the room, going to the toilet, saying "Hello" to someone you pass on the street are excellent opportunities. Traveling by car also presents fine opportunities for microgoal self-remembering. "I will sense, look, and listen until I reach that billboard on the next curve. Good, I'm there, I've done it. Now I will try sensing, looking, and listening until I reach the freeway overpass I see ahead," and so forth.

Breadth-of-Focus Reduction

Sometimes it is difficult to sense the whole pattern of sensations in your arms and legs while actively looking and listening. The pattern may be too diverse, or you may just be having difficulty focusing on it. Trying harder is always worthwhile, but sometimes you still don't get anywhere. In such cases, simplify.

While actively looking and listening, simultaneously sense just the sensations in your arms; don't worry about your legs. If even that's too much, sometimes just simultaneously be aware of the sensations in one hand while you actively look and listen. Then, as you get better at it, you can expand to include more of your arms and legs. Remember, only about 5 to 10 percent of your attention is going to sensing your arms and legs anyway; you're mainly looking and listening.

A similar way to reduce the effects of overload is to narrow your external goal. If you can close your eyes without creating any problems, you could practice just sensing and listening for a while. Or you might try focusing on sensing your arms and legs while looking at people's body movements, but letting the listening go for the time being. These reductions are temporary measures, though, for we want to develop an increased ability to take in the world while remembering ourselves.

There will be times when you naturally increase the breadth of bodily focus. I have emphasized sensing your arms and legs because they are neutral areas of your body, their sensations exist in the here and now, and so can help anchor you to the here and now. Sensations from more central body areas like the gut may come in at times. When they occur naturally, it is perfectly all right to include them in the part of your attention that is being used to sense your arms and legs, or you may put them in the foreground of attention, as contrasted with simultaneous sensing of your arms and legs, in order to perceive them more clearly. But don't force attention on central body sensations at this early stage of practice. We sometimes have traumatic memories associated with central body sensations that we may not be ready to deal with yet, and also there are psychological and emotional "control points" in the central body that we do not want to inadvertently activate in our current state of poor self-knowledge.

THE UNIVERSALITY OF SELF-REMEMBERING

Self-remembering, like self-observation, is intended to be a universally applied practice. *Every* aspect of life is to have sensing, looking, and listening applied. The same rule holds for self-observation. Eating, walking, talking, swimming, making love, arguing, urinating, praying, feeling good, feeling bad—all are material for sensing, looking, and listening.

You will be tempted to practice sensing, looking, and listening selectively, perhaps doing it when something nice is happening to enhance the pleasure, or trying it when in emotional pain to see if it will reduce the pain. This is especially likely when you first begin these practices and still have too low an idea of what you are capable of. It is better that you are at least self-remembering then rather than not doing it at all. If we keep up such selective practice, though, we have given up the pursuit of truth for the pursuit of pleasure, and are distorting the practice in a way that will cause trouble and suffering later. Recall once again:

> There is no God but Reality.
> To seek Him elsewhere
> Is the action of the Fall.

Whenever your attitude is that you want to know what really is only as long as it is what you like, you set yourself up for trouble.

SELF-OBSERVATION AND SELF-REMEMBERING

I have described self-observation and self-remembering as distinct practices. They are different in some ways, but in others they are rather similar, such that self-observation can start to become self-remembering. Both involve the deliberate use of attention, and both can give you clearer perceptions of your world and yourself. The major difference is in the source of the attention.

Self-observation can be done from the level of false personality. One "I!" observes aspects of its behavior. In the case of partial or full co-consciousness of "I!"s, something likely to come about with dedicated practice, one "I!" can observe some of the functioning of other "I!"s. Ordinary mind pays attention to ordinary mind. You can see something more clearly than normal but may not see the biasing characteristics you bring to the observation or notice that you are getting absorbed in the observation.

Self-remembering can observe the same contents of world and experience, but the level or source of observation is different. The deliberate volition employed in splitting attention, so that you are observing much better than ordinarily while keeping something else in attention simultaneously, such as the sensations in your arms and legs, creates functioning on a level outside of your ordinary mind. You do not get absorbed in what is happening; there is a way in which *you*, in a much greater sense of the term than it is ordinarily used, exist independently.

The words I use to describe this difference are not very satisfactory. I know what I mean through direct experience, but our language is not satisfactory for conveying it.

Our parable of the horse, carriage, and driver can be helpful here. Sometimes the driver notices qualities of the carriage, or that his clothing is not stylish and will make a bad impression on other drivers. He notices them from the kind of perspective that is innately his as a driver. At other times the horse notices aspects of the driver's behavior, but it notices them from a horse's perspective. The body odor of the driver may convey very clear things to the horse, for example, that are not even noticed by the driver, but the style of the driver's clothing means nothing to the horse. This is like self-observation: we bring much of our ordinary, automated, consensus trance, false personality perspective to it. This is not to say it isn't useful: it is very useful and absolutely necessary as a starting point in the Fourth Way.

Self-remembering is like the Master arriving on the scene and observing it. The Master is outside of, different from, the transportation system of horse, carriage, and driver, even though he may use it and be affected by it. The Master can observe and involve himself with it, but continues to know he is something different from the horse, carriage, and driver. From this superior, external position, he may see and do things that are impossible for the horse or the carriage or the driver or the combination of them. In self-remembering you are more vitally yourself than ever, and yet you are more than, somehow distinct from, your ordinary self.

Again I am not satisfied with these words. Yet I know they will communicate quite well to someone else who has some experience in self-remembering. I am trying to communicate some knowledge that, to refer back to Chapter 1, is partly state-specific. So take as much as you can from this description, but make it real by practicing self-remembering.

This chapter has discussed the beginnings of self-remembering practice. Sensing your arms and legs while actively perceiving your world is a technically convenient way to begin. The ultimate aim is to remember *all* of your self. This *all* is beyond our knowledge at this point, but we have a beginning.

I do not like the melodramatic sound of it, but the truth is that long-term practice of self-observation and self-remembering can totally change your life.

19

Higher Levels of Consciousness

We began this book with a definition and brief discussion of states of consciousness. Let us quickly review that.

We defined a discrete state of consciousness for a given individual as a unique configuration or system of psychological structures. The parts or aspects of the mind we can distinguish are arranged in a certain kind of pattern or system. There is always some variation in the exact way our mind functions at any moment, but one of these overall patterns can persist for some time and remain recognizably the same. There is an overall "feel" or "taste" to the pattern of a state.

The structures operative within a discrete state of consciousness make up a system whose parts stabilize each other's functioning by means of feedback control, so that the state maintains its overall pattern of functioning in spite of some changes in the environment. Yet when certain key environmental stimuli come along, the pattern can break down and be replaced by another, as when some personal remark causes a transition from one identity state to another.

A state is an altered state if it is discretely different from some baseline we want to compare things with. Since we usually take ordinary waking consciousness as our standard of comparison, a state like nocturnal dreaming is thus an altered state. Other well-known examples of altered states are the hypnotic state, states induced by psychoactive drugs such as alcohol, states centered on strong emotions such as rage, panic, depression, and elation, and states induced by meditative practices.

We commonly speak about our ordinary state of consciousness as if it were one. Given our discussions of identity states, we now can see that ordinary consciousness is a collection of identity states. Since most identity states function within the allowable limits of consensus consciousness, they are not recognized as altered states in the way some obviously different state like hypnosis is. Each identity state is an aspect of consensus trance. Using ordinary consciousness as a baseline to declare other states as different or altered may be the best we can ordinarily do, but it lacks much precision.

The formal definition of states of consciousness that I gave in Chapter 1, drawing from my earlier scientific work, has a characteristic that was deliberately chosen for its original usage: it is free of values. It is intended to be an accurate and purely technical description of the mental and emotional functioning of consciousness, whether the particular state being described is that of someone buying a pair of shoes, a saint at his devotions, or a depressive adrift in the slough of despond.

Since I originally introduced this definition of states of consciousness as part of my attempts to legitimize the study of altered states within the scientific community, this value-free approach was necessary. Many scientists believe science should not deal with values, as this will distort "objectivity." This is true in many instances, but becomes a dangerous half truth when it is interpreted to mean we should never deal with emotions or values in any way.

We definitely need to not confuse evaluations with observations. If you think you are talking about the factual form of events when you are really talking about your feelings and values, you are doing poor science—or living your life poorly. You make a similar mistake if you believe you are discussing values when the issue is one of external facts.

At the same time, values are not just *subjective*: they are observations and conclusions of the emotional brain. Depending on the quality of functioning of your emotional brain, they may be neurotic fantasies or they may be the most important aspects of a situation. To ignore them is to ignore parts of reality. As discussed in Chapter 14, this leads to the wrong work of the three brains and distorts our functioning. It has also led to a great distortion of our view of the universe in modern science. Because it ignores the emotional and intuitive side of life and pretends to an objectivity it doesn't have, modern science is full of implicit, hidden, and often debilitating emotional assumptions and values that have injured the human spirit. My study of the hidden assumptions of Western psychology will be useful to readers wanting to pursue this.[1]

A totally value-free orientation, especially when it is based on fear and poor understanding of the functioning of the emotional brain, will not work if we want a comprehensive science of life. It certainly is not desirable for us here, given the practical orientation in this book. Our discussions have often had a technical flavor, yet have repeatedly dealt with questions of finding greater happiness and fulfillment in life.

How can I clear up the distortions in my life, wake up from consensus trance, transcend my culture's limits, and discover the reality of the world and of my own essence? How can I be more effective in improving the quality of life in this world? How can I attain unity instead of my current fragmentation of many "I!"s? Such aims contain a set of values: clear perception is better than distorted perception, freedom is better than bondage, and so on. From this perspective, various states of consciousness are better or worse, helpful or hindering, higher or lower. The state the saint is in may be much more helpful, higher, than that of the buyer of shoes or the depressive, at least, as we discussed in Chapter 1, when appropriately used.

FOUR LEVELS OF CONSCIOUSNESS

Gurdjieff described consciousness as capable of functioning at any of four major levels. Various states can exist within each level. We can call these levels (a) ordinary sleeping and dreaming; (b) consensus consciousness or ordinary waking, more aptly called consensus trance when we value states; (c) genuine self-consciousness, characterized by self-remembering; and (d) objective consciousness. They constitute, among other things, a progression from fragmentation to unity.

Ordinary Sleeping and Dreaming

The level of ordinary sleeping and dreaming is just what we usually think it is—our mental activity (or lack of it) in bed at night. Gurdjieff seldom bothered to distinguish the sleeping state from the dreaming state within the level of sleep. He did not work with nocturnal dreams, except as an analogy: when we wake from nocturnal dreaming into consensus trance, we generally feel that our mind is so much clearer than it was while we were dreaming. Similarly, when self-remembering, when in a state of genuine self-consciousness, our mind is as much clearer than consensus trance as consensus trance is much clearer than nocturnal dreaming.

Nocturnal dreaming is a state involving very high levels of simulation of reality. A whole dream world is created. Compared to consensus

trance, our experience covers a much wider range in nocturnal dreaming. This is because the simulator is not constrained by external stimuli
to any significant degree. There is no visual pattern coming in through
the eyes that has to be included in the simulation, so any visual scene can
be simulated. The only constraints seem to be internal, given by false
personality characteristics and defense mechanisms, and these constraints are more relaxed than in consensus trance. The quality of "I!"
can be added to almost anything, hence the "uncharacteristic" actions we
sometimes find ourselves doing in dreams.

Consensus trance is a level of consciousness in which we can practice
the activities of self-observation and self-remembering, and so is a much
higher level than the blankness of nocturnal sleep or fantasies of nocturnal dreaming.[2] There is a very real sense, though, in which nocturnal
dreaming is a much safer state than consensus trance. In nocturnal
dreaming our physical body does not carry out the actions we dream
about. Jumping off a dream cliff or hurting dream people does not result
in broken bones or having an enemy when we wake up!

Modern sleep research has demonstrated that there is actually an active paralysis of our muscles when we dream, so that we can't act out our
dreams. There is no such protection in consensus trance, however. As
we have seen, we have only a partial orientation to the actual reality of
the physical world, other people, and our own feelings. We are living in
a waking dream. The world simulation process is going on in consensus
trance, just as it is in dreaming. There are more restrictions on it than in
dreaming, for there is massive sensory input that has to be fitted into the
simulation. Our various false personalities have been thoroughly
enculturated, further limiting the range of our simulations, our thoughts
and feelings, whereas our dream selves have been largely left alone after
initial invalidation. But we can act on the basis of our distorted perceptions, thoughts, and feelings, affecting ourselves and other people in the
process. The reactive consequences of our external actions in consensus
trance are a major cause of useless and stupid suffering.

Consensus Trance

About one-third of our lives is spent at the level of nocturnal sleeping
and dreaming, the remaining two-thirds in consensus trance. Consensus
trance is actually a collection of identity states. Here we walk and talk,

make and break promises, make love and war, and *imagine that we are in the third state of consciousness, genuine self-consciousness.*

We have already discussed the characteristics of consensus trance in detail throughout this book, but I want to stress this one additional aspect here. We already believe we are genuinely self-conscious, that we know what we are doing, that we make our own decisions, that we understand our own minds, that we are one. These particular illusions are especially pernicious, for if we don't know how much we lack genuine unity, self-consciousness, self-understanding, and volition, it doesn't occur to us to seek these things. Further, when we do hear of them, we tend to reduce them to ordinary levels of thought and so destroy their potential power to transform us.

Sometimes in the writing of this book I have thought, "This whole effort is wasted. No one will believe he has to work very hard to create faculties he believes he already has!" Yet the need to do this is crucial for our survival: will automatons in consensus trance bring peace to our planet? Certainly argument alone, no matter how cleverly I do it, will not really communicate our condition, but if I have enticed you to begin practicing self-observation and self-remembering, your own experience will get my points across.

Genuine Self-Consciousness

The third level of consciousness, the state of self-remembering, is our natural birthright. In it we would have the qualities we falsely ascribe to ourselves in consensus trance. We would be genuinely self-conscious of our actions and internal states, see the world clearly, have all three of our brains functioning well and harmoniously, comprehend our essence desires, and have true will to do what we wish. We are finally one. We can genuinely say "I am," for there is a real self there that is far more alive and important than the passing identity states of consensus trance.

For most people this third state, unfortunately, occurs only as rare flashes interrupting consensus trance, and is almost immediately forgotten as we sink back into sleep. I hope this statement is or will become false for you as a result of practicing the self-observation and self-remembering exercises in the previous chapters.

As you will understand from earlier chapters, and even more from your own attempts to observe yourself and to awaken, it is difficult for people to realize that they are in consensus trance. Indeed, a special perverse reaction further insulates people from this knowledge; if you tell someone he is not genuinely self-conscious, he will probably partially wake up for a second and be closer to some kind of self-consciousness as he denies that he is unconscious! Stress sometimes has the effect of making us focus much more strongly on the here and now, thus taking energy away from our illusions and bringing us closer to reality, making us feel more alive. This is why dangerous sports are popular with some people: better to be alive and in danger than dead to reality and essence. It is even better to learn to be more alive by self-remembering!

An important distinction should be made here between self-remembering as a practice and genuine self-consciousness as a level of functioning that may or may not result from the practice at any particular time. Self-remembering is a process, a particular kind of mental action you carry out, trying to create an observing and integrating part of your mind so you know what you are doing with yourself. You can work hard or less energetically at it, and you can have varying degrees of success. The *state* of self-consciousness may be a *result* of your attempts at self-remembering.[3]

At times you make the attempt to self-remember and immediately attain the state of genuine self-consciousness. A clarity of perception of both the external world and your own inner processes occurs, and a hard-to-describe quality of genuinely existing in a new, real way. Self-consciousness, this third state of consciousness, may last for only a moment or for longer periods. When the individual instances of it occur more and more frequently and each lasts longer and longer, it is more clearly recognizable as a distinct state of consciousness.

There are other times, far more frequent when you first begin practicing self-remembering, when the main experience you have is not of a new and wonderful clarity but a realization of how difficult it can be to get clear, of the power of the automated thought processes that are driving your life. There has been a shift in your depth *within* the level of consensus trance, or clear observation of it, but no attainment of the altered and higher state of genuine self-consciousness.

An analogy I find quite apt is underwater swimming. It is as if my mind were a swimmer in a river. Thoughts, feelings, sensations, and external events are waves and currents in the river. Some are very minor, some are very powerful. Sometimes I am near the surface of the river, near the light that comes from above, and can see more clearly. At other times I am way down in the depths, where the currents are very treacherous and powerful and the water very muddy.

Self-remembering is like trying to swim toward a definite goal instead of being passively swept along by the currents of the river. There are times when my attempts to remember myself, to perceive where I am and swim toward a goal, only show me that I am in dark bottom waters, caught in powerful, murky currents, hardly able to fight them at all, much less make progress toward my chosen destination. At other times I am better able to remember myself and find myself in clearer, calmer water, able to perceive my surroundings much better and to make some progress swimming toward my goal. And there are moments when my head breaks water and I get a lungful of wonderful, pure air, rejoice in the joy of being alive, and see my goal clearly and swim toward it.

Self-remembering is the swimming. The light and the world above the river are the goal of genuine consciousness. The mud and currents of the river are our own automated minds and the pressures of consensus reality that function to keep us in consensus trance. The moments of self-remembering in which we only see how deeply in the murk we are and how little we can do are discouraging. Yet they are vitally important, for we are trying to swim, developing the will to swim, and learning how to swim. It is analogous to building up your muscles. You can't do any feats of strength at first, and the effort in training is unpleasant, but one day you find you are much stronger and do things that would have been a great strain with almost no effort.

This analogy fits some of my own experience very well. It often feels as if I am battling powerful and murky currents of thought and feeling when I attempt to self-remember.

Objective Consciousness

Gurdjieff defined the fourth state of consciousness as a state in which *you see things as they really are*. It has all the qualities of the third level of consciousness, such as the unity and integration of the three brains, but makes them more permanent by resulting from a change of *being*, not just conscious functioning. More specifically, you perceive and understand a whole new range of realities about yourself and the world because two new centers or brains begin to operate. You can begin to understand some aspects of the fourth level of consciousness from the third level; you can understand very little from the second level of consensus trance.

Thus this discussion is a pointing to the fourth level, not a definition or accurate description of it. Take it as inspiration, or a reminder that our possibilities are far greater than ordinarily thought, but do not take it literally!

In Chapter 14 we discussed man as a three-brained being, as having emotional and bodily/instinctive centers for taking in and processing information which are just as much "brains" as our intellectual functioning. Gurdjieff claimed that in addition we have two more centers, the higher emotional center and the higher intellectual center. Each of these higher centers is tremendously more powerful and intelligent than the ordinary emotional and intellectual centers, and each operates far more rapidly than the ordinary centers. The higher emotional center includes what Gurdjieff called "real conscience," as opposed to the relative, conditioned morality of consensus trance. Both of these centers are part of our natural heritage as human beings and are fully developed and operational, but it takes great work on one's development to create the third-level foundation for contacting and utilizing them. They are already taking in and processing information about our selves and our reality. *But* our ordinary selves are disconnected from their output. We ordinarily don't even know they exist. It reminds me of a saying attributed to the Buddha following his enlightenment, on the order of "Wonder of wonders! All men are enlightened, but they don't know it!"

The Computer Analogy to Higher Centers

Living in the computer age, we have an excellent analogy for this situation. Each of us has a little personal computer of our own. It runs slowly, has only a small memory for data, and very little data stored in it. It uses three rather primitive programming languages for computing: Intellectual Basic, Emotional Basic, and Bodily/Instinctive Basic. It can function very well for many of the needs of ordinary life if we use it efficiently. We rightly love and admire this little personal computer, for it is a marvelous, even if limited, machine. Indeed, we have identified with it: we think its thoughts are our thoughts.

What we have forgotten, in our attachment to and dependence on our little personal computer, is that there is a way of programming it so that it will act as a terminal to connect us with a giant supercomputer. This supercomputer runs far faster than our personal computer, has an enormous memory full of vital facts ordinarily unknown to us, and uses two very sophisticated and powerful languages for computing that solve all sorts of important problems that can't be adequately dealt with in Intellectual Basic, Emotional Basic, or Bodily/Instinctive Basic. These languages are Higher Emotional and Higher Intellectual.

The most important questions of our lives could be answered if the supercomputer worked on them in Higher Emotional and Higher Intellectual, drawing relevant knowledge from its vast data banks. But alas! We aren't connected. We try to solve these vital problems on our little personal computer, but we can't solve them in any of the various Basic computer languages. Just as certain jokes in Hungarian may not translate into English without losing their essence, their funniness, certain things make sense only in Higher Emotional or Higher Intellectual. This is the kind of state-specific knowledge we talked about in Chapter 1.

INEFFABILITY OF HIGHER STATES KNOWLEDGE

The ordinary, level-two knowledge we have about objective consciousness comes from the little we know about altered states of consciousness and the unusual moments we vaguely call "mystical experiences" that can occur in them. People have insights into their own nature and into the universe that are experienced as the most important things in the world, understandings that can totally alter the directions of their lives. But to describe them to others, and even to themselves once they are back in ordinary consensus consciousness, they must use ordinary thoughts and languages. "All life is one," for example, or "God is love," or "All reality is both void and full."

The better reporters agree that their consensus understanding and descriptions, which may be the best they can do, are not very good and may even be badly misleading, *especially to people who have not had similar experiences themselves.* The knowledge and insight that are perfectly clear when expressed in, say, Higher Emotional, are badly garbled in Emotional Basic or Intellectual Basic. The poor reporters confuse the garbling and distortion of these higher-level insights by their automatized minds with literal truth.

This is what is meant when we say that certain knowledge is "ineffable." It is not comprehensible in ordinary consciousness, in consensus trance, but it is quite comprehensible, sensible, in some nonordinary state of consciousness. The reality and importance of state-specific knowledge is what led me to propose creating sciences to study it some

years ago, a proposal which may be of great interest to technically inclined readers and research scientists.[4] Gurdjieff claimed that there are
people around who, through their efforts, can reliably function at the
fourth level of consciousness: such people would be able to communicate quite clearly with each other.

State-Specificity of Higher Centers

Although Gurdjieff describes these two new centers as "higher," my
knowledge of altered states makes me suspect that they are also specialized
and state-specific. Because of this, our computer analogy breaks down
when pushed too far. In the ordinary world you could use a big mainframe
computer to balance your checkbook, just as you could use a small personal computer or a hand-held calculator. The mainframe can duplicate all the
functions of the personal computer, even though it can do far more. I
doubt that the higher intellectual center would really be useful for balanc-
ing your checkbook, though: it's designed to handle very profound
problems that can't be solved at all by the ordinary centers.

Our insistence that everything of importance should be understandable
in consensus consciousness terms is another kind of example of the wrong
work of centers. Ordinary centers, even if brought up to a level of proper
functioning instead of staying at their usual uneducated and neurotic level,
probably can't solve certain problems. My research with altered states
suggests this very strongly: ultimate questions about the meaning of life
and death cannot be adequately answered in ordinary consciousness.

If a person has been totally blind from birth, he may reason about vision.
He may come to some clever, partial understandings, but he will never really understand the beauty of a sunset. Until we have at least flashes of
objective consciousness, we will never fully understand the nature of life.

It is tempting to write at length about altered states of consciousness
and the fascinating possibilities (as well as traps) they have for us, but this
book is primarily focused on waking from consensus trance and reaching
the third state of genuine self-consciousness, so I shall write no more here.
Further, I have also found, as Gurdjieff stated, that until we clean up and
refine the functioning of our three brains and achieve a goodly measure of
self-understanding and genuine self-consciousness, both the personal experiences and secondhand knowledge about altered states or objective
consciousness we have can be so badly distorted that we can sometimes be
better off without them.

Ideally we should be thoroughly prepared in this way before experiencing any altered states, much less fourth-level states. Unfortunately, our culture is now so disspirited, so lost in its scientistic world view, that we desperately need inspiration, flashes of the higher levels, to remind us that there is something to work for. Even at the risk of distortion of higher-level knowledge, I believe some experience with altered states is essential for many people.

Spiritual Reality, Work, and Prayer

Work as if everything depends on work.
Pray as if everything depends on prayer.
—G. I. GURDJIEFF

Gurdjieff's ideas contain so many useful psychological understandings and techniques that it is possible to study them on a purely psychological level. That is, you can profit from them without any interest in or acceptance of "spiritual" ideas, ideas that we are more than our physical bodies.

In some ways this is fine. So much nonsense has been promulgated in the name of the spiritual that our culture's aversion to it has many healthy aspects. At the same time I am convinced that there are vital spiritual realities, and if we do not come to terms with them and spiritually evolve, we and our civilization will die. To believe anything and everything because it is labeled "spiritual" is the height of foolishness. To automatically disbelieve anything and everything associated with the idea of the spiritual is just as foolish. Intelligence, discrimination, and personal experience are what is needed, not blind belief or disbelief.

I focus on Gurdjieff's teachings as a psychology in this book because that is how I best understand them. I do not want to give the impression that that is all there is to Gurdjieff, though. His psychological ideas were imbedded in a very elaborate and sophisticated spiritual system. In common with many great spiritual systems, it is a world view that sees the entire universe as an integrated, meaningful, and alive manifestation of the Absolute. Man has a place and a function in this alive, evolving universe. His function interlocks with those beings higher in the scale of the universe, beings who would be considered "nonphysical" or spiritual in ordinary terms. That man has fallen into the insanity of consensus trance and lost touch with his true possibilities and functions is a tragedy. The Fourth Way is not just a way of optimizing programming in your organic biocomputer: it is a system of spiritual growth, eventually going beyond organic, physical life as we know it so that man can regain his true function and happiness.

I will not attempt to explain Gurdjieff's cosmological and spiritual ideas any further here. Much has been written about them in the works cited in Appendix A, and my own understanding of them is meager: they are not the sorts of things easy to test in everyday experience. I must present several of Gurdjieff's idea as "Gurdjieff says . . ." statements in this chapter because they go beyond my personal experience; it is a presentation I have largely avoided in the rest of this book, but it would give too incomplete a picture if I did not do so.

What I shall do in this chapter is present an interesting example of the kinds of events that are truly "higher" than our ordinary functioning, an example associated with my attempts to share some of my understanding of the human situation. It is time we had a respite from the necessary focus on the pathology of consensus trance anyway. I shall then use this example to illustrate something about the idea of prayer.

MARY'S DREAM

In November of 1981 I began an experimental program for applying some of what I had learned about awakening from Gurdjieff and other sources. It was called Awareness Enhancement Training, and I worked with it for two and a half years. It consisted of teaching people basic processes for self-observation and self-remembering, providing evening meetings to allow sharing of the problems encountered and insights discovered, and a weekend retreat in the country each month for intense group work. The weekend group work entailed a variety of physical work activities (in conjunction with self-remembering) connected with the construction and maintenance of the retreat facilities.

More than a year and a half before I began this Awareness Enhancement Training work, one of the people who would later become a student, Mary, had a dream. She had been keeping a regular dream journal at the time. The following dream made no particular sense to her when she had it, but she recorded it and forgot it for almost three years. Here is Mary's dream.

It's a hot summer day. I am riding in a van with a group of people.

We arrive at a building, sitting on a kind of terrace in the country. It's being restored, people are working on it. A man steps down from a long ladder leaning against the outside wall which faces south. He carries a paint bucket, and I comment on the chestnut color of the paint, because it seems to have a tinge of purple in it.

We are led into a rather bare kitchen, with an original old, rusty-looking stove. Some food is cooking and the owner, who met us there, allows me to dip my finger in it for a taste—gooey stuff. He is nondescript and wears nondescript gray clothes.

We look around the kitchen, there's not much to see, then go through the back door outside. I am a bit confused because we have been inside the house, yet have only seen a sort of kitchen.

Outside it's gorgeous, high, brittle summer grass, trees, and rolling hills, above blue skies and a blazing sun. It feels very good.

We walk behind the house, it's shady there, and we are told that the previous owners are buried there. One woman in the group gets pretty hysterical, saying they are not in coffins, but mummified bodies covered with some mulch. I tell her there's no reason to be afraid of the dead, and go to have a look myself.

There are two "graves," a man's and a woman's. I stand in front of the man's grave. I can see the outline of his body through the thin layer of soil. I feel very much at ease. In some way I communicate with him and know for sure he is going to talk to me. After a while there are breathing movements that ripple through the soil over his face, then an undulating movement goes through the mulch covering the whole body. He jumps up, shaking off the dirt, laughing, and saying he was hired by the owner to act out the authenticity of this place, and that this was the reason for our coming here.

Mary had been working at Awareness Enhancement Training for over a year when on one weekend retreat she suddenly realized that she had been at the place of her dream, working on reviving from "death," from consensus trance, for over a year! Consider these striking parallels:

It's a hot summer day. I am riding in a van with a group of people.

- Even though the training program's first weekend retreat was in November, it was a warm, beautiful day, and most weekends were like that. Summer days at the retreat center in Mendocino

County are usually hot, in contrast to typical summer days in Berkeley, where Mary lived.

- Students often car-pooled, coming up in one of the students' vans.

We arrive at a building, sitting on a kind of terrace in the country. It's being restored, people are working on it. A man steps down from a long ladder leaning against the outside wall which faces south. He carries a paint bucket, and I comment on the chestnut color of the paint, because it seems to have a tinge of purple in it.

- The retreat building is a large rectangular building, built on a prominent, artificial terrace on a hillside.
- The group was constantly working on it, both maintenance and new construction, since it was not fully functional when the training program started.
- There was much work on ladders on the outside walls. As several students were afraid of working on ladders, this ladder work was emotionally salient and often talked and kidded about.
- The most striking external feature of the building is its long, south-facing wall, which has numerous floor-to-roof translucent windows.
- The building is painted a deep, rich brown. Painting jobs were a frequent part of the group work.

We are led into a rather bare kitchen, with an original old, rusty-looking stove. Some food is cooking and the owner, who met us there, allowed me to dip my finger in it for a taste—gooey stuff. He is nondescript and wears nondescript gray clothes."

- The kitchen is at one end of the twenty- by sixty-foot building, which is all open inside except for a small sleeping loft at the end opposite the kitchen. It is bare compared with a normal home kitchen. The gas stove is an antique, a little corroded and rusty.
- The students rotated cooking among themselves and usually produced what can best be described as feasts. The quality of the food was generally so interesting and delicious that there

was frequent kidding that in addition to Awareness Enhancement Training (AET), the group was devoted to Eating Awareness Training (EAT)!

- I, the owner, almost always wear old, nondescript jeans and a faded grayish-blue work shirt when I am in the country, including the times when I worked with my group.

We look around the kitchen, there's not much to see, then go through the back door outside. I am a bit confused because we have been inside the house, yet have only seen a sort of kitchen.

- The inside of the building is open, fourteen feet from floor to ceiling, and largely unfinished and in the process of further construction. By ordinary standards it is ambiguous as to function, except for the kitchen area, which is clearly defined and fairly conventional.

Outside it's gorgeous, high, brittle summer grass, trees, and rolling hills, above blue skies and a blazing sun. It feels very good.

- A perfect description of the setting, and the usual feelings about being there.

To this point we have had a strikingly accurate and rather literal description of the physical characteristics and surroundings of the retreat center. It is these parallels that called attention to the dream. In investigating psychic dreams in the past, I have noted that they sometimes begin with such an obvious physical parallel to a situation in order to call attention to themselves, and then get on with a more meaningful and emotional message.[1] The remainder of the dream is easily seen as dealing with Mary's deep feelings toward the work of awakening.

We walk behind the house, it's shady there, and we are told that the previous owners are buried there. One woman in the group gets pretty hysterical, saying they are not in coffins, but mummified bodies covered with some mulch. I tell her there's no reason to be afraid of the dead, and go to have a look myself.

- Gurdjieff described many people as dead, even though they walk and talk, because their essence is effectively dead. The purpose of the Awareness Enhancement Training work was to wake the students up, revivify them, restore the life that was buried when essence was drained of energy by false personality.

- Students often brought up fears and ambivalences about waking up, giving up the security of the known and attending to the unknown.

There are two "graves," a man's and a woman's. I stand in front of the man's grave. I can see the outline of his body through the thin layer of soil. I feel very much at ease. In some way I communicate with him and know for sure he is going to talk to me. After a while there are breathing movements that ripple through the soil over his face, then an undulating movement goes through the mulch covering the whole body. He jumps up, shaking off the dirt, laughing, and saying he was hired by the owner to act out the authenticity of this place, and that this was the reason for our coming here.

- A major function of the retreats was that I and the students would serve as "alarm clocks" for each other, to wake each other from consensus trance, and to model a state of greater awareness and aliveness. The authenticity of the place indeed lay in showing how one could arise from the living death of consensus trance.

What are we to make of Mary's dream? Let us first discuss prayer.

PRAYER

Prayer is not a fashionable topic in contemporary intellectual and scientific circles. Meditation, preferably of an interesting and exotic Eastern variety, may be in with the avant-garde in some intellectual circles, but prayer? That is left for the uneducated who need superstitious practices to comfort them.

Although people often use the terms *prayer* and *meditation* interchangeably, this causes confusion. An atheist can meditate, even if he cannot logically pray to a nonexistent God. Meditation properly refers to internal psychological practices whose intent is to change the quality or state of consciousness of your mind. Its efficacy comes exclusively from the skill of the meditator. Prayer, on the other hand, is effective insofar as there is a "supernatural" or nonordinary order of Being or beings who might respond to it. Some practices, which may be termed either meditation or prayer in common conversation, have the qualities of both meditation and prayer as we are using the terms.

Petitionary Prayer

The most typical kind of prayer can be more accurately termed petitionary prayer, a petition to someone more powerful than the one who prays, a being who has the power to grant a request through nonordinary means if it is so inclined. In our culture, that "someone" usually means God, Jesus, a saint, or an angel. Saints don't receive that title until they have been long dead in Catholicism, so petitionary prayer is almost always addressed to a nonphysical being. Since Scientism (the function of science as a dogmatic religion) long ago rejected the existence of nonphysical beings, prayer, by definition, cannot be heard. Even if there were other intelligences in the universe existing in some physical form, how could they hear thoughts that exist only in the mind?

Scientism, in its most charitable mood, sees prayer as nothing more than a subjective effort of possible psychological or psychiatric interest, perhaps doing something useful for the person who prays. In its more typical mood, Scientism sees prayer as a degraded example of superstition and nonsense that we would be much better off without.

Scientism's attitude toward prayer is not based on what I would describe as extensive and high-quality scientific research on its effects. Indeed, there has been almost no research at all on prayer (if we don't count research on extrasensory perception or psychokinesis). A genuinely scientific attitude toward prayer would be to admit that factually we know almost nothing about it, and that dogmatic and a priori rejection of the possibility that prayer has effects beyond the psychological is not good science.

A Mechanism for Prayer

While there is almost no scientific research on prayer per se, there is an extensive body of research data on *psi* (pronounced *sigh*, like the Greek letter), the general name now used to cover manifestations of both extrasensory perception (ESP) and psychokinesis (PK). Although it is ignored and rejected for largely irrational reasons beyond our scope of discussion here, a body of more than seven hundred careful parapsychological experiments has shown that humans occasionally show three kinds of ESP as well as PK. Briefly, telepathy, mind-to-mind communication, is one kind of ESP. Clairvoyance, the direct perception of the state of matter without the use of the physical senses, information that is not known to anyone at the time, is the second kind. Precognition, the prediction of future events that have not yet been determined, is the third kind. Psychokinesis is the direct influence of mind on matter without the intervention of known physical agents, such as influencing the fall of dice by wishing alone or, as is common in experimental research today, biasing the operation of electronic random-event generators by wish alone.

What is quite interesting and relevant to our discussion of prayer is evidence that people can use psi without knowing that they are doing so. Experimental demonstrations have shown that a person may unknowingly scan a situation by ESP and discover that if he "just happens" to do a certain thing out of many likely possible actions, he will end up in a more favorable situation than if he doesn't.[2] Enough people end up doing the right things that we know some sort of unconscious ESP is being used.

If we see prayer as a way of contacting "nonphysical" (in terms of our current concepts of what is physical) levels of reality or beings, ESP is the obvious communication mechanism, and some sort of PK is the means for changing reality so that a person is "lucky." To the extent that we can use these psi abilities unconsciously, we have a mechanism for unwitting prayer, for our hopes and fears can then affect our reality in an unusual and psychic way, as well as in usual ways.

Laboratory manifestations of psi are usually very small in size, small deviations from chance outcomes, and are usually quite unreliable. This can be partly attributed to lack of skill in trying to use psi, but another part may be due to the inconstancy and inconsistency of our desire. Gurdjieff claimed to have performed some very impressive psychic feats as a result of having learned to integrate and unify his being, but he did not put any emphasis on psychic abilities. Compared to the goal of awakening, conscious control of psychic feats is of small importance, and the many crazy ideas we associate with them in our culture may act as further barriers to awakening. My point in briefly introducing psi here is simply to show that we have some basis for prayer, and for the unwitting use of prayer, in laboratory research.[3]

Attitudes toward prayer probably derive mostly from personal experience in both scientists and laymen. We may pray to be granted something that we want very much. Sometimes we get it, sometimes we don't. If we think that prayer should be infallible, especially if it's fervent prayer stem-ming from strong desires, we are terribly disappointed if we don't get what we want, and may then reject prayer. Failed prayer can be a deep emotional hurt and color our attitudes for the rest of our life. Answered prayer can similarly affect us in a positive way. Experiences of apparent answers or lack of answers to prayer are especially formative in child-hood, when emotional intensity is high, so that an experience then can fix a lifelong attitude, an automated view.

Efficacy of Petitionary Prayer

Gurdjieff looked at the efficacy of petitionary prayer as a function of the intensity and consistency of a person's desires, whether they were de-liberately praying or not. Although he did not spell out the psychic mechanisms of connection to higher levels of reality or higher beings, he believed that our thoughts and feelings can have effects on such higher levels. Thus a consistently held desire for something acted as an unwitting "prayer," a petition or direction of intention to higher levels of reality, whether that desire was expressed as a formal petitionary prayer or not.

The man who thinks about getting money all the time is in effect pray-ing for money with unwitting prayer, whether he thinks of himself as a religious person or not, whether he gets down on his knees and formally asks God for money or not. The man who imagines tragedies befalling him is effectively praying for them. Our habitual attitudes affect our life in many ordinary, psychologically understandable ways, of course, but un-witting prayer is another way in which we create our life, sometimes with tragic (even if wished for unconsciously) consequences. As Gurdjieff fre-quently expressed it, your being attracts your life. Many other things affect your life, of course, but your attitudes and identities affect your world in many ways that tend to create reflections of themselves.

Effective petitionary prayer for Gurdjieff, then, is intense and consis-tent desire and thought. However, most petitionary prayer, formal or unwitting, has almost no effect.

First, because the ordinary person is plagued by shifting identities that have disparate and often conflicting desires, the unwitting prayers of various identities tend to contradict and largely cancel one another. Random alternations of "I desire X" and "I'm not interested in X, give me Y," and "I hate X" do not give any consistent message to higher levels of the universe.

Second, an obstacle to effective prayer is our inability to be *consciously intense*. Ordinary emotions, triggered by external events and reacting predictably and mechanically with our automated false personality patterns, may temporarily produce strong desires, strong formal or unwitting prayers, but external events change and the instigating desires disappear.

A person in a life-threatening situation may genuinely and intensely pray, "Dear God, save my loved one's life and I will never sin again!" The loved one recovers (an event that may or may not have any relation to this prayer), the stress disappears, and the promise never to sin again fades away. We do not remember (all of) our selves. This lack of control over emotions is related to the alterations in our false personalities, of course, since most false personalities have specific emotional cores.

Effective petitionary prayer would be much more possible to a person who was genuinely conscious, who, at will and for extended periods, deliberately summoned up the intellectual and emotional intensity to pray consciously without distraction. If he prayed from his more integrated and constructive subpersonalities or from his essence, better yet. Praying from the third level of consciousness, remembering yourself while you pray, is the most effective of all.

WHO OR WHAT ANSWERS PRAYER?

Consider Gurdjieff's somewhat paradoxical statement:

Work as if everything depends on work.
Pray as if everything depends on prayer.

Gurdjieff felt strongly that we must work on understanding and transforming ourselves with no expectation of any sort of outside help, natural or supernatural. Only *I* can transform myself, only *my* efforts count. The strength I have is the strength that comes from making efforts. I cannot grow stronger muscles by just wishing for them, nor can someone else magically make my muscles stronger. I have to push and pull and strain, pushing myself to and a little beyond my limits over and over again: then I get stronger muscles. Why should psychological growth be any different? From a strictly psychological point of view it seems obvious that wishing and praying are fantasies that divert us from what we actually need to do. We are better off to just get on with the work.

Yet Gurdjieff also said to pray as if everything depended on prayer. We must ask for help from a higher level, recognizing that our work efforts will come to nothing unless we are helped from above.

In his practical teaching, he emphasized work effort, not prayer. His students generally had so many distorted and incorrect ideas about "higher" ideas like prayer that there was no point in teaching much about it until they had done enough psychological work on themselves to clean out the aspects of false personality which would otherwise sabotage most efforts at genuine prayer.

STATE-SPECIFIC VIEWS ON PRAYER

The paradox between the injunctions to work as if everything depended on effort and to pray as if everything depended on prayer can only be partially resolved in our ordinary state of consciousness. I have found that a fuller resolution requires considerations derived from altered states of consciousness.

In proposing the idea of state-specific sciences some years ago, I noted that our ordinary state of consciousness is limited and arbitrary in many ways.[4] In our ordinary state we do not have access to the full range of human perceptions, logics, emotions, and possibilities of action, but only to a specialized selection of them. This selection is generally useful for everyday problems of survival and fulfillment in our particular culture, but quite inadequate for other human issues that go beyond the everyday. We have discussed these limitations in detail in earlier chapters.

From the point of view of my ordinary consensus consciousness it is perfectly obvious that everything depends on my own efforts. Realistically I also recognize that the effects of my efforts are modified by the desires of others, by the limits imposed by physical laws, and by chance. I can pray for a million dollars to materialize in the middle of the floor so I can finance my next research project. It's a worthy project, I'm sure! But nothing happens. I'd be better off reading books on how to raise funds through normal channels. Funny things sometimes happen, but I can write them off as luck (whatever that means) or chance. If I seriously consider the possibility that higher levels intervene, they do so rarely and in ways that are often contradictory to what I want. Ordinary consciousness makes it obvious that we are separate, finite, quite undivine beings who had better depend on our own efforts.

The Altered-States View

As I write this in my ordinary state of consciousness, though, I can dimly and partially remember insights and understandings I have had in some altered states of consciousness. At times it has been perfectly obvious to me that we are not separate, isolated beings, that we are a part of a divine plan, that our prayers come from our deeper selves, which are also a part of that plan, and that our prayers are answered in the ways that are best for our evolution. The lack of answer to a prayer from some aspect of false personality can be the best possible answer. From the altered-states perspective I know how limited my ordinary-state perspective is and how foolish I am, in my ordinary state, to identify completely with my ordinary-state perspective as if it were all of the truth.

I stress that these are *dim* memories. If I completely identify with my ordinary-states perspective, I can easily talk myself out of them: they were strange ideas in states of temporary "craziness" and are best ignored. How could I possibly believe, for example, that there is a loving purpose for a world in which concentration camps ever existed? Yet I know that the next time I consider these ideas while in an altered state they will not be dim; they will be as clear and obviously truthful as the ideas I have now in my ordinary state. So I have learned to try to remember that they are part of my overall understanding and should not be simply ignored, even if they may not be immediately applicable to everyday life, even if paradox seems to be part of the reality I must live with.

This does not mean, incidentally, that altered-states knowledge is always necessarily true, just that it is part of our overall knowledge base as fully functioning human beings. Recall that we defined *states* as different, but not necessarily better or worse, configurations of consciousness. Each state has its strengths and weaknesses. You can be insightful or deluded in any state, and your degree of this is the quality of within-state enlightenment we discussed in Chapter 1. Also, knowledge from a higher *level* of consciousness may not always be applicable to this level. Altered-state and altered-level knowledge, like ordinary knowledge, needs to be constantly tested, refined, and developed. Yes, this feels like a revelation and I like it. Now I need to take it as a *possible* truth and see how well it fits with the rest of my experience, and how much I can use it.

The paradox between work being all and prayer being all, then, is a paradox only when viewed from the limitations of a single state of consciousness. When I use my intelligence either in my ordinary state or in an altered state to remember that there are other points of view, and that all these points of view may be fragmentary rather than any one being "truer" than any other, the paradox disappears.

CONSCIOUS PRAYER

Gurdjieff described a process of "conscious prayer." It is one of those practices mentioned earlier that partakes of the qualities of both meditation and prayer. Conscious prayer is a psychological process of *recapitulation*, in which we consciously remind ourselves of intentions and knowledge. The effectiveness of such recapitulation is a function of the degree of consciousness we bring to it. It is best done from a state of self-remembering.

> . . .These prayers are, so to speak, *recapitulations*; by repeating them aloud or to himself a man endeavors to experience what is in them, their whole content, with his mind and his feelings. And a man can always make new prayers for himself. For example a man says—"I want to be serious." But the whole point is in how he says it. If he repeats it even ten thousand times a day and is thinking of how soon he will finish and what will there be for dinner and the like, then it is not prayer but simply self-deceit. But it can become a prayer if a man recites the prayer in this way: He says "I" and tries at the same time to think of everything he knows about "I." It does not exist, there is no single "I," there is a multitude of petty, clamorous, quarrelsome "I"s. But he wants to be one "I"—the master; he recalls the carriage, the horse, the driver, and the master. "I" is master. "Want"—he thinks of the meaning of "I want." Is he able to want? With him "it wants" or "it does not want" all the time. But to this "it wants" and "it does not want" he strives to oppose his own "I want" which is connected with the aims of work on himself. . . . "To be"—the man thinks of what to be, what "being" means. The being of a mechanical man with whom everything happens. The being of a man who can do. It is possible "to be" in different ways. He wants "to be" not merely in the sense of existence but in the sense of greatness of power. The words "to be" acquire weight, a new meaning for him. "Serious"—the man thinks what it means to be serious. How he answers himself is very important. If he understands what this means, if he defines correctly for himself what it means to be serious and feels that he truly desires it, then his prayer can give a result in the sense that strength can be

added to him, that he will more often notice when he is not serious, that he will overcome himself more easily, make himself be serious. . .[5]

The kind of topics for conscious prayer will obviously be rather different most of the time from what a prayer from some aspect of false personality would be about. As our understanding of our true nature and needs grows, our prayers could become far more appropriate.

In many ways Gurdjieff's description of conscious prayer fits the definition of meditation given at the beginning of this chapter better than the definition of petitionary prayer. Indeed, Gurdjieff states that the focused, conscious attention and recapitulation in consciously praying something like "God have mercy upon me!" may well have the effects that God is being asked to provide. This throws us back to the paradox: work as if everything depends on effort, pray as if everything depends on prayer. From the psychological point of view, the effort of conscious prayer lawfully produces beneficial results, including possible connections to higher levels of our selves. From another point of view, our efforts may be "pleasing" to or "resonate" with higher aspects of being and attract help and blessings. Probably these two views are both true and untrue, depending on your state of consciousness and being.

WHAT DO YOU WANT?

My personal experience has convinced me of the reality of higher levels of being, and that these higher levels can be of assistance. To use them as any sort of excuse for not working, however, is foolish.

Consider Mary's dream. More than a year before she began working on awakening along Fourth Way lines, she dreamed a strikingly accurate portrayal of the place of work, followed by a depiction of happiness, overcoming of death, and authenticity. Did her desire to awaken call out to something higher, something outside our ordinary conceptions of time? Is this "something" some higher aspect of her own self with precognitive abilities, the Master? Is it something beyond the self? At that level does it make sense to draw distinctions between the self and the not-self? Did that something or someone give some kind of assistance? Gurdjieff spoke of "magnetic center," something innate in people that would help guide them toward useful teachings when they sincerely desired them. Is this a partial illustration of the functioning of such a magnetic center?

I will not attempt to answer these questions here, but I want to leave this unfinished example of possibilities in your consciousness as we move on to discuss the nature of group work for awakening. I also want to leave a vital question open in your mind. If your being attracts your life, what are you attracting? What are your most consistent desires, conscious or unconscious? Your most persistent beliefs about yourself and your world? Do you really want to get what you believe in and wish for in consensus trance? A constant examination of wishes and beliefs is in order.

Group Work and Teachers

Many readers of Gurdjieff's and Ouspensky's works have been inspired by the ideas of self-observation and self-remembering, and have immediately resolved to begin work on themselves. Striving to be aware of being aware, to be present to the reality of the moment, they may immediately discover a certain kind of clarity resulting from this which directly demonstrates the importance of this kind of practice.

As I described earlier, this happened to me in 1965 as a result of reading Ouspensky's book *In Search of the Miraculous.* An immediate clarity resulted, a partial awakening, strengthening my resolve to practice self-remembering. Three months later I realized that after a few seconds of self-remembering I had stopped doing it and, indeed, had forgotten all about doing it. I had not actually self-remembered since then, *even though I had continued reading about it.*

Our ordinary intentions are easily swept aside and forgotten in the rush of automated mental and emotional processes characteristic of consensus trance. One subpersonality makes the intention to self-remember, but then it is gone as another subpersonality is conjured up by the force of circumstances interacting with our conditioned patterns of mind. The intention to self-remember is effectively dead until the blind play of circumstances happens to reanimate the original subself.

The situation can be worse than this. Ordinary intention tends to create a habit, an automated use of attention and particular ideas and memories. Even though the intention to self-remember may again be activated, it is easy for it to become an automated rehashing of some *idea* about self-remembering. This is what had happened to me. By my ordinary consensus trance standards, I had "understood" the idea of self-remembering, so my mind was satisfied and filed it away. It took a new experience and abstracted it into an idea instead of exploring its reality.

Much later, when I had had more experience of self-remembering, I found the process could also be aborted by becoming an automated re-creation of some sensation associated with an earlier experience of or attempt at self-remembering, rather than the actual process of paying attention to attention. Genuine self-remembering is a fuller awareness of the present moment, a deliberate attention to attention, and can never become a "habit," can never be automated. It *always* requires a small but definite act of will, a bit of consciousness deliberately used to produce more consciousness.

This situation is discouraging, but I go over it not to discourage you but to sketch the typical background against which real work takes place. Discovering how much of the above description is true of your *personal* mental processes is an important task of self-observation.

The automated nature of our ordinary life is a major enemy of self-observation and self-remembering. Automated life can use up all of our attention/energy. Cultivation of self-observation and self-remembering can lead to an understanding of exactly how this automated loss of your energy works in you personally, and thus eventually lead to the recovery of enormous amounts of energy you can use for the benefit of your own true, essential nature.

ALARMS

Ouspensky, using Gurdjieff's analogy of ordinary consciousness as a form of sleep, argues that we need "alarm clocks" to wake from sleep. An alarm is a sudden stimulus, different enough from ordinary input that it shocks us out of sleep, like the sudden ringing of an alarm clock in an otherwise silent bedroom.

You can actually set a physical alarm to help you self-remember. I have used the "beep beep" sound my digital watch makes on each hour as a reminder to "Wake up!" You can resolve to use particular kinds of events as alarms: "Every time I talk to my grocer, I will remember myself!"

This use of physical events as alarms only works for a while, though. Just as a very heavy sleeper may learn to not hear the alarm going off beside his bed, and may even incorporate the sound of the bell into his ongoing dream and sleep even more deeply, we can habituate to our self-remembering alarms so that we don't actually wake up and remember ourselves, we just have fantasies about being awake. My watch can sound the hour and I can have a pleasing thought like "I'm practicing an esoteric discipline," or "I'm awake now," without actually remembering myself or becoming more aware of my surroundings. The thought "I'm awake now" can occur while I am asleep in consensus trance. When I actually remember myself, it is quite different from just thinking about it.

One way to deal with this habituation problem is to change our physical alarms frequently. Use them for a while, but as soon as you show signs of habituation to them, use something else. This can be useful, but eventually stops being effective. We need a more effective kind of alarm than physical events that we select. Gurdjieff frequently said that a person can do nothing by himself. A special group to assist you in working on yourself is needed.

FUNCTIONS OF THE WORK GROUP

A "work group" is a group of people trying to observe and remember themselves, so they can become more alive and awake. A primary function of a work group is to act as an alarm, as a reminder to individual members of their goal of waking up. It can do this in a variety of ways. We will examine some basic functions of a work group in this chapter.

Because others are usually less predictable than your own mental processes, and even likely to clash with your automated desires, they function as alarms that are harder to habituate to. Indeed, people whose ordinary manifestations irritate us can sometimes be the best sort of people to be in a work group with. Their constant stimulation of our false personalities will keep us from settling down into a deep, comfortable sleep. We will look at the positive functions of the work group in this regard.

Reminding by Social Contrast

Because our social instinct makes us want to belong, to be accepted, we tend to automatically and unconsciously imitate the people around us. Because they also want to belong and be accepted, they reinforce us for being like them. We are in a situation of mutual positive feedback.

Ordinarily we are surrounded by sleeping people, people who neither know nor care about the idea of awakening. Thus we are automatically rewarded for continuing to sleep, for maintaining consensus consciousness. Simply by being in a different social grouping than we ordinarily function in, the work group can lessen the automated power of ordinary social norms. You are in a group of people who are not there for ordinary social reasons, nor are you there for those reasons.

Reminding by Example

Self-remembering means, among other things, paying clear attention to the immediate world around you. When you are in a work group meeting, this means the people around you are a major part of your immediate sensory world. If these people are themselves working on self-observation and self-remembering, as you are, this will sometimes manifest in observable aspects of their behavior. Your observation of these manifestations can serve as a reminder to you of your goals.

This does not mean that people in a work group act in any obviously strange ways. There are no turbans or robes, mysterious ritual gestures or secret handshakes. Some jargon may be present, but this is normal for any group of people who have worked together for some time. Ordinary activities are done in relatively ordinary ways most of the time. People can chat over coffee, paint the house, trim the shrubbery, sweep the floor, plan an outing, and so forth. It takes close observation to reveal that all of these ordinary activities may be done in a subtly different way that hints at the inner work going on.

Take sweeping the floor as an example. Ordinary sweeping typically involves thinking about something other than what you are actually doing, something "more important." The sweeping activity itself is usually hurried, more forceful than necessary, sometimes with an angry quality about it. The sweeper often has a slightly glazed look in his eyes, as his mind is elsewhere, "out to lunch."

A person who is remembering himself could also sweep the same floor. A careful observer might notice a certain "present" look in his eyes and a deliberate looking at the floor to be swept, suggesting that the sweeper's mind is present. The force of the sweeping might be just right for the job. The sweeper might turn the broom ninety degrees on the backstroke to raise less dust. Or the sweeper might sweep with a variety of deliberate strokes if he were experimenting with different ways of using his body. All in all, an impression might be created of someone actually present who is deliberately and consciously sweeping.

The physical tasks used extensively in work groups are very important in providing opportunities for students to observe one another in a wide range of situations, as well as in educating the body/instinctive brain. Too often in life we mainly see one another sitting still, or in interactions quite limited in range by the definitions of jobs and roles we are accustomed to. The various physical tasks let you see bodies in motion, which is quite revealing and very educational for our body/instinctive brain. The unusual and wide range of tasks in working together can function similarly. What does body language say, for example, when you ask someone to climb a ladder and bring up a load of shingles? What reactions occur in your body? Or what do the bodies of the man instructed to clean the kitchen and the woman instructed to repair the lawn mower say about their identities?

By looking around at the people in your work group, by working on becoming more sensitive to more subtle aspects of behavior, then, you see things that the ordinary observer misses. That person wiping off the table has a certain look that makes me think he is remembering himself, which reminds me that I'm here to remember myself, so *I do it*. Members of a work group serve as reminders, as alarm clocks for each other.

It is not just the "good" things people do that serve to remind us of our goals by example, but also the "bad" things. It is much easier to see others' negative manifestations than to see your own. When you are committed to self-observation in the work group, however, the consequence of seeing these things in others is liable to be that you see them in yourself also, thus furthering your own self-knowledge.

Reinforcing Awakeness

It is very satisfying to interact with someone who is relatively awake. There is a rewarding quality that intuitively feels as if it is based on realistic perception. You feel that you are being given real attention by the other, as well as giving real attention to yourself and the other. Ordinary attention from others, by contrast, feels as if you are something of a peripheral stimulus to someone's fantasy process.

Further, there is usually a "pure" or "clean" quality to this kind of attention. It is free of hidden agendas: *you* are being perceived more as you really are, to the best of the other's ability. This kind of attention is inherently nourishing. It feels as if it feeds the real, essential you rather than any of your false personalities. This is all very rewarding.

Another nourishing aspect of work group interaction stems from the fact that a primary rule for members of such groups is that they must be absolutely honest with each other and with the teacher of the group. This is far from easy, of course, but the struggle to be completely honest in your interactions (as if you were very awake, even if you can't fully self-remember while you are doing it) provides much material for self-observation and a quality of interaction that is much more fulfilling than the automatic dishonesty of so much of consensus trance. One way of implementing this rule, which I found helpful in my Awareness Enhancement Training work, was to remind people frequently to speak from their experience, not just from their intellect. If people can self-remember while speaking too, much of the nonsense and fantasy of ordinary conversation automatically disappears.

The more intensely you are self-remembering, the more awake you are, the more you can detect manifestations (or lack of them) of awakeness in others, and the more satisfying interactions become. Thus work on self-remembering is specifically reinforced in group work.

We have considered the individually rewarding effects of interaction when you are more awake. In addition to this there is a general social effect: the work on self-remembering by each individual uplifts the tone of the whole group, which further affects the individual. This effect should not be confused with another ordinary-level effect, namely the good feeling that comes from identifying oneself as a group member. This happens with any group in which you are accepted and fulfills a basic need. It may help to a limited extent in mobilizing energy in a work group, but must eventually be transcended if the work group is not to sink to the level of an ordinary social group.

Sharing Techniques, Problems, and Triumphs

There are many little "technical tricks" that can aid self-observation and self-remembering. The "microgoals" technique in Chapter 18 is an example. As other work group members share the individual techniques they discover, your own repertoire is increased.

Discrimination is necessary here, of course. What is a useful technique for one person may not work for another, or may even be a hindrance. The experimentation that reveals this can lead to valuable insights.

Students' discussion of their problems in applying Fourth Way work in their lives is often quite valuable. Each of us tends to think of our own problems as relatively unique, and often shameful, as if we were the only one who would have such a "bad" or "shameful" or "silly" aberration. Hearing about others' problems and struggles can often correct this fallacy. The realization that "I'm not weird and crazy; lots of people are like that!" frees up energy. When others solve those same problems, it is encouraging to us.

Fear as a Reminder

In addition to the positive reminding functions a work group can perform to help you remember to self-remember, there are some reminders that are based on lower functions like fear. Properly used, they can be helpful, but they are tricky and must ultimately be transcended.

Low levels of fear are common in most social situations. You could say something stupid or embarrassing, people might not like who you are, they could reject you. Even when not expressly felt, fear is potentially there. Fear can also be a common element in work groups. We are afraid of the condition of consensus trance we find ourselves in, of being like automatons, afraid that we won't learn to self-remember and will thus fail in our goal, afraid that others may see how badly we are doing and reject us.

If these kinds of fears are intermittent or of a low intensity, they can be used as motivators to work on yourself. You must remind yourself of something like this: "I'm afraid I'm not self-remembering enough: I do not deny my fear, but now I use it as a reminder to self-remember *now!*" Or "I fear the other people who are watching me will reject me because I don't look like I'm self-remembering. I do not deny that I am experiencing fear but will use it as a reminder to self-remember *now.*" In the latter case it's important to use the fear as a stimulus to actually self-remember, not as a stimulus to try to act externally as if you're self-remembering without actually doing it.

Notice that an essential part of using a negative emotion like fear positively is that you don't deny the experiential reality of it. Self-remembering involves self-observation, so denying that you feel fear when you actually do is fantasy, not self-remembering. Further, actively denying an emotion sometimes has the effect of giving it more energy. But you want to have energy to use for self-observation and self-remembering, not tie it all up in struggling with your fear.

Self-remembering as a result of a fear stimulus may actually diminish or banish the fear. While you are not fighting or denying the fear, you are deliberately putting your energy into self-remembering, so there is less free energy available for the fear to feed on. The insights you gain into the precise nature of your fears by observing them may also have the effect of dissolving them, creating a permanent energy gain.

These remarks about fear apply to other negative emotions, like anger and envy.

Reminding by Silence

A common rule in Fourth Way groups is that the student is not allowed to tell outsiders about what goes on in the group. One function of this rule is to show us what chatterboxes we are. We want to run out and tell everybody about everything exciting we have learned, right away. By agreeing not to do this, you have increased your necessity to observe yourself in order not to automatically start talking about the work. The rule also provides an opportunity to observe your motives for wanting to talk about the work. Does the thought of secrecy bother you, seem wrong? Fine. Observe *in detail* everything about it that bothers you. Are you trying to impress people that you are different? Put them down because they are not doing what you're doing? Feeling the need to save every soul you come in touch with?

Another function of this rule of secrecy is to provide a safe space for members of the group to talk about their feelings and experiences. You are not going to share your deepest feelings if you think they will be broadcast all over town. This kind of confidentiality is used in almost all growth groups.

The secrecy rule is also used because your understanding of the real aims and processes of the work is usually very bad, especially at the beginning of the work. That is the time when you are most likely to want to tell everyone about it, of course. By not speaking of it to outsiders, you do not give them distorted versions that may make it difficult or impossible for them ever to benefit from the work themselves if they later want to join in it. In my own work I asked students to keep the practices and events in the group a secret temporarily. When the time came that were sure they deeply understood some aspect of the work, that it was their own experiential knowledge, instead of outside learning, then they were free to speak of it with others if that might help others. This requires, of course, considerable self-observation as to what you really know.

Secrecy is also useful because most people are not interested in these ideas. Recall our discussions in earlier chapters about how we already believe we have unity, permanent identity, self-consciousness, and real will. To push these ideas on people who have not developed a real desire for them from personal experience is generally useless.

Reminding by Direct Injunction and Questioning

Last, but hardly least, other members of a work group can command you: "Observe your internal processes!" "Wake up!" "Pay attention to both yourself and the world simultaneously!" Or they may occasionally ask you, "Are you remembering yourself right now?"

There is trickiness here when such commands or questions become unconsciously used as part of ordinary social manipulation. Then "Are you awake?" or "Wake up!" become tools of social manipulation. If I have to ask you if you are awake, I, in my superior position, must have perceived that you, in your inferior position, were asleep. Ordinarily in work groups this direct injunction or question procedure is only used by the teacher or more advanced students.

Let us now consider the functions of the teacher.

THE NEED FOR A TEACHER

Gurdjieff believed we are so lost in the fantasies of consensus consciousness that it is almost impossible for any individual to make much progress in waking up without the assistance of a teacher who is substantially more awake than the pupil. Because of his or her superior level of awakeness and psychological understanding, a teacher can often see when a student is lost in fantasies about awakening and give the student specific techniques to try to work out from under these dead ends and fantasies. You are very lucky to find a competent teacher, as they are rare in a world of sleeping people.

Resistance to the Idea of a Teacher

I spend a couple of class periods on Gurdjieff's ideas when I teach my course on humanistic and transpersonal psychology at the university. The idea that we need a teacher to awaken evokes strong resistance from the students every time. They frequently get so caught up in this resistance that it blocks their access to other ideas of Gurdjieff's.

A major source of resistance is our enculturation as Americans: we believe we are rugged individualists and we can do anything we want to do on our own. As a good American I sympathize with and often share this feeling. Further, it often comes out that the students don't want to become dependent on anyone, even for psychological and spiritual growth. This is a particularly salient issue for most college students, as they are not finished with their personal struggles of becoming independent of their parents.

A third major source of resistance is the elitism inherent in the idea that if you don't have a teacher, you can't evolve very much. Again, our American background usually produces an automatic surface rejection of things associated with elitism. It is surprising to them when I remind them that as students in a major university they are part of an elite. They have gone through numerous selection processes in the course of schooling that allowed them to become students of one of the best universities in the country. By being there, they are supporting the practice of elitism. Nevertheless, they still don't like the idea that one needs a teacher for growth, nor the idea that such teachers are not readily available.

A fourth source of resistance is the students' knowledge of various cult leaders and the terrible things that they have done to people while claiming that they were enlightened teachers. They are quite right to be concerned about this, of course. Many people are called spiritual teachers, by themselves or their followers. Yet some of them are outright charlatans, some are madmen, some are insecure neurotics, some are well-intentioned but ineffectual figureheads. A person who has the status of a teacher but insufficient real knowledge may at best only waste people's time, but at worst delude and harm them.

Another source of resistance is the idea of paying a teacher. The spiritual is about loving and giving, so everything about the spiritual should be free, shouldn't it?

A sixth possible source of resistance is seldom verbalized: if you were working with a real teacher, he or she might make you actually change instead of just talk about it.

Resistances or not, we are social creatures. It is immensely helpful (and quite dangerous, as we shall see in the next chapter) to work in a group and to have a teacher, so let us look at some of the functions of a Fourth Way teacher.

Exemplar Function

A primary function of a teacher is to be an example to his students of what being more awake is all about. Part of the students' work of paying precise attention to the world around them is to study their teacher, thus gaining some idea of what a more awake person acts and looks like from the outside. How does he use his body? How does he stand and walk and talk? How does he react under stress? How do other people react to the teacher?

This is not to say that there is some fixed and learnable way that an awake person acts. Indeed a more awake person would be flexible and less predictable than someone in consensus trance, although the differences are often rather subtle. By studying the behavior of the teacher in the context of observing and remembering yourself, however, you see new possibilities in situations other than those that flow mechanically from the machinations of your false personality. This gives you an opportunity to further study your personality and to pick up a certain "feel" for flexible, more aware functioning.

Ideally the teacher should be someone who is completely awake, who self-remembers every moment, who represents the highest possible stage of human evolution, whose permanent being is that of the fourth level of consciousness. Then his or her every action would be a lesson, and his or her simple, natural being would be the teaching. In this less than ideal world, such teachers are rare, and the probability of meeting one is low (ignoring the functioning of magnetic center, discussed in Chapter 20), especially at the beginning of your work on yourself. Indeed, if you think you have a perfect teacher, the chances are high that you are seriously distorting your perception, for reasons to be discussed in the next chapter.

Practically, the basic requirement for a useful teacher is that he or she be fairly awake and developed with respect to the level of his or her students. If your child needs tutoring in spelling, there are many good spellers around who can help: you don't need to hold off getting any help at all for your child until the head of the most prestigious university English department in the country agrees to personally do the tutoring. Thus a mildly awake person might be an adequate teacher for those who are almost completely asleep, provided that teacher's own understandings and control of his own psychodynamics and personality pattern were good enough to avoid serious distortions entering into his teaching.

As we noted in discussing the alarm function of group work, there is a sort of "contagion" or catalytic effect of being around other people who are working on awakening. This applies to the teacher's role also. Simply by being around and being substantially more awake than his pupils in his actions and interactions, a teacher sets up a kind of "field effect" that can promote the students' efforts and successes.

Understanding Students

Another basic function of a teacher is observing and understanding his students. The teacher wants to be effective in imparting his knowledge and stimulating his students. To be effective, a Fourth Way teacher has to transcend fixed forms. To simply lecture in a traditional way in "time-honored" words or to perform demonstrations or exercises the way "it has always been done" is often to lose much effectiveness. Individuals can be very different from one another. The general structure of people's consensus consciousness in the same culture can vary greatly from generation to generation. A formulation or exercise that was very effective for your own teacher or for you may now work well for some people but be completely ineffective or even misleading for others.

Many spiritual traditions have become fossilized in this way, assuming rigid forms that no longer adapt to the time, place, and people currently using them. Gurdjieff described the Fourth Way as appearing at a time and place when people and conditions were judged right, then disappearing when the teaching could no longer be effective there. Those who hadn't learned the essence of the teaching would still remain, and they often preserved the outward forms of the teaching without having understood the inner core.

Thus the teacher must constantly study his students and try various methods to see what works best. Gurdjieff himself certainly experimented this way. Some experiments, of course, don't work, they don't produce the intended results. It is quite possible that some of the methods used by followers of Gurdjieff today are such fossils.

Just as the teacher must study individual students, he must also study the work group. Are his interactions with the students producing an atmosphere that is conducive to self-observation and self-remembering? Are the interactions of the students supporting this? If there is a certain amount of low-level fear among some students, for example, that may be providing a kind of "fuel" for their self-observations? On the other hand, the fear may be too strong for some and may be inhibiting their work. The teacher needs to monitor and adjust the group dynamics.

Motivating and Pushing

Another function of a teacher is to motivate the students. Certainly students come to the work strongly motivated to understand themselves and to wake up. Unfortunately, the subpersonality that is so motivated will frequently be displaced by other subpersonalities that have no interest in the work, or may even dislike it or try to use it for nongrowth reasons.

The teacher must help strengthen the genuine growth motivation. Gurdjieff expressed this as helping strengthen those subpersonalities that are interested in the work at the expense of those who aren't.

Sometimes a crucial development stage is reached in self-understanding where the student bogs down. Resistances to knowing and other defense mechanisms are activated, so the student avoids facing crucial things in himself or stays away from situations that might force him to face these things. The teacher may choose to wait until the student is ready, but sometimes it appears that the student may never be ready on his own. The subpersonalities interested in growth are not strong enough to overcome this obstacle. The teacher was employed by one or more subpersonalities in the student who really wanted to grow, though, in spite of resistance from other parts of false personality. Now the teacher must push the student in spite of resistance.

This is a delicate and sometimes dangerous moment. If the teacher is wise and knowledgeable with respect to the student, clearly understands the problem and the resistances, and has a good idea that a certain kind of psychological pressure might get the student over the hump, even if it is painful, he will push. I doubt that such psychological pushing is ever a sure thing. There is always a risk that the teacher's understanding is faulty or that the push won't be effective and may even backfire and increase resistance, or that the pain involved in pushing through may be too much for the student, so he will quit the work rather than see it through.

Gurdjieff thought that the risks of pushing were well worth it, as the alternative was to leave someone in consensus trance, possibly for the rest of his life. He was very rough on people when he thought they needed a push: better to upset someone, even to risk permanently damaging him by consensus trance standards and/or take a chance on losing him as a student, than to deny him the opportunity to really grow. Gurdjieff was harsh in this way, an attitude that made sense in terms of his belief that ordinary, mechanical man would die like a dog, having served only the lowest functions possible for a human in life. He was also very awake and knowledgeable about his students. I doubt that we will ever know if his pushes were always justified and effective.

Imparting Knowledge

Now we consider what is usually discussed first in thinking about teachers: the teacher's job of teaching in the ordinary way. There are ideas to be presented, questions to be answered, assignments to be given, "tests" of many kinds to see what students have absorbed or misunderstood. But because of the factors mentioned above, there cannot be a totally fixed curriculum for these. To impart knowledge as effectively as possible, the teacher frequently modifies and experiments with the teaching to maximize effectiveness.

Certain ideas, for example, should not be given to particular students until they have reached a certain level of development. Otherwise the premature idea will not make sense to them, or will be misunderstood and produce wrong effects. A good teacher would also try to maximize the "shock value" of ideas, giving them at a time and in a form when they would get maximal attention from a student by clashing with his automated habits of thinking and feeling.

Here we have the basic functions of group work: reminding students to observe and remember themselves, providing social support for doing so, nourishing both our essence and our higher aspirations by rewarding quality of interactions in the group, and sharing useful techniques, problems, and triumphs.

You can have a preparatory work group without a teacher: a sincere group of students working on talking about these ideas and sharing their understandings can be helpful to one another. It is especially important to try to be as honest as possible and speak from personal experience, not just intellectual considerations, in such a group. Such a leaderless group cannot go very far, unfortunately.

When a teacher, an advanced student of Gurdjieff's ideas, is available to lead a group, much more can be gained. By being significantly more awake than the students, the teacher can give useful ideas at opportune times, act as a model for an awakened person, and motivate, and push students to take steps they might never take on their own. When a genuinely awake Teacher is available . . .

Group work is not a simple process. Valuable and indispensable as it is, it carries risks. We shall look at these in the following chapter. My intention in doing so is not to discourage anyone from group work, but to make the process less likely to be distorted by alerting you to the potential pitfalls.

22

Problems with the Work Process

The work process has very high aims. These include greatly enhanced self-understanding; balanced development of mind, emotions, and body-instinctive intelligence; development of essence so that it, rather than false personality, is dominant; awakening, the development of a permanent higher state of consciousness as a result of self-remembering; and other aims that are beyond the psychological scope of this book.

The work process takes place under very difficult conditions, however. On the learning side, the students are almost completely entranced in their personal version of consensus consciousness, their understanding of what must be done is incomplete and often dangerously distorted, and the cultural setting we live in encourages consensus trance, not awakening. On the teaching side, since "perfect" Teachers are rather difficult to find, and may have better things to do than work with us in our present condition, real human beings with shortcomings of their own act as our teachers. They may inadvertently bring some of their own problems into the work situation.

At its best, the work process produces real progress toward its high aims in at least some students. At its worst, the work process can increase the depth of trance students are in and amplify their and/or the teacher's psychopathology. In between these extremes the work process may simply be ineffective: high ideas are discussed, practices are followed, but no real change takes place in the students, and the whole process is only a way of passing time. This kind of marking time may do no real harm, but by desensitizing students to the power of work ideas, it may sometimes decrease their chances of future benefit if they later enter a more effective work situation. This chapter will consider the problems that interfere with the success of group work toward awakening.

CONFLICTS BETWEEN HIGHER AND LOWER NEEDS

One of the safety and security needs we all have is a need for stability: things seem safer if only the anticipated happens. There are no surprises, no changes. Indeed, we will often put up with unpleasant things for long periods of time (sometimes a lifetime) rather than take a chance on the unknown. This conservative safety need is often coupled with specific fears of what might happen, or with semiconscious or unconscious traumas associated with change.

This need for stability and fear of change are in conflict with our essential curiosity, our inherent desire for self-actualization. How can I observe myself or my world accurately and objectively unless I am willing to see whatever is there, whether I like it or not? How can I wake up unless I will see and take responsibility for my reality? Abraham Maslow spoke of constant conflict between our safety needs and our growth needs that results in an oscillation. When safety needs are predominant, we may *talk* of growth, but actually take no chances and strengthen our psychological defenses. When our lower needs are reasonably well filled, our growth needs can become stronger and we will take chances and venture into the unknown. This is a general, not an absolute picture: sometimes dissatisfaction of our lower needs can be the force that activates higher ones.

This conflict between safety and growth needs is why Gurdjieff insisted that the Fourth Way starts from a reasonable level of success (by commonsense standards) in the ordinary world. The householder, the successful malcontent, has lots of imperfections and craziness in an absolute sense, but by common standards has mastered the tasks of staying alive and reasonably comfortable. He or she has a solid base to start from, and that successful base, satisfaction of lower needs, allows the essential curiosity and desire for self-actualization to emerge.

Any time a group of people spend time together, there is a possibility of satisfying ordinary social needs. As social beings we need to receive attention from others, we need to feel secure that others will not attack or otherwise reject us, and, more positively, we need to feel that we have friends, are accepted, belong. When these needs are reasonably well met, higher needs can emerge. One of the functions of a teacher is to select students for a work group who are at this reasonably successful level so that higher needs can predominate.

Ideally all of these ordinary social needs would be met outside the work group context, so that nothing would be needed from the work situation but assistance with the higher aims of the work itself. This ideal can only be approximated at best, for all we have occasions when we haven't gotten enough attention or acceptance from our ordinary social interactions, and so will find ourselves looking for attention or acceptance in a work situation ostensibly aimed at something higher. Indeed, *if we are sufficiently self-aware to know we are doing this,* it can be a very valuable learning experience when this happens in the work group situation: we may be able to observe these needs and learn more about their precise functioning in ourselves than we might be able to do in ordinary social groups.

When these ordinary social needs are too strong, and/or we are not able to observe or control them adequately, the real function of the work group may be lost. We may imitate the work practices externally, but internally we keep distorting them. If we notice that people working on self-observation or self-remembering have certain movement styles, for example, we may imitate those styles *so that other people will think we're like them,* so that we can be accepted, rather than focus on the inner practices that might lead to those outer manifestations.

THE WORK GROUP AS MINICULTURE

Whenever a group of people spend a lot of time together, regardless of the reasons they consciously have for doing so, their social needs interact and they form a group that is semi-independent of the larger groups and overall culture around them. Thus a work group is a sort of miniculture. It will tend to develop its own perceptions of itself and its members, of the "outside" world, and its own set of values and norms.

A Gurdjieffian work group is particularly apt to do this because of the explicit teaching that consensus reality and our normal state of consciousness are a kind of sleep or trance. You should not, of course, accept this statement on faith, but only as a focus for self- and world-observation; you should *test* this idea rather than just accept it. Nevertheless, the statement easily constitutes an implicit permission from authority to reject many or all of the cultural norms you normally live by and develop new ones that suit you better.

This is socially unusual for us. If you join a sports club, a professional group, a great-books discussion group, or a political party, for example, you expect that a certain amount of in-group jargon will be developed, and some specialization in the way you see the world while with the group, but these changes are usually expected to be minor and *subordinate to your culture's overall world view*. When they are not, the culture usually calls such groups "deviants" or "cults." Such groups in turn usually overtly reject the culture around them by such means as overtly attacking it or dressing and acting in an obviously different fashion.

Gurdjieff demanded that you question everything about your culture, but at the same time he suggested not making any major changes in your external lifestyle. This was so that you would have years to observe yourself carefully in the situations in which your false personality was formed and maintained, and thus come to a *precise* understanding of the workings of your mind before attempting any changes. Even after such precise understanding was attained, you might or might not make obvious external changes in your life: if your essential goals could be reasonably approached in a conventional lifestyle, you would be foolish to generate the social static that acting unconventionally would generate.

Still, the injunction to question all, the implication that much of what you have automatically lived by is wrong, gives an enormous amount of freedom and creates a great potential danger to a work group. For all its shortcomings and craziness, our culture is an integral part of our psychological support system, and the source of values that make life reasonably smooth.

We are taught to be polite to others, for example, and whether that is mindless conditioning or not, it does mirror the profound principle of consideration for others, and it regulates social behavior in an adaptive fashion. The injunction to question all can be turned into a specific idea: "I don't have to be polite to anyone. I can be nasty, and that may be more honest since it works against my conditioning."

As a *time-limited experiment*, working against conditioned norms of politeness can be very valuable to your growth. Observing what happens internally and externally when you act impolitely, observing the resistances to change that come up in you, seeing how you deal with the rejection and hostility of others when you are impolite to them, can be very valuable. If you develop the genuine ability to *not* be polite, and then you *consciously choose* to be polite out of consideration to others, that is a highly moral and meaningful act. Conditioned politeness, as we discussed earlier, has no moral significance.

Recall the situation of the work group as a miniculture, though. It is quite possible that someone experiments with nonpoliteness as part of self-observation, but others imitate it because they want to be accepted in the work group. Nonpoliteness can become an automatic habit, a part of a new consensus trance state based on the implicit consensus spreading through the work group. Nonpoliteness can become a group norm rather than an experimental tool. An important aspect of the work has become distorted and loses its effectiveness.

Things like this happen in ordinary groups, of course. It can be fashionable to be snappy and "tell it like it is," for example. As group norms that are different from general social norms accumulate, though, group members feel uncomfortable; they don't want to become too "different" and turn into cultural outcasts. The group variation is restricted by the overall normative system of the culture. In the work group, however, this restriction may not hold, since all of the cultural norms are in question. There is no set of powerful standards that says a little deviance is OK, but you mustn't go beyond certain clear limits. Thus the work group culture has the possibility of drifting further and further from standards of "normalcy," and eventually becoming very deviant indeed.

To the extent to which the work group members are fully conscious of and learning from this, there is no problem other than responsibly accepting the consequences that come from social rejection responses. To the extent to which lower needs for social acceptance are dominant over real consciousness, though, the work group members can simply create a different form of consensus trance than the socially dominant one, even though they call it "waking up," and perhaps become more entranced than they were before.

A major function of the teacher is to prevent a work group from turning into a culture with a different trance state. It is possible that a teacher may not be awake enough to fully prevent this, however, or may not fully recognize its dangers, especially if, as discussed elsewhere, the teacher's own flaws are being magnified in a positive feedback loop.

POSITIVE FEEDBACK LOOPS

The engineering sciences have a very useful concept of feedback. You take a device that has an input and an output and feed part of its output back into its input, and this affects the device's performance. Instead of just input at one end flowing straight through the device to output at the other end, part of the flow loops back on itself—the system starts to feed on itself.

Psychologically, positive feedback is like the principle of reward in learning. If you do something and are rewarded for it, you are liable to do it more strongly and more frequently. A classical demonstration of this, which also shows that consciousness is not necessary for learning, has been done in many classrooms through the years. The students conspire to reward some infrequent mannerism of the lecturer, say a wide sweeping motion of the right arm to emphasize a point. Perhaps the lecturer only makes a partial sweep four or five times in a lecture. Now the students nod and smile every time he makes the gesture. Several lectures go by, and soon the lecturer is making dozens of big arm movement gestures in every lecture. Reward. Positive feedback.

In physical devices like amplifiers, too much positive feedback is destructive: it changes the device from an amplifier into an oscillator. Anyone who has ever heard a public address system turned up too loud and then breaking into a horrendous scream as the sound from the speakers feeds back into the microphone has observed the effects of too much positive feedback. It actually can burn it out if it is not stopped soon. Psychologically, a similar thing can happen. The infrequent but appropriate action can become dominant and inappropriate, interfering with action instead of helping it.

The teacher of any spiritually inclined group, Gurdjieffian or otherwise, can get into a positive feedback loop that can be quite dangerous.

Because the teacher is supposed to be quite advanced in the spiritual discipline in comparison to his students, there is a tendency for his every action to be interpreted as a teaching. Insofar as the teacher is more awake than the students, studying (including conscious, deliberately experimental imitation) the teacher's every action can be a profitable source of insight. What does the teacher eat? How does he dress? What kind of jokes does he tell, or does he avoid jokes? How does he treat "outsiders"? What sorts of looks does he give people? He is never, as it were, "off camera."

If the teacher were a perfectly evolved and awake person, without the slightest trace of consensus trance, stupidity, ignorance, or neurosis ever manifesting in his actions, the students' close study and imitation of the teacher would not go wrong. Insofar as it is unrealistic to expect total perfection of real teachers, though, students will see actions based on ignorance, unrefined habit, consensus trance, and neurosis, as well as actions flowing out of wakefulness and development. If they cannot tell them apart, this tendency to see every action as a teaching will result in many distorted and incorrect ideas. For example, the teacher may not like card games because of unresolved childhood experiences of being beaten at them. Observing him turning down invitations to card games, some student may mistakenly conclude that this is a teaching about the immorality of card games.

This misguided overinterpretation of the teacher's actions by his students can involve the teacher in a dangerous positive feedback loop. We all need and like attention and approval. The teacher gets lots of attention and approval, not just for the skilled and deliberate actions of his teaching, but for everything, including the mistakes. Thus the teacher's mistakes and flaws can get amplified, and a teacher who is not fully on top of the situation can be ruined.

Consider some of the Eastern teachers who have come to the United States and initially taught very valuable spiritual material to their Western students, but eventually had their groups turn into "cults." Positive feedback, students rewarding the teacher for everything, day after day after day. The public address amplifier that could reproduce vital teachings becomes a device that gives off an ear-splitting squeal.

UNREALISTIC PERCEPTION OF THE TEACHER

There is a special difficulty in the role of the teacher that adds great power and danger to the work process, namely that the teacher so easily becomes a Teacher to the students, but not in reality.

A teacher is a person who is skilled at something you would like to learn. You respect his knowledge, are willing to pay or otherwise reimburse him for the time he takes instructing you, and, within reasonable limits, you will open yourself to unexpected and possibly painful methods of teaching if you are assured this is necessary. If you want to learn to speak a foreign language, for example, you select a teacher who speaks that language and has some credentials as a teacher. You know he has to make a living, so you pay him a fair wage for putting his skill at your disposal. He may make you do pronunciation drills when you'd rather do something else, but you understand that what you get out of his teaching will depend on what you put into it, and the teacher knows more about what is needed than you do.

You can generally tell when an ordinary teacher is failing to teach properly. If you can't carry on a conversation with native speakers of the language you are learning after years of effort, and you know you have a reasonable aptitude for languages, you can legitimately doubt your language teacher's ability. If your language teacher asks you over late at night for "special lessons," locks the door, and suggests that you take off your clothes, you may or may not appreciate this sexual advance, but you know it's not language teaching. If you don't like your teacher's performance, you can fire him.

You can learn enormous amounts from a teacher. How much more could you learn from a Teacher?

In reality, there may be Teachers, people who have so mastered themselves and attained such heights in the psychological/spiritual realms that they are indeed drastically different from ordinary people like you and me. Gurdjieff taught that there were indeed such people, those who were qualitatively as well as quantitatively beyond us, living at the third or fourth levels of consciousness. In the world of the sleeping and the entranced, the fully awake man is king, with powers resulting from his vision that see instantly through illusions and delusions that blind and bind the rest of us. If you could be guided by such an awake person, have such a Teacher, you would be lucky indeed.

Transference and Countertransference

One of the most important contributions of psychoanalysis was the discovery and exploration of transference. Earlier we discussed how absolute, powerful, and godlike our parents are to us when we are very young. In these formative years we automate the attitude of regarding our parents as incredibly knowledgeable and powerful, and many emotions and other attitudes are connected with this. Other influential people in our childhood may also be perceived in almost mythic ways.

Transference refers to the fact that in later life we often unconsciously transfer this attitude we had toward our parents or other childhood figures to other people. Bosses, colleagues, spouses, even relative strangers can be the objects of transference. This gives them an emotional charge in the unconscious parts of our minds and thus makes them much more powerful than they are. Unresolved problems with our parents may be projected onto the other as part of the transference, so the anger you feel toward some action by your boss, for example, may have only a little to do with what your boss actually did and much more to do with some unresolved feeling toward a parent. Transference reactions keep us deeply asleep, deep in our individual versions of consensus trance, for they consume energy that could be used for constructive purposes and seriously distort our perception of reality.

Some interactions in life have little or no elements of transference involved in them. Transference is more likely if the person or situation you are involved with has some resemblances to your parents or to unresolved situations that involved your parents. If your boss looks somewhat like your father or acts somewhat like him, transference is more likely than if there is little or no resemblance. If you want something that seems magical from your ordinary point of view, like awakening, like being taught by a Teacher, that may also evoke transference reactions.

Countertransference refers to a transference that is a reaction to a transference. You unconsciously start treating your boss as if he were your father. He doesn't know this consciously, but unconsciously he reacts and starts treating you as his child. Now you are both much deeper asleep, in a folie à deux.

Any teacher of any discipline, from baseball to auto mechanics, is potentially subject to some degree of transference from his students. After all, our parents were our first teachers, so all teachers are easy marks for transference reactions.

The intensity and power that come from a transference reaction are a two-edged sword. On the one hand, when a student has strong, positive transference onto his teacher, it gives the teacher enormously greater power to affect the student than he would otherwise have.

Without the transference, a suggestion by the teacher that the student practice a certain mildly unpleasant physical and mental exercise regularly is just that: a suggestion. It will be intellectually evaluated and is likely to be ignored in the face of discomfort or realistic, alternative conditions. The same suggestion when transference is operating takes on a magical quality in the unconscious. It is a command from the omniscient and omnipotent god or goddess. Hidden emotional forces reinforce it, and the student may carry the exercise out vigorously and rigorously, gaining the benefit that he would otherwise have missed. Initial progress in learning can be especially fast with the boost that transference can give, with the student seeming to transcend his natural limits and resistances. The student will see the teacher as the Teacher and be a devoted, enthusiastic, loyal disciple. The Teacher is so wise, so understanding, so powerful! The student's simulation of reality is badly distorted.

Such a transference reaction could be projected onto a teacher or a Teacher, whether he wants it or not.

On the other hand, if the negative aspects of transference reactions predominate, the student may resist and sabotage the work that is suggested to him, even though consciously he wants to do it and it would be good for him. A straightforward, obviously sensible suggestion from the teacher becomes, on the unconscious level, another command from a hated parent figure. If your pattern was not to directly resist, since your parents were so powerful, but to sabotage, the suggestion becomes consciously accepted but unconsciously sabotaged. You "forget" to do the exercise, or you keep "misunderstanding" the directions and do it incorrectly.

Transference is tricky because inexplicable (by conscious standards) reversals can happen. Some seemingly irrelevant situation triggers a powerful unconscious response, and a wise and deeply beloved (for transference reasons) Teacher who is doing wonderful things for you can suddenly be perceived as a treacherous, manipulative charlatan. Your growth gains can suddenly be lost because they were built on false foundations, and you can feel as if you are worse off now than before you started working on yourself. In reality the teacher's behavior and attitudes may have shown no significant change at all.

If the teacher develops a countertransference onto one or more of the students, the whole situation can get very powerful and very crazy. Combined with the problem discussed earlier of the positive feedback loop that a teacher and students can get caught in, transference and countertransference reactions can take any spiritual group and make it downright crazy. Cults flourish on this kind of thing, of course, but real work does not.

When a student first starts working on himself, but has not gained much knowledge yet, some transference onto the teacher may be inevitable. In the long run, though, transference is inherently crippling, for it keeps the student in a state of dependence. Essence must grow to a state of intelligent, independent adulthood, not stay fixated in a realm of childish fantasies and dependencies, even if that realm feels wonderful. The teacher who accepts or encourages long-term transference relationships from his students is probably caught in a countertransference reaction and can have his whole teaching effort aborted as a consequence.

I believe that the understanding of transference is one of the greatest gifts of Western psychology to the spiritual traditions. You can see strong manifestations of transference in some Eastern systems especially, where

it is explicitly called guru worship. You can see how genuine love and respect for the higher teachings being manifested through the guru are
involved here, as well as genuine love and respect for the person of the
guru. The transference mixed in with this, however, is a serious distortion
of reality.

Some systems do not seem to recognize the transference aspects of this
situation or any need to eventually resolve it, while others seem to assume
that the experience of higher states of consciousness will automatically take
care of any problems. Gurdjieff's emphasis on *constant* self-observation and
self-remembering will, if practiced well, make manifestations of transference fairly apparent to students, but they may still need specific
psychological help to resolve transference manifestations.

Daniel Goleman, a psychologist with considerable expertise in spiritual
development work, has summarized some very practical indicators of
problems in group work.

> Spiritual groups—like families, corporations, therapy groups, and
> marriages—are susceptible to the full range of human foibles. Vani-
> ty, power-seeking, and looking out for Number One are as likely to
> show up in a spiritual organization as any other. The very nature of
> such groups often makes it difficult to notice or acknowledge that
> something is awry. Group collusions such as "It's all part of the
> Teaching" are invoked to alibi for meanness of spirit and pettiness.
>
> Wandering the spiritual path by no means protects us from the
> normal dose of folly that accompanies any other human endeavor.
> Spiritual work is perhaps all the more ripe for foibles because of the
> excellent coverup self-deception lends for the use of the spirit in
> the service of the ego, libido, and pocketbook.
>
> As a spiritual freelancer for many years who has been at the
> center or periphery of a variety of such groups, I've had ample op-
> portunity to note or fall prey to some of the typical pitfalls listed
> below. Of course, in one or another context each of these signals
> may be a false negative—a benign symptom with no underlying
> pathology. More often than not, they mean that an open-minded,
> skeptical enquiry is called for.
>
> Be wary when you notice the first signs of:
>
> • Taboo Topics: questions that can't be asked, doubts that can't be
>   shared, misgivings that can't be voiced. For example, "Where
>   does all the money go?" or "Does Yogi sleep with his secretary?"

- Secrets: the suppression of information, usually tightly guarded by an inner circle. For example, the answers, "Swiss bank accounts," or "Yes, he does—and that's why she had an abortion."

- Spiritual Clones: in its minor form, sterotypic behavior, such as people who walk, talk, smoke, eat and dress just like their leader; in its much more sinister form, psychological stereotyping, such as an entire group of people who manifest only a narrow range of feeling in any and all situations: always happy, or pious, or reducing everything to a single explanation, or sardonic, etc.

- Groupthink: a party line that overrides how people actually feel. Typically the cognitive glue that binds the group. E.g., "You're fallen, and Christ is the answer"; or "You're lost in samsara, and Buddha is the answer"; or "You're impure, and Shiva is the answer."

- The Elect: a shared delusion of grandeur that there is no Way but this one. The corollary: you're lost if you leave the group.

- No Graduates: members are never weaned from the group. Often accompanies the corollary above.

- Assembly Lines: everyone is treated identically, no matter what their differences; e.g., mantras assigned by dictates of a demographical checklist.

- Loyalty Tests: members are asked to prove loyalty to the group by doing something that violates their personal ethics; for example, set up an organization that has a hidden agenda of recruiting others into the group, but publicly represents itself as a public service outfit.

- Duplicity: the group's public face misrepresents its true nature, as in the example just given.

- Unifocal Understanding: a single world view is used to explain anything and everything; alternate explanations are verboten. For example, if you have diarrhea it's "Guru's Grace." If it stops, it's also Guru's Grace. And if you get constipated, it's still Guru's Grace.

- Humorlessness: no irreverence allowed. Laughing at sacred cows is good for your health. Take, for example, Gurdjieff's one-liner: "If you want to lose your faith, make friends with a priest."[1]

Group work, then, is a powerful amplifier of individual aims and energies. When it works correctly it can enormously assist your individual efforts. If it is distorted by unresolved psychological problems like transference, though, it becomes another form of entrancement, not the road to awakening. It takes constant vigilance, self-observation, and self-remembering on both the teacher's and students' parts to prevent distortions of the work process from occurring. This requirement, of course, is just fine. It provides some additional pressure and motivation for awakening.

There has been so much discussion of pitfalls on the path to awakening in this book, because the pitfalls are there, and knowing about them can lessen the danger. Let us now turn to the positive side of dealing with pitfalls, though—the art of developing compassion. Not only compassion for others but, just as necessary, compassion for oneself.

23

Compassion

I have attempted to practice the kind of mindfulness inherent in Gurdjieff's practice of self-remembering for some years. Even though I have not developed it to the degree I would like, it has been very valuable to me, as I have become more fully and realistically aware of the world around me and of the workings of my own mind. The major lack of self-remembering practice for me, though, has been that it does not deal directly with the heart.

I understand intellectually how, in the long run, the clearing away of obstacles to natural functioning through self-observation and self-remembering will allow a natural development of love and compassion, and I have seen some growth in myself in this way. Since I regard myself as too intellectual and too lacking in love and compassion to begin with, though, I am impatient and have always wanted to encourage the growth of these aspects of myself more actively.

Most Gurdjieff work does not encourage active development of love and compassion until after years of practice of more basic work. If love and compassion were cultivated at the beginning, before you had much understanding of your own mind and feelings, it would probably result in the growth of more illusions that would further support false personality.

We considered an analogy in the introduction of a person who wanted to grow beautiful flowers and nutritious vegetables. He had heard of "powerful fertilizers" and wanted some. When you looked in his back-yard, though, you saw it was overgrown with weeds. In such a case there was no point in discussing fertilizers and varieties of seeds: there was a lot of work in getting rid of weeds that had to be done first. Indeed, to tell such a person about fertilizers before he had gotten rid of the weeds would be worse than doing nothing. The idea of "fertilizers," of spiritual practices, is exciting, not just to our essence but to many parts of our false personality. The application of fertilizer at this stage would just make the weeds worse.

This reasoning makes perfect sense to me, both intellectually and from personal experience. There have been too many occasions in my life where actions I thought of as using and developing love and kindness turned out to be fertilization of the weeds of my unconscious, of the automatized parts of my false personality. Mindfulness, self-understanding, and self-remembering are clearly necessary. A balanced development of all three major aspects of our being—body/intuition mind, intellectual mind, emotional mind—is also necessary. The kind of self-observation and self-remembering advocated by Gurdjieff, as well as some kind of body work, facilitates the development of body/intuition and intellectual mind directly, and, because insight removes energy from the automated operation of false personality, it also sets the stage for the growth of the heart. Yet I have always felt a lack of more direct development exercises for the heart in the basic Gurdjieff work that I have been exposed to.

In 1984 I had the good fortune to attend two lectures by the venerable Sogyal Rinpoche, a leading teacher of Tibetan Buddhism in the West. The emphasis in Rinpoche's lectures was on mindfulness, not just as a special meditative practice but, more important, mindfulness in everyday life. The parallels with Gurdjieff's focus on self-observation and self-remembering were clear, but of even greater interest to me was his specific emphasis on the active development of compassion within the overall context of the cultivation of mindfulness. I do not fully understand the ideas he presented in terms of their comprehensive development in the Tibetan Buddhist tradition, but I want to share my personal understanding of them here, combined with my psychological knowledge of compassion, in the hope that they may be of value to others.

Note that these ideas and practices are embedded in a general cultivation of mindfulness. I suspect the concepts and methods described below would not have the same effect if used outside a personal commitment to constantly expand your mindfulness of yourself and the world. They might not be as effective, and sometimes they might amount to putting fertilizer on the weeds, so treat them with caution.

What is compassion? Standard dictionaries trace its origin to the Latin roots *com*, "with," and *pati*, "to bear or suffer," and define the word as meaning a sympathetic consciousness of the suffering of others and a desire to help them. It is a sad commentary on our times that a major encyclopedic dictionary of psychology I turned to for more clarification doesn't even list *compassion*, a lack reflected in most introductory psychology textbooks.

We can't really define compassion in any exact sense, of course. It is primarily a quality of emotional intelligence, and words relate primarily to intellectual intelligence. We can say a few things about it that can resonate with appropriate feelings, though.

Breadth of Self-Knowledge

Compassion requires the development of several qualities. One is breadth of self-knowledge: if you don't experience, recognize, and understand a wide range of human experiences in yourself, it will be difficult to recognize and understand them adequately in others. If you never acknowledge anger in yourself, for example, you can't adequately understand what it is and how it functions in someone else, or sympathize with the way it can constellate other contents of the mind so that they are perceived as reasons to justify the initial anger and fuel further anger.

Empathy

A second requirement for the development of compassion is empathy. Empathy is a recognition of a feeling/thinking state in another, *plus* an ability to at least partially experience that same state in yourself. Thus empathy ties in with self-knowledge. To recognize that someone is "depressed," for example, could be done in a cold, intellectual way. You could learn that certain facial expressions, body postures, and styles of speaking usually mean that a person is "depressed." To also emotionally know what it is like to feel depressed from your own experience leads to the experience of empathy. This does not necessarily mean that you must feel as depressed as the depressed person you are empathizing with, but the basic emotional knowledge must be readily available to consciousness.

Modern psychology has thought of empathy as a late developmental function, but recent research suggests that it begins to develop within the first few years of life. We could say it is an innate part of our essential nature. It may be partly related to bodily/instinctive intelligence also, such that mimicking others' postures and expressions helps us feel what they feel.

Desire to Help Others

A third requirement for compassion is the desire to help suffering beings find relief from their suffering. My own feeling is that this desire is natural, a part of our essence that is naturally aroused by the empathic perception of others' suffering. It is the defenses we have erected around ourselves, discussed below, that keep us from being aware of this natural desire to help others.

Effective Compassion and Intelligence

A fourth requirement for *effective* compassion stems from the fact that compassion should work in concert with intelligence. Compassion is not just an exaggerated empathy in which you feel another's negative emotions very strongly. If that were all there is to it, compassion would be a crippling emotion, adding others' sufferings to your own and probably getting you caught up in some of the maladaptive behaviors suffering people often engage in which prolong or worsen their sufferings. Intelligent, effective compassion thus involves:

- The open self-knowledge and maturity that give you intimate, experiential knowledge of a wide range of human suffering (and abilities)
- Empathy that allows you to correctly perceive the nature of another's suffering
- A basic caring for others, a motivation and commitment to help alleviate their suffering
- The application of intelligence (mental, emotional, body/ instinctive, spiritual) to eliminate the *cause* of another's

suffering, rather than just lessen the symptoms. This last aspect is important for efficacy of results.

To illustrate, suppose you see someone drowning near the shore. Assuming you are a good enough swimmer to rescue someone in these particular circumstances, compassion would lead you to jump in and tow him to shore. But suppose you weren't sure that your swimming abilities were good enough for this particular situation. To jump right in anyway would be noble but stupid, probably leading to two drowning tragedies instead of one. The addition of intelligence to compassion would lead you to look around before jumping in. Perhaps there's a life preserver or other buoyant object that could be thrown to the person in the water or towed out by you to protect both of you. Is another person who is a better swimmer close enough to ask for help?

Suppose you jump in and rescue the person. He is very grateful, and you naturally feel wonderful about your noble and compassionate act. A week later you again see him shouting for help in the water, and again rescue him. Suppose you find out that this person often gets rescued from drowning because he won't bother to learn to swim well and/or keeps taking foolish chances. Will it be compassionate to keep rescuing him if that means he won't come to terms with the consequences of his foolishness?

Immediate and Root Causes of Suffering

The immediate cause of the swimmer's suffering, in this instance, is being in the water and in danger of drowning, but the root cause of his suffering is not learning (or refusing to learn) about the dangerous consequences of taking chances in the water when he is a poor swimmer. By continuing to rescue him, you compassionately save him, but on another level, you are keeping him from facing the root cause of his suffering. If he does not face the root cause, chances are that someday he will take a chance when no one is around who can save him, and he will drown. Would it be more compassionate to tell him that the next time you will *not* attempt to rescue him, so he had better learn to swim better and/or to not take chances? Or perhaps you might rescue him the next time but take a risk by taking your time about it, so he will go under a few times and have a fearful and painful experience that might force him to become more intelligent by facing and changing the deep cause of his suffering.

Is it worth taking the risk that he will actually drown if you try waiting (out of compassion) until he's gone under a few times?

These kinds of questions do not have easy answers. I am using this example to illustrate that intelligent and effective compassion must deal with issues of sometimes letting people suffer if it will make them deal with the root causes of their suffering.

SOME OBSTACLES TO COMPASSION

To be compassionate is both natural and satisfying, yet it is all too rare a part of human behavior. Why? Let's look at some of the obstacles to compassion.

Childhood Rejections of Our Love

We have all had experiences of loving someone and trying to give to him or her, but finding our love and generosity rejected. Such experiences embitter us greatly, especially when we are children. Consequently, we are all emotionally scarred (and scared) when it comes to acting openly from love and generosity. Indeed, to avoid the pain of rejection of this tender, vital, loving part of ourselves we create active defenses to live behind.

The Vulnerability of Openness

When you give from your essence, you are open and vulnerable. You are being your deep self. When that giving is rejected, you feel rejected on a very deep level. Suppose as a child you loved your mother so much that you suddenly gave her your most prized possession to show her how much you cared. Your prized possession happened to be the dead frog you had been hiding in your bedroom drawer for a week. To you the frog is beautiful and you are wide open, functioning from pure love. To your mother the partly decayed frog is filthy and disgusting, and she yells at you: "Take that filthy thing out of the house this minute and throw it in the garbage! Then go wash your hands! You're a disgusting little boy! When will you learn how to behave!"

An experience like this can be devastating. From your current adult perspective you can understand why your mother acted like that and forgive her, but you weren't an adult when it happened, and you understood and learned quite different things as a child. You learned that acting spontaneously from love gets you into trouble. That you must be mistaken about what you think love is, or you wouldn't get such a reaction from someone who, you believe, must have loved you. That you can't depend on your own judgment in important matters. That you are a disgusting little boy. That you are dumb, since you are much too slow in learning how to behave. That being spontaneously loving leads to great rejection, pain, and confusion. That spontaneity in general is dangerous.

Many of our childhood experiences are this dramatic, and there are many more that aren't as dramatic, but make up in frequency what they lack in individual intensity. Is it any wonder that you wall off your essential self? That you lose touch with your essence and replace it with "safe" behaviors, habits, learned feelings? The "safety" of your defense is an illusion, of course, for any position that isolates you from knowing what is really happening in your world leads to actions that are flawed. And your life now has a constant undercurrent of anxiety from a new worry: suppose the defenses break down?

Attempts at Invulnerability

You try to become invulnerable so you won't hurt so much. Unfortunately you usually do too good a job of it, walling off your natural love and compassion so well that your life becomes dry and stale. The many defense mechanisms, Gurdjieff's "buffers," discussed in Chapter 13, come into play and your natural vitality is stolen and automatically channeled into the habitual perceptions, thoughts, feelings, and body movements of false personality. In adult life you may then want to be compassionate and loving, you may try to be that way, but you feel nothing. Worse yet, you are led astray down the subjective paths set up by false personality, experiencing the pathologically distorted versions of "love" you were conditioned to accept in childhood, so that true compassion and love are absent. To note that this leads to a sterile life with much useless, stupid suffering is to put it mildly.

Avoiding the Pain of Incompetence

There is another important reason for staying defended and closed down. As children, and as adults, we had experiences where we were compassionate, we felt another's suffering and tried to help, and *it didn't work*. Lacking skillful means, our efforts to help were to no avail, and all we did was suffer without accomplishing anything.

How easy to build up a feeling of "Don't notice, don't feel, then you won't get hurt," the all-too-prevalent modern theme of not getting involved.

REDUCING "I!" AS A WAY TO COMPASSION

In earlier chapters we discussed the psychological process of identification, the way in which unconsciously and habitually adding the feeling of "I!" or "This is me!" to some contents of the mind gives those contents greatly increased psychological and emotional power. Information about, say, selfishness, can be looked at much more effectively and objectively when I am thinking about some stranger's selfishness rather than my own.

We have a huge amount of stored information in our minds. Some of this information has the "I!" tone attached to it, as, for example, "This is *my* valuable understanding of the sacred," rather than "This is one understanding among many about the sacred." Our defense mechanisms were initially developed to defend our vital, essential selves, but over the years they begin to automatically defend almost anything that has this "I!" quality attached to it. What was once an essential maneuver by a relatively powerless child to protect its essence has become an automated style of (largely unconscious) emotional and mental functioning that unnecessarily constricts our being.

As an adult, then, you want to be open and compassionate but you don't know how to. Our fears and our ingrained habits of mental and emotional functioning cut us off from the parts of our essential selves that generate love and compassion. While you can try to deal with obvious, conscious fears about openness, the ingrained habits and unconscious fears are more difficult to deal with. They require various combinations of mindfulness, vulnerability, psychotherapylike growth, and reduction of the process of identification.

Mindfulness

Becoming mindful, observing and remembering yourself, being increasingly sensitive to the exact nature of your reactions to the world, allows increased insight into the functioning of false personality, as well as greater sensitivity to your genuine, essential feelings. Such mindfulness gradually dissolves some obstacles to compassion: many of our automated constrictions and defenses fade away when exposed to the light of greater consciousness. It may also highlight other aspects of your self that need more specific work. As we have discussed mindfulness at great length in this book, we need not discuss it further here.

Vulnerability

Vulnerability seems most undesirable and yet is absolutely necessary to fully recover your essential self. When you were a little child you were tremendously vulnerable in real ways. As we have discussed in earlier chapters, your physical survival, as well as your psychological well-being, depended on your parents. Your lack of experience of the world gave an *absolute* quality to what your parents said and did, which enormously increased their power to love and their power to (consciously or unconsciously) hurt you. With your own resources so small and your parents' power so huge, was it any wonder that the times they hurt you were so incredibly bad? Such that sometimes you thought you would die from the pain of psychological wounds? Friends and strangers, often acting from far less love or even anger than our parents felt, hurt us very badly at times too. It is not surprising at all that the defenses you created were so powerful: you felt you were fighting for your life—and in many ways, you were.

The psychological habit of fighting for your life is still with you in unconscious and habitual ways. It is as if you received blows from giants and so encased yourself in thick armor for protection. You are still wearing that thick armor, but you have grown into a giant yourself and it's very cramped inside!

Suppose you are walking in the woods with a loved one today and you see a fascinating-looking dead frog. Biology fascinates you, and you were fortunate enough to not have the particular childhood experience used as an example above, so you pick it up and show it to your beloved, a spontaneous gesture of sharing one of the fascinating things of the world. You may get another version of "Take that filthy thing away from me this minute and throw it away and clean your hands! You're disgusting, like a little child! When will you grow up?" To the degree that the automatic defense mechanisms of false personality operate, the armor closes a little tighter around what's left of your essential self, and you may yell back and start a fight, or coldly withdraw and feel hurt and/or angry. But in reality: (a) You're not a little child, you're an adult. (b) You're a competent adult who can take care of yourself, and need not feel more than mildly hurt by this attack. (c) Compared to your current, adult resources, this is a very minor attack, you can directly experience the rejection. If you are vulnerable, you don't need to deny what you feel. It doesn't feel good, but you can handle it. Indeed, you can handle far more intense attacks than this. Armor, defense mechanisms, aren't needed. (d) By using empathy, intelligence, compassion, you can understand how your loved one feels, make a good guess why he feels this way (social conditioning and/or traumatic personal experience), and, without denying the reality of his feelings, realize that he can't help it. There is no need to feel deeply attacked, as it is not really that much of an attack on you *personally*, any more than rain falling on you is a personal attack by nature. Your loved one is reacting mechanically as a result of conditioning.

Intelligent compassion would allow you to empathize with your loved one, take the frog away to stop the immediate upset, and then skillfully apologize and, perhaps, help your beloved understand why he is so bothered by dead frogs. Perhaps the root cause of this particular suffering might be eliminated.

Allowing yourself to be vulnerable, then, removes the need for much of your automatic defensiveness and so allows much greater openness to and compassion for other people.

Therapeutically Aided Growth

Sometimes mindfulness and vulnerability are not enough. Some kinds of attacks, even if they really are quite minor in reality, cause such intense hurt that you can't keep your attention in reality or feel compassionate; you must retreat or attack, for your defenses take over despite your intentions. Sometimes help and understanding from a friend can get us over these blocks, but sometimes not. This is where Western-style psychotherapy techniques can be helpful.

A good therapist is a trained person who is "outside" your delusions and problems, so he or she has a more objective perspective on them. With the help of such an outside expert, a therapist who is empathic and intelligent, you can be led to see things you can't otherwise see and feel things you can't otherwise feel. In return for the immediate pain of facing the unfaceable, you get at its root cause and eliminate the years of suffering you would otherwise have.

Reducing the Sense of "I!"

Because our defenses spring into operation when "I!" am attacked, reducing the intensity and frequency of the identification process creates a more relaxed style of mental/emotional functioning that allows our natural compassion, love, and intelligence to function more effectively. Two ways of reducing our sense of "I!" are self-remembering and many kinds of meditation.

Self-remembering reduces the intensity of the identification process. Under ordinary circumstances, you only have so much attention to give. If you exercise little voluntary control over that attention, then it largely goes where the circumstances of the moment, predictably and automatically reacted to by false personality, take it. We are "stimulus-driven," to borrow a term from conventional psychology, reactive rather than genuinely active.

When you self-remember, you voluntarily direct your attention so that you simultaneously pay active attention to what is happening outside you and inside you, as well as keep some reference object (such as your arms and legs) in mind. The simple act of voluntarily putting attention where you want it means that there is generally less attention/energy available to power your false personality and your identification processes and defense mechanisms. Quite aside from specific changes in the functioning of your mind, this reduces the automatic defensiveness that comes from too much "I!" and allows greater empathy and compassion toward others. The traditional Buddhist practice of keeping part of the mind always watching your breath, even in daily life, similarly reduces the sense of "I!" by diverting energy from the identification process.

Deliberate meditation practices, done at times specially designated as meditation time rather than ordinary life, can also lead to a temporary lessening of the identification process. If you spend fifteen calm minutes just observing your breathing while sitting still, for example, you have fifteen minutes in which your mind has been filled with the simple, emotionally neutral experience of breathing, rather than the typical mental/emotional activities that reinforce false personality and its multitudinous identifications. In his lectures Sogyal Rinpoche emphasized that right after meditation is one of the best times to try to practice compassion. Indeed, for the beginner (practically all of us) this may be one of the few times when compassion can be successfully practiced.

THE CULTIVATION OF COMPASSION

We have looked at the obstacles to openness and compassion at some length, for understanding the obstacles to doing something automatically suggests ways of circumventing or dismantling those obstacles. Learning to meditate in some fashion that reduces our sense of "I!" is a way of indirectly setting the stage for more compassion to manifest naturally. Learning to be mindful in everyday life, trusting your self enough to be more vulnerable, and using the type of help developed for psychotherapy to work on specific obstacles to free mental and emotional functioning, similarly set the stage for more frequent and natural functioning of compassion. What more can you do?

It would be wonderful if you could just decide "I will be compassionate and open from now on," but, as you know, it isn't that easy. That is why Sogyal Rinpoche used the phrase "courting compassion." You will have more luck if you try to gradually work your way up to being compassionate than if you try to get there all at once.

REMEMBERING LOVE: A PRELIMINARY PRACTICE

One of the practices Rinpoche suggested invokes a feeling of compassion by building on earlier experiences when you were loved by someone else. Here is an outline of the practice. As discussed above, it is best done when your identification process is not working so intensely, so right after some meditation practice that has succeeded (remember, meditation doesn't always work) in producing a calm state of mind is a good time, as is the time after a successful period of self-remembering.

1. Think about someone who loved you a lot. Parents are tricky to use for this purpose, as many of us have unresolved psychological tensions about our parents, but a grandparent is often excellent. Think about the ways this person loved you and was kind to you.
2. Realize that you must be a worthwhile person to have been

loved by another. Focus on that rather than any doubts you have about yourself.

3. Experience the feeling of being loved, of how that person felt in loving you.

4. Now experience the feeling of loving. Then call up images of other people and give your love and compassion to them.

   a. At first use images of other people who have been good to you.

   b. As you get successful at this, extend the giving of love to images of people who have treated you neutrally.

   c. As you get more practiced, extend your love to images of people who have treated you badly.

   d. When you get good at the above, extend the love to images of people with whom your relationship was mixed and complicated, such as your parents.

   e. Now extend your love to all beings.

When you first do this practice you may not get beyond step 2, or you might go directly on without difficulty to step 4a. Don't try to jump directly to the most advanced steps if you're having difficulty with earlier steps: that might set you up to have a failure experience and reinforce all that early defensiveness that closed you up in the first place. You needn't be perfect at each step, but experience some success at it before you go on to the next one.

The Dalai Lama recommends a similar practice for actively developing compassion.[1] His Holiness's version starts with recognizing the incredible kindness your mother performed in giving birth to you and raising you, and then trying to see all beings as mothers, so you will feel kindness and closeness toward them. I understand the principle involved here, but my psychological knowledge of the two-sided nature of the mother-child relationship leads me to prefer Sogyal Rinpoche's suggestion. Base this exercise on a person who was more one-sidedly positive toward you than many people's mothers were toward them, lest you have negative, unconscious associations implicit in your model of a loving person.

TONG LEN

Tong Len is a Tibetan practice Sogyal Rinpoche described for developing greater openness and compassion. It can be used as a way of reviewing unpleasant or problematical events of the day to open your mind to compassionate options for future events. As with the preliminary practice described above, doing it just after a successful meditation or self-remembering period, when your sense of "I!" is less, is a good idea.

1. Recall the specific problem or unpleasant situation that this Tong Len practice is to focus on.

2. Reflect on the various aspects of the problem situation, its atmosphere, as well as its specifics. Accept the problem, don't deny any aspect of its reality. See the multiple sides of the situation, the positive as well as the negative aspects.

3. As you reflect on these positive and negative aspects of the situation and the people involved, as you "breathe them in," also keep track of the equanimity, happiness, and compassion you experienced to some degree in your meditation, and give these positive feelings to the problem situation and people. "Breathe out" your happiness as an *unconditional* gift to them. You are not denying the negative, you are simply loving everything and everyone in the problem situation anyway.

4. Reflect on yourself with regard to this situation. We are all wondrously complex, many-sided beings, so reflect on how different parts of you are responding to the situation. Don't deny anything you see about yourself, even if it's fearful or shameful. Accept all these different aspects of yourself, the "good" sides and the "bad" sides, and give your happiness as an unconditional gift to them.

5. Don't force changes, but if aspects of your self change as a result of putting the positive and negative together, giving your love to all sides, accept the change.

I believe the Tong Len practice or similar practices can significantly restructure your mind. Instead of having a steadily growing store of totally negative memories of situations in which you were not compassionate—which will, of course, increase your convictions that life is unpleasant and that you are not and cannot be a compassionate person—you have processed memories to allow for compassion. The negativity is not denied—that would be pathological—but it is put in a context where compassionate alternatives are seen.

The ultimately important effect, of course, is to sensitize yourself to compassionate alternatives so that they become available in real time, when the next unpleasant situation is starting to happen, rather than only later.

And now for the difficult part. . . .

DEVELOPING COMPASSION FOR YOURSELF

It is often difficult to develop just plain tolerance for many other people, much less compassion: they can be so difficult! It is a real accomplishment to bear the negative manifestations of others without always having to try to correct them or being unnecessarily caught up in them. We can learn great and realistic tolerance, though, and even develop our capacity for compassion.

The more difficult accomplishment, however, is to accept yourself and develop compassion for yourself.

I have given students difficult and trying assignments for self-development, often involving observation of their negative sides, which can be very unpleasant. I am always impressed by how hard students will work at this. There were also times when I have given students assignments of being nice to themselves, something just as important for self-development. These were no big deals, just little things, like looking in a mirror and smiling at themselves for a moment, or thinking nice thoughts about themselves for five minutes a day.

The resistance to being nice to oneself is enormous! Students forget all about doing the exercises. Even after being forcibly and repeatedly reminded, they come up with all sorts of reasons (rationalizations) why they don't have time to be nice to themselves for five minutes a day. Work on the feelings behind these resistances usually shows they have a deep-seated set of feelings to the effect that they don't deserve to have *anyone* be nice to them. "Anyone" includes themselves, often especially themselves, because of feelings of lack of self-worth. Some people have much stronger feelings like this than others, but almost everyone has them to some degree.

That we harbor strong dislike for and rejection of ourselves is not surprising in light of what we have discussed about the enculturation process. We all went through rejection, rejection that made no sense to us. We had our essential feelings invalidated many times, and we learned to identify with socially desirable aspects of ourselves and disidentify with those that didn't fit into consensus reality. It was natural to develop a general feeling like "What I basically am is not good enough, is bad. I can only be accepted and loved if I am careful to do the right thing and don't act spontaneously." This general negative feeling acted in conjunction with specific negative feelings toward particular aspects of ourselves that we felt were bad. We are strongly defended against important parts of our essential nature.

Gurdjieff observed this same kind of resistance to letting go of the apparent security of false personality and consensus trance. He reported that his students would gladly do unpleasant tasks requiring heroic efforts, taking on deliberate, conscious suffering in the hope of growth, but when he asked them to give up their suffering, that was another story!

In discussing false personality and essence in Chapter 15, we noted that essence has to be nourished and cared for so that it can begin growing again. The practice of self-observation will allow you to start contacting neglected aspects of your essence, distinguishing them from false personality. Then you have to give them energy and attention deliberately, so they will grow. You have to be nice to yourself! When resistance occurs, it is to be observed and understood, and eventually overcome.

The practices of self-observation and self-remembering are a general way of giving attention to essence. Attention is energy, so deliberately paying attention to your essential self is a way of nourishing it. After all, you only pay attention to what is valuable, so *you* must be valuable if you give yourself attention.

To have compassion toward yourself is vital. Self-observation, in its various forms, eventually leads to a depth of understanding we seldom dream of. A vital part of that understanding will be of how pure and marvelous you essentially are. There will be resistance to self-understanding on the way, as you see negative parts of yourself, but the process is worth it.

Until you learn to understand and have compassion toward yourself, all your tolerance, love, and compassion toward others rests on a very shaky foundation.

NOURISHING ESSENCE

I will not attempt to give detailed advice about emotional development, as I am an overintellectualized person, but I will suggest a couple of basic but powerful exercises that are helpful in nourishing your essence, in promoting self-liking.

These exercises are to be done occasionally, once a week or so. They generally produce quite pleasant experiences. That is fine, but remember the goal is awakening, achievement of genuine self-consciousness. That requires prolonged self-observation and self-remembering. Since much of that means looking at unpleasant aspects of yourself and reality, neither reject pleasure nor substitute it for genuine knowledge. Remember again,

> There is no God but Reality.
> To seek Him elsewhere
> Is the action of the Fall.

The Musical Body

This exercise should be done lying down in a warm, reasonably dark, and comfortable place where you will not be disturbed.

This musical body exercise can sometimes create very powerful emotions. You should, if necessary, modify the directions as you go along to keep any emotional reactions within the range where you can learn from them.

Pick one of your favorite musical selections that lasts for about fifteen to twenty-five minutes. Don't use vocal music, as you don't want to get involved in verbal meanings. Flowing, peaceful music that is relatively even throughout is best.

Start the music, and take a minute or two to just relax.

Now listen to the music in both of your feet. Put your attention on whatever sensations are in your feet and gently let the music be there too. Don't force it: there isn't some very specific sensation you're trying for and must have. As in the morning exercise described in Chapter 18, gently put your mind in your feet. Sense whatever is there, and "hear" the music there.

Don't worry about intellectual arguments that you really hear with your ears, not your feet. You really don't, anyway: you hear with your *mind*. By wishing to hear in any specific part of your body, you will have the experience of hearing/sensing there, and that's what matters. The music helps you focus attention and a pleasant, positive feeling in the part of your body you are listening in. Enjoy the music in your feet and the sensations in your feet.

After about a minute, move your attention up into the calves of your legs, from the ankles to the knees. Pay attention to whatever sensations are there, and hear the music there. *Enjoy* the music in your calves and the sensations in your calves.

Again in a minute or so (timing is not crucial) move your attention to your thighs and sense and listen there.

At about one minute intervals, go through your body in the following order: genitals; pelvis, with particular attention to an area about two finger widths below your navel and about three finger widths in; belly; chest and back (don't focus strongly on your heart yet); shoulders; upper arms; forearms; hands; neck; and face and scalp.

Then focus on the inside of your head for a minute or so.

Then listen to the music in your heart. Strong positive feelings will probably result here, especially if your choice of music has been appropriate. Immerse yourself in and enjoy these feelings.

Finally, spread the sensing and the listening to the music and any positive feelings associated with your heart throughout your whole body. After a minute or two of this, let your attention relax and just drift into a relaxed state for a few minutes until the music ends.

When the music ends, get up slowly; jumping up from a relaxed state can make you faint. Start practicing self-observation and self-remembering again. Live!

The above sequence for listening with the body is not the only one that is useful, so feel free to try different sequences. Just include all of the body.

For those who would like more specific guidance with this exercise, I am creating a cassette tape with appropriate music and directions. Information on the tape is given on page 300.

The Morning Liking Exercise

This is a modification of the morning exercise described in Chapter 18. It is to be done about once a week. It is particularly useful to notice any resistances you have to doing this morning liking exercise.

Just before starting the morning exercise, think "I like me." Feel it a little. Put a little smile on your face.

Now, all through the regular steps of the morning exercise, keep that little smile on your face; emotionally smile at your body parts as you sense them. As with the musical body exercise, don't force too hard or try to overdo it. Just a gentle physical and emotional smile, a gentle liking, not a big deal.

So many of us have such little liking for ourselves that it can actually be a big deal indeed to spend a few minutes deliberately paying attention to yourself and deliberately liking yourself, but it is within everyone's ability to like himself or herself at least a little—and eventually quite a lot.

Both the morning liking exercise and the musical body exercise can be made much more powerful by asking that you *love* yourself, instead of just liking yourself. That might trigger too much resistance, though, so just like yourself. When you can practice this as loving yourself, you will be well along the way to developing compassion, for yourself and for others.

The development of compassion, for yourself and others, is essential for properly understanding the idea that false personality must die.

24

Selecting a Spiritual Path

> If a man could understand all the horror of the lives of ordinary people who are turning round in a circle of insignificant interests and insignificant aims, if he could understand what they are losing, he would understand that there can only be one thing that is serious for him—to escape from the general law, to be free. What can be serious for a man in prison who is condemned to death? Only one thing: How to save himself, how to escape: nothing else is serious.
>
> —G. I. Gurdjieff[1]

When people become concerned with searching for psychological and spiritual truths beyond the ordinary, it is natural to assume there are paths to knowledge or teachers and exemplars of such knowledge that may have the answers to many of our questions. We hope we can get useful assistance from those who've taken the path before us.

As we begin searching, we find that there are multitudes of teachers and paths around, yet many of them seem to contradict one another or not make sense. Who has the truth? Do they all have all the truth we need to know? Do some paths have some of the truth, but lack important parts of it? Do some teachers have dangerous errors mixed in with what they know of truth? What is the minimally acceptable ratio of truth to error that makes a path or teacher worth following? Which path is *best*? Even more important, which path is best for *me*?

In ordinary life we can often get fairly reliable answers to similar, ordinary questions. If I need the services of an electrician, for example, I can hire any electrician who is state-licensed and be reasonably sure that he or she possesses a certain minimal level of competence, probably enough to handle my job. If I want to learn computer programming, I can take a course at a state university and be reasonably certain that whoever the university hires to teach the course knows what he's talking about. I may not get the *best*, but I'll get basic competence. If I want to buy a new washer, I can read *Consumer Reports* and get an objective appraisal of the faults and virtues of various models, balance these against my needs, and make an intelligent decision as to which model to purchase.

If only it were like this in the "spiritual marketplace"! Where is the licensing board that guarantees a basic level of competence for spiritual teachers? Where is the "Spiritual Consumer Reports" that, after objective testing, might make statements like:

> For seekers of extroverted temperament and personality traits A, B, Q, and T, Zen meditation produces rapid progress toward enlightenment. It is definitely Not Acceptable if you have traits C or R, however. Seekers with trait C should investigate the new Gestalt Sufism. Unfortunately, no satisfactory spiritual path has yet been discovered for those with trait R, who are better off in this lifetime in artistic vocations.

I think one of the things a more enlightened science could do for spiritual paths would be to develop something like a "Spiritual Consumer Reports." That is a huge project for several generations of researchers, but it would be possible to assess the characteristics of many people, let them become involved with various spiritual paths, and then see what kinds of outcomes occurred for what kinds of people. It is only a part of the answer, but it would help.

BASES FOR SELECTION

Selecting the best from among the many is a real problem, even if you're only reading about spiritual matters. It is even more important when you are ready for serious practice. We have conflicting claims, many paths implicitly or explicitly consider others inferior, and there is no objective authority to turn to for guidance. What can an intelligent person do?

First, we must realize that selecting a spiritual path is not just a matter of verbal, intellectual intelligence; it is also a matter of our feelings and our instincts. We must use all three of our brains. For most individuals in our culture, our intellectual intelligence has been highly developed, but our instincts and our feelings have been grossly neglected and often suppressed and distorted in their functioning. As we have seen, this distorted functioning of our instincts and feelings in turn can distort our intellectual functioning, so that much "rationality" is actually rationalization. Part of our approach to choosing spiritual paths, then, should be based on a continual effort to understand and mature our emotional and bodily/instinctual nature.

To illustrate a problem I doubt is unique, one of the reasons I was attracted to several spiritual paths in my past was that I had an immature need to feel superior to other people, in order to mask feelings of inferiority in myself. That was *my* problem, not one necessarily inherent in any of those various paths. Yet there are teachers and systems around that have lost touch with their original spiritual impetus and now cater to those sorts of immature emotions. Continual increase in our self-knowledge is essential. *Why* am I interested in a certain path or teacher?

Second, intelligence requires us to recognize our current limitations and practice humility. While I would like to believe that I can assess the real quality of various spiritual paths and teachers, I know that's too grandiose to be true. I, and you, can certainly recognize some of the charlatans, at one extreme, and we can sometimes recognize (intellectually and/or emotionally and/or instinctually) higher ideas and actions. So we can do our best to choose, but sometimes we will be wrong. If we learn from our mistakes, we have little objective cause for regret.

Third, choosing a spiritual path will, it is hoped, depend on more than "rational" choice, even if that choice is emotional as well as intellectual. In Chapter 20 we noted that Gurdjieff spoke of a "magnetic center," something analogous to a compass in us that would help us navigate. The analogy refers to something essential in us, something from our essence or higher aspects of our selves that could recognize truth when it found it. Thus genuine higher teachings will possess a certain appeal above and beyond rationality.

The idea of magnetic center is a dangerous one, however, as it is easily subverted into the idea that anything mysterious and emotionally appealing must always be a higher teaching. The *a*rational must be paid attention to, but it can easily be confused with the *ir*rational and the erroneous. Thus the necessity of self-study, to learn exactly how the machinery of your mind works, what its illusions are, and how to distinguish them from the arational but valid intuitions we may have.

I am a pragmatist and a scientist as well as someone interested in spiritual growth, I want to know what the actual outcome of something is, regardless of all the talk and theory surrounding it. When I encounter a spiritual system or teacher, I try to "listen" and evaluate with my mind, my heart, and my instincts, drawing on what I think I know, and remembering that I've made mistakes before and will probably make more in the future. If I decide I can learn from a system or teacher, or do something useful for myself or others by getting involved, I get involved.

ARE GURDJIEFF'S IDEAS OUTMODED?

G. I. Gurdjieff was one of the first people to make a systematic attempt to translate knowledge and wisdom he acquired from Eastern teachers into a form that would be suitable for Westerners of his time. He realized that what may be an efficient formulation of psychological and spiritual knowledge for one culture may not work properly in another, so he experimented with forms of teaching that would effectively transmit his knowledge. Similarly, what is an effective path for some people in our culture may not be effective for others. I have little patience for people who believe "This Way is the only Way", whether it is a particular Gurdjieff group or any other path. Obviously I have found Gurdjieff's ideas very useful, otherwise I wouldn't have written this book. But you must find a path or paths that are effective for *you*.

I am familiar with a variety of claims about what path is superior. These include the Sufi claim (via Idries Shah) that Gurdjieff's ideas were useful but are now outmoded.[2] There are counterideas to this, the feeling among some followers of Gurdjieff that Shah's Sufi stories are useful but limited. Oscar Ichazo, founder of the Arica training, supposedly claims that his Arica training comes from the secret school that was behind both Gurdjieff and Sufism, and supersedes both of them.[3]

I have immense respect for the teachings of Gurdjieff, Shah, and Ichazo: all of these systems have been of great value to me and friends of mine. I recommend Shah's books of teaching stories all the time, for example, his *Tales of the Dervishes*. Since I don't know the address of the "spiritual licensing bureau," though, I can't check on who really has legitimate credentials and who doesn't. Nor have I been able to locate the issue of "Spiritual Consumer Reports" that gives the "objective" evaluation of these systems, or rates one or more as a Best Buy! As a limited

being, I can only conclude that all these (and many other systems) probably have something to give to at least *some* people, and I hope that the
right people will get involved with the right path for them.

Although I have studied several spiritual traditions, this book focus-
es on Gurdjieff's ideas. Why Gurdjieff? Because he was a genius at
putting Eastern spiritual ideas and practices into useful forms. His influence on Western culture, although largely behind the scenes, has
been great, helping to open the way for current spiritual interests. His
basic formulations of psychological and spiritual ideas are still some of
the best around today, and cover important areas often untouched in
other traditions.

ARE GURDJIEFF'S IDEAS FOR YOU?

If you have read this far in this book, you probably find my understanding of some of Gurdjieff's ideas fairly interesting, and perhaps you
want to go further. The advice above is applicable to getting involved
with any spiritual group, including Fourth Way groups, but let's consider some specifics for Gurdjieff's ideas.

To begin with, remember the injunction at the beginning of this book:
don't believe the ideas herein. Test them. See if they are real for you.
This is not easy, of course. A few of them can be directly observed and
tested with little difficulty. Others can only be tested as a result of prolonged work and observation, and you have to build a strength of focus
and attention to do that. Others will be accepted or rejected for unconscious reasons. Some ideas will have to be accepted or rejected through
some kind of "experimental faith." Accepting things on temporary, experimental faith is fine, as long as you remember to recheck every once
in a while: is something you accepted on faith now testable?

This brings us to an important problem: how far can you test and uti-
lize these ideas and practices on your own? Considering the things about
the importance of group work and work with a teacher discussed in
Chapter 21, don't you need to join a group and find a teacher if you want
to go very far with these ideas?

I believe the answer is yes, although I don't like to admit it. I like to
learn from books and solitary reflection, and haven't resolved all of my
concerns in relating to others, so I have some resistance to the idea of
needing a group. I can theoretically imagine an individual who is alert
and observant enough to go a very long way with these ideas on his own.

In practice, though, we are so strongly affected by our interactions with others that we need the support, stimulation, frustration, and challenge of working with a group and a teacher. We gain great power and advantages from that. We also put ourselves in a different kind of danger than the dangers of ordinary life, as discussed in Chapter 22, but the advantage can be well worth the risk.

FOURTH WAY GROUPS

Gurdjieff was undoubtedly a genius, and a man far more awake than we are. If he were alive today, I would try to accept him as a teacher (I know I would have many personality clashes!) and want to study in a group under his direction.

When a genius who has started a new line of endeavor dies, a social process occurs that seems inevitable. His students and disciples feel a great need to carry on his work. There is usually harmony among these students for a while—sometimes only a few days, sometimes years—and then the splits begin, especially if the founder did not clearly designate a successor. Now you have two or more branches of the original work. At its best, each branch modestly and rather objectively claims that it is specialized in some aspect of the work. At its worst, each branch claims that it has the only true version of the Founder's Teachings and that the other groups are ignorant imitators at best and irresponsible charlatans at worst. The various branches may engage in doctrinal quarrels, ignore each other, undermine each other's work, sue each other, and so forth.

When Gurdjieff died in 1949, he had not clearly designated anyone as his successor in a way accepted by all his students. Today someone interested in his teachings will find many groups claiming to have them, all claiming authenticity. Some will point to continuity with Gurdjieff because some of his oldest disciples were members of this group; others will speak of secret authorizations from Gurdjieff and claim the older disciples did indeed study with Gurdjieff for a long time, but did not really understand and develop as the founder of this branch did. Some did not study with Gurdjieff or any of his senior disciples, but claim spiritual inspiration from Gurdjieff, sometimes figuratively, sometimes literally.

To make matters worse, Gurdjieff's ideas readily lend themselves to authoritarian interpretations that turn work based on them into cults (in the worst sense of the term), giving great power to a charismatic leader.

Some of the problems of group work discussed earlier, especially those involving transference, are relevant here. Some of these leaders are deluded about their level of development but are very good at influencing others. Some are just plain charlatans who appreciate the services and money available from devoted followers.

What to do?

It is dangerous to get involved with any group teaching Gurdjieff's ideas. It may be led by a charlatan, it may be only a social group with no real teaching effect, it may be riddled with pathological group dynamics that hurt its members. It may also be an effective group: the techniques, which go well beyond those mentioned in this book, are often very powerful and may force change in spite of your resistance. That is, it can be dangerous because it may work: you will be forced to grow in spite of your resistances.

It is also dangerous *not* to get involved in some sort of intense spiritual search, Gurdjieffian or otherwise. Ordinary life is not safe. Clinging to the ordinary, trying to ask no questions and change nothing, is not safe. Look at the armaments race, the mental illness figures, the overpopulation problem, pollution, the suicide rate, the vast numbers of people only getting by with a steady diet of tranquilizers. Ordinary life is not safe. And ordinary life does not provide us with enough meaning after a certain point: we must look for self-actualization, for spiritual growth, or experience the living death of emptiness.

There are many Gurdjieff-oriented groups in the world, as well as other spiritual development groups. There is no external guarantee of which are good, which bad, which indifferent. Some advertise and are easy to find; others never advertise and you must use your intelligence to find them. I have discussed finding groups in Appendix B.

Shopping around, looking at many spiritual paths, is quite appropriate. Read about paths X, Y, and Z. Try a weekend workshop with C, do a few months of Sunday meditations with Q, hang out with people involved in P, and see what kind of feel you get. Is one of these paths speaking to something vital in you?

MAKING A CHOICE

At some point, though, mixing a little of this and a little of that is no longer appropriate. Most paths will affect you in direct proportion to the amount of energy you put into them, so you will have to really focus on one and give it large amounts of energy. You can't go in several directions at once if you want to go a long way.

So choose a path that has heart for you, whether it's a Gurdjieff group, a Zen group, or whatever. Accept the fact that your choice is made in relative ignorance and in consensus trance, but that's all right; you have to choose from where you are. Recognize this: you are making the best choice you can for who you are now. But also recognize that you may change, new facts may come to light, reality is change, so your sincere and best choice at this moment may not be the best choice in the future. Believe in the choice you are making so you can give it energy, but accept your beliefs as part of an experiment.

All genuine experiments are subject to evaluation, leading to a new level of knowledge. Give your commitment and your time to the path of your choice, but as you start down it, I strongly recommend that you make a contract with yourself about making your choice an experiment. Since our memories can be rather fallible, I suggest a written contract along the following lines. It commits you to give your best but limits you to a specified time commitment (six months may be plenty for a first path, two years is plenty for any path) with a commitment to evaluate your experiment at the end.

THE SPIRITUAL COMMITMENT CONTRACT

I, _____, wish to grow beyond my present boundaries toward that which is the highest possible. Insofar as I can understand my nature and my possibilities, the goals I wish to work toward and the things I really value are:

(List your important goals and values.)

I recognize that while I must change myself, I believe I can also profit from teaching and guidance from someone more advanced in attaining the above goals than I currently am, and I can profit from being part of a group that provides social support for the attainment of these goals. To help me attain my goals, I am now committing myself to study with _____ (name of teacher) and his/her group _____ (name of group) for a limited period of _____ (time commitment).

During this commitment period I shall give as much of myself as I can to learning and understanding what is offered and to helping others, even when the directions I am given seem contrary to my expectations or arouse my resistances. I shall do this within the broad limits of not harming myself or others, because I understand that what I get is in proportion to what I give.

I also recognize that my imperfect understanding at this time may mean I have chosen a path, group, or teacher that is not really the best for me, or one that may be useful for a time only, or one that may contain elements that are harmful to me or others. Thus my wholehearted commitment is of the nature of an experiment. No matter how the experiment turns out, I will learn from it by honestly evaluating it.

I recognize that becoming immersed in a path may lead to loss of perspective and forgetting of my goals. Therefore, to evaluate this experiment in commitment, I promise myself that at the end of the commitment period specified above I will withdraw from the group and teacher, go off by myself for a period of at least two months to allow the immediate influence and habits of thought of the group to diminish, and then evaluate the experiment in the light of the goals and values listed above.

Because I may forget this commitment, I have given a copy of this contract, in a sealed envelope, to my good friend _____, who has promised to deliver it to me at the end of the commitment period, even if we are no longer friends.

I will probably have changed at the end of the commitment period. Given the goals and values listed above, do I like this change? Is the group and teacher helping me meet my goals or hindering me? Do I see that some of my earlier goals and values aren't important or were misguided? Is this a genuine perception of my deeper self or merely the fashions of the group or teacher I have been with? Have I changed in unexpected ways? Do I want to increase these unexpected changes or not? Am I a better person as a result of my work, or do I simply feel superior for being part of a "special" group? Can I get useful feedback from old friends who are not part of the group on how I have changed? (Beware of putting them under pressure to say you've improved to justify the time you've put in.) Am I more able to help my fellow humans? Have I cut myself off from my fellows by thinking of them as inferior to my friends in my group?

After prolonged reflection on these and similar questions, do I want to continue with that teacher and group, or find something different? If I continue with this path, or begin another one, I will make another contract with myself like the present one.

I ask the highest powers in the universe to assist and guide me on my journey.

We began this book with a look at the possibilities of enlightenment, a wide range of understandings and abilities that would help to make life more meaningful, effective, loving, and peaceful. The reality of our situation made us focus on the obstacles to enlightened abilities. They are many, but they are not insurmountable. Awakening from consensus trance is not easy, and yes, there are dangers in attempting it, but the rewards for yourself and others are very great. I hope you will find the effort worthwhile, and find the Light. I wish you good luck on your journey of discovery!

25

Reality and God

There is no God but Reality.
To seek Him elsewhere
Is the action of the Fall.

APPENDIX A

Recommended Readings

READINGS USEFUL FOR WAKING UP

This appendix lists some of the more useful books on Gurdjieff's ideas, as well as a few more general writings of mine that supplement and expand the themes in this book. This is only a small selection of what is available. If you get very interested in this sort of material, you will find more as you read.

I want to emphasize again, however, that *reading* per se is only a small part of the process of understanding yourself and beginning to awaken. It is helpful to have some intellectual framework, but only if that intellectual framework is a provisional tool for working with deeper experiential data. The map can be a useful guide to the territory, but it is not the territory. Indeed, having a good map when you are too far from the territory is dangerous, for we are easily charmed by clear maps and think we know too much.

Note too that Gurdjieff's work was intended to be passed on primarily by direct contact between teacher and student, so the books are often deliberately incomplete.

Several times I have stressed that you should not accept the ideas in this book just because they seem clear or clever or appealing, or because they come from people who are supposed to be authorities on consciousness. Test them for yourself, modify them as needed, and accept only what works out in your experience. Even then, make such acceptance provisional: if your further experience doesn't fit with the ideas, they may need to be revised. Be particularly wary if you find yourself passionately defending any idea, as such an action often indicates that at a deeper level you are not at all sure about it yourself and are afraid to look at it clearly.

This same advice applies to all the readings cited here.

BOOKS ABOUT THE GURDJIEFF WORK

For most of us, books about Gurdjieff's ideas and practices are easier to begin with than Gurdjieff's own writings. Opinions vary greatly among people who espouse Gurdjieff's ideas as to the authenticity and usefulness of the various books in this category, however. Some use the criterion that having studied directly with Gurdjieff is a prerequisite for writing an accurate book, and judge later books by their consistency with the writings of such direct pupils and Gurdjieff's own writings. This makes a fair amount of sense. Others feel that this attitude tends to become dogmatic and is an attempt to preserve an "ideological purity" that fossilizes what should be a living teaching. This also makes sense.

In making a selection of readings, I assume that almost any book by any person (including me and including Gurdjieff) will be a mixture of wisdom and error, and it is up to the reader to discriminate. The books I mention below are such mixtures but, I believe, have much more wisdom than error in them. I also have some bias toward books that focus on the psychology, rather than the cosmology, of Gurdjieff, as I can more easily understand and validate the former than the latter. The ones listed here have been useful to me, and will, I hope, be useful to you. The editions cited are the most recent at the time of writing.

In Search of the Miraculous: Fragments of an Unknown Teaching by P. D. Ouspensky (New York: Harcourt Brace Jovanovich, 1977) is generally considered one of the best and most comprehensive expositions of many of Gurdjieff's ideas. Gurdjieff approved the book as being an accurate exposition of the ideas he was teaching at the time Ouspensky studied with him. I have returned to it many times for clarification. It is not an easy book, but it is well worth attempting to master. It presents Gurdjieff's cosmological theories, which may be profound or incorrect: I cannot tell which.

In reading this book, note that Ouspensky did break with Gurdjieff and so indeed presents fragments, not a complete system, as he honestly indicated in the book and in its subtitle. Ouspensky was a brilliant intellectual, probably in the unbalanced way described in Chapter 14, and I believe the break came when he could no longer deal with the emotional aspects of Gurdjieff's work. Try to compensate for the overly intellectual tone of the book as you read it.

Ouspensky also wrote a much shorter introduction to Gurdjieff's work, *The Psychology of Man's Possible Evolution* (latest edition, New York: Random House, 1981). I recommend reading this before starting *In Search of the Miraculous*. When you are familiar with these two books, you may want to read Ouspensky's *The Fourth Way: A Record of Talks and Answers to Questions Based on the Teaching of G. I. Gurdjieff* (New York: Random House, 1971).

Another brief introduction to Gurdjieff's ideas is a chapter by Kathleen Riordan (Speeth) in my *Transpersonal Psychologies* (El Cerrito, Calif.: Psychological Processes, 1983). She later expanded this chapter into a small book, *The Gurdjieff Work* (Berkeley: And/Or Press, 1976).

John Bennett spent some time working with Gurdjieff, as well as studying other sources of psychological and spiritual teaching. His books have impressed me as intelligent and honest attempts to understand Gurdjieff, rather than just a repetition of Gurdjieff's ideas. His major work, *Gurdjieff: Making a New World* (New York: Harper & Row, 1976), is a combination of the presentation of some of Gurdjieff's ideas with historical background for those ideas and speculation about their meaning.

Robert deRopp's *The Master Game: Pathways to Higher Consciousness beyond the Drug Experience* is a useful introduction to Gurdjieff's ideas in the context of the psychedelic revolution of the late 1960s, giving a broader context than the usual Gurdjieff book. There is a strong streak of negativity toward ordinary people running through deRopp's writings which may need to be filtered out in reading. When I read deRopp's autobiography, *Warrior's Way: The Challenging Life Games* (New York: Delacorte, 1979), I understand the roots of his attitude and admire his personal triumph over the horrors life can put in our way.

Maurice Nicoll was a psychologist who trained with Carl Jung before becoming involved with Gurdjieff's ideas. His five volumes of *Psychological Commentaries on the Teaching of Gurdjieff and Ouspensky* (Boston: Shambhala Publications, 1984) are valuable and stimulating. He also was interested in the relation of Gurdjieff's ideas to early and esoteric Christianity, and put forward some ingenious ideas of their relationship in *The Mark* (Boston: Shambhala Publications, 1985), and *The New Man* (Boston: Shambhala Publications, 1984).

Michel Waldberg's *Gurdjieff: An Approach to His Ideas* (London: Routledge and Kegan Paul, 1981) is a useful and brief introduction, as is Kenneth Walker's *A Study of Gurdjieff's Teaching* (New York: Samuel

Weiser, 1974), and Jean Vaysse's *Toward Awakening: An Approach to the Teaching Left by Gurdjieff* (San Francisco: Harper & Row, 1979).

For the reader who wants to track down everything written about Gurdjieff, the authoritative reference work is *Gurdjieff: An Annotated Bibliography*, by J. Walter Driscoll and the Gurdjieff Foundation of California (New York: Garland Publishing, 1985). With 1,146 references to English-language references to Gurdjieff, 581 in French, and some miscellaneous ones in other languages, this is as complete a scholarly reference as we could hope for. Many of the references are merely passing mentions, but all the substantial references are there. The evaluation of some of the references as misleading or worthless from the authors' point of view sometimes comes through the attempt at scholarly neutrality.

GURDJIEFF'S WRITINGS

Gurdjieff gave the inclusive title *All and Everything* to a series of three books that were intended to be an exposition of his major teachings. The first volume of the series was entitled *Beelzebub's Tales to His Grandson* (New York: Dutton, 1978). Written as an allegory, it takes the form of stories by a very high cosmic personage/"devil"/angel, Beelzebub, told to his grandson to illustrate the way the universe works, particularly with reference to humanity on Earth.

In writing this volume Gurdjieff tried an experiment based on the idea that the harder you work for something, the more you appreciate it. He would write a chapter and read it to his students. If they understood it, he would rewrite it to make it more difficult. Full of elaborate, multisyllabic words invented by Gurdjieff, this is a difficult book. I have heard stories that Gurdjieff decided in later life that this experiment hadn't worked—students did not necessarily have a better understanding because of the deliberate difficulty. I am not sure whether you should force your way through it. In some branches of the Gurdjieff work it is treated like a sacred gospel whose every word is absolutely true. This has the negative effect of making those who don't clearly understand it feel guilty and inadequate.

The second volume of the series, *Meetings with Remarkable Men* (New York: Dutton, 1969), is very readable. You can breeze through it like an interesting novel, as an allegorical account of some of Gurdjieff's travels, but it has deeper levels.

Life Is Real Only Then, When "I Am" (New York: Dutton, 1982) is the third volume of the series, and very provocative. I would suggest this as later reading, after gaining thorough familiarity with Gurdjieff's work.

Views from the Real World (New York: Dutton, 1975) is a collection of talks of Gurdjieff as recollected by his pupils.

The Herald of Coming Good: First Appeal to Contemporary Humanity (New York: Samuel Weiser, 1971) strikes me as one of Gurdjieff's experiments that he quickly decided wasn't going right, as he withdrew it almost immediately. Of primarily historical interest.

RELATED WRITINGS

The following recommended readings deal with psychological possibilities for us that fit with the theme of waking up of this book.

If you like the style of presentation of material in this book, you may want to subscribe to my quarterly essay/newsletter, *The Open Mind*. I will continue writing about waking up in there, as well as discussing altered states, parapsychology, and related topics. Additionally, the newsletter lists my forthcoming lectures and workshops around the country. Subscription information on *The Open Mind* can be obtained from Box 37, El Cerrito, CA 94530.

I have been asked whether I will set up another working group on waking up for Northern California people, similar to the Awareness Enhancement Training group I ran several years ago. I have not made any decision yet, but if you are interested in such a group you can write me at the address for *The Open Mind* given above. If I do so, it will be announced in *The Open Mind*.

A more formal scientific presentation of my understanding of the mind, particularly as mind manifests in various altered states of consciousness, is presented in my *States of Consciousness* (originally published by Dutton, 1975, now in print with Psychological Processes). This book will be of particular interest to psychologists and researchers. My *Altered States of Consciousness* (New York: Doubleday, 1971) is a collection of research articles on topics like hypnosis, dreaming, lucid dreaming, meditation, and psychedelic drug effects that offers further background. *Transpersonal Psychologies* (originally published by Harper & Row, now in print with Psychological Processes) develops the parapsychological background for taking spiritual development seriously and has chapters by several authorities that present the psychologies inherent in a number of major spiritual systems (Buddhism, Yoga, Gurdjieff, the Arica Training, Sufism, Christianity, and the Western Magical Tradition). These books are available from Psychological Processes at Box 37, El Cerrito, CA 94530, as is the musical body guidance tape mentioned in Chapter 23.

The books I am currently working with intensively in my personal search are a three-volume set, *A Course in Miracles* (Tiburon, Calif.: Foundation for Inner Peace, 1975). Gurdjieff said that we all have to come to terms someday with the religion of our childhood, and the course is forcing me to do this. Its inspiration/authorship is attributed to the Christ Consciousness, something not subject to ordinary validation, and an attribution likely to evoke many resistances, but its content clearly comes from a level that, for want of a better term, we might say is the higher emotional center. It represents an extremely high level of psychological sophistication, while speaking directly to the heart. For example:

> Perception can make whatever picture
> the mind desires to see.
> Remember this.
> In this lies either Heaven or hell,
> as you elect.

or:

> When I have forgiven myself
> and remembered who I am,
> I will bless everyone and everything I see.

I am just a beginner at understanding the course, and I have enormous resistances to accepting it (which suggests something about my unconscious beliefs). Some aspects of it fit in with and expand many of the ideas in this book; some are beyond my power to fit in at this point. If you are ready to struggle with our Judeo-Christian heritage, I recommend it highly.

GENERAL BIBLIOGRAPHY ON CONSCIOUSNESS AND TRANSPERSONAL PSYCHOLOGY

When I published my *Altered States of Consciousness* in 1969, reliable, scientifically oriented information about these drastic, fascinating, and important changes in the way our minds can function was difficult to find. I hoped that my book, by providing a central source of information on altered states, would be a contribution toward legitimatizing altered states as a field of psychology. Developments since that time have been very encouraging. There has not been as much progress as I had hoped: I thought my *Altered States* book would be outmoded within a decade, but it is still the standard reference book in the field. There are still many questions, but we do know more than before.

An extensive bibliography on older literature on altered states of consciousness, transpersonal psychology, and related topics can be found in *Altered States of Consciousness*, but this naturally only goes up to the late 1960s. I am happy to say that the field is now so extensive that it would take far more time than I have to prepare a really comprehensive bibliography. This one lists books that have appeared since the late 1960s that deal with altered states, transpersonal psychology, and related areas. These are books I have in my personal library and so can recommend as generally reliable and worthwhile. They are listed alphabetically, by author. I have put a (t) after those that are rather technical.

Ajaya, Swami. *Psychotherapy East and West: A Unifying Paradigm*. Honesdale, Pa.: Himalayan Publishers, 1984.

Barber, T. (ed.). *Advances in Altered States of Consciousness and Human Potentialities*, vol. 1. New York: Psychological Dimensions, 1976.

Cade, C., and Coxhead, N. *The Awakened Mind: Biofeedback and the Development of Higher States of Awareness*. New York: Delacorte, 1979.

Carrington, P. *Freedom in Meditation*. New York: Anchor, 1977.

Castaneda, C. *The Teachings of Don Juan: A Yaqui Way of Knowledge*. Berkeley: University of California Press, 1968.

_____. *Tales of Power*. New York: Simon & Schuster, 1974.

_____. *A Separate Reality: Further Conversations with Don Juan*. New York: Simon & Schuster, 1971.

_____. *Journey to Ixtlan: The Lessons of Don Juan*. New York: Simon & Schuster, 1972.

_____. *The Second Ring of Power*. New York: Simon & Schuster, 1977.

_____. *The Eagle's Gift*. New York: Simon & Schuster, 1981.

_____. *The Fire from Within*. New York: Simon & Schuster, 1984.

Davidson, J., and Davidson, R. (eds.). *The Psychobiology of Consciousness*. New York: Plenum, 1980.

Davidson, R.; Schwartz, G.; and Shapiro, D. (eds.). *Consciousness and Self-Regulation: Advances in Research and Theory*, vol. 3. New York: Plenum, 1983. (t)

Deikman, A. *Personal Freedom: On Finding Your Way to the Real World*. New York: Grossman, 1976.

_____. *The Observing Self: Mysticism and Psychotherapy*. Boston: Beacon Press, 1982.

Dixon, N. *Subliminal Perception: The Nature of a Controversy*. New York: Macmillan, 1971. (t)

Dychtwald, K. *Bodymind*. New York: Pantheon, 1977.

Ellwood, R. *Religious and Spiritual Groups in Modern America*. Englewood Cliffs, N.J.: Prentice-Hall, 1973.

Emmons, M. *The Inner Source: A Guide to Meditative Therapy*. San Luis Obispo, Calif.: Impact Publishers, 1978.

Ferguson, M. *The Aquarian Conspiracy: Personal and Social Transformation in the 1980s*. Los Angeles: J. P. Tarcher, 1980.

Furst, P. *Hallucinogens and Culture*. San Francisco: Chandler & Sharp, 1976.

Garfield, P. *Creative Dreaming*. New York: Simon & Schuster, 1974.

_____. *Pathway to Ecstasy: The Way of the Dream Mandala*. New York: Holt, Rinehart & Winston, 1979.

Galyean, B. *Mind Sight: Learning through Imaging*. Long Beach, Calif.: Center for Integrative Learning (767 Gladys Ave.), 1983.

Goleman, D., and Davidson, R. (eds.). *Consciousness: Brain, States of Awareness, and Mysticism*. New York: Harper & Row, 1979.

Grinspoon, L., and Bakalar, J. *Psychedelic Drugs Reconsidered*. New York: Basic Books, 1979.

_____. (eds.). *Psychedelic Reflections*. New York: Human Sciences Press, 1983.

Grof, S. *Realms of the Human Unconscious: Observations from LSD Research*. New York: Viking, 1975.

_____, and Halifax, J. *The Human Encounter with Death*. New York: Dutton, 1977.

_____. *LSD Psychotherapy*. Pomona, Calif.: Hunter House, 1980.

_____, and Grof, C. *Beyond Death: The Gates of Consciousness*. London: Thames & Hudson, 1980.

Halifax, J. *Shaman: The Wounded Healer*. New York: Crossroad, 1982.

Hampden-Turner, C. *Maps of the Minds*. New York: Macmillan, 1981.

Harner, M. *The Way of the Shaman: A Guide to Power and Healing*. San Francisco: Harper & Row, 1980.

_____. (ed.). *Hallucinogens and Shamanism*. London: Oxford University Press, 1973.

Hendricks, G., and Weinhold, B. *Transpersonal Approaches to Counseling and Psychotherapy*. Denver: Love Publishing, 1982.

Hillman, J. *Revisioning Psychology*. New York: Harper & Row, 1975.

Hoffer, A., and Osmond, H. *The Hallucinogens*. New York: Academic Press, 1967. (t)

Hoffman, E. *The Way of Splendor: Jewish Mysticism and Modern Psychology*. Boulder: Shambhala, 1981.

Houston, J. *The Possible Human*. Los Angeles: J. P. Tarcher, 1982.

John, Da Free. *The Transmission of Doubt: Talks and Essays on the Transcendence of Scientific Materialism through Radical Understanding*. Clearlake, Calif.: Dawn Horse Press, 1984.

Johnson, D. *Body*. Boston: Beacon, 1983.

Johnson, W. *Riding the Ox Home: A History of Meditation from Shamanism to Science*. London: Rider, 1982.

Larsen, S. *The Shaman's Doorway: Opening the Mythic Imagination to Contemporary Consciousness*. New York: Harper & Row, 1976.

Lee, P.; Ornstein, R.; Galin, D.; Deikman, A.; and Tart, C. *Symposium on Consciousness*. New York: Viking, 1976.

Leonard, G. *The Transformation: A Guide to the Inevitable Changes in Humankind*. Los Angeles: J. P. Tarcher, 1972.

Lilly, J. *The Center of the Cyclone: An Autobiography of Inner Space*. New York: Julian Press, 1972.

Mann, R. *The Light of Consciousness: Explorations in Transpersonal Psychology.* Albany, N.Y.: State University of New York Press, 1984.

Master, R., and Houston, J. *The Varieties of Psychedelic Experience.* New York: Holt, Rinehart & Winston, 1966.

Naranjo, C. *The One Quest.* New York: Viking, 1972.

———, and Ornstein, R. *On the Psychology of Meditation.* New York: Viking, 1971.

———. *The Healing Journey: New Approaches to Consciousness.* New York: Pantheon, 1973.

Needleman, J. *The New Religions.* New York: Doubleday, 1970.

———, and Baker, G. (eds.). *Understanding the New Religions.* New York: Seabury Press, 1978.

Ornstein, R. *The Psychology of Consciousness.* San Francisco: W. H. Freeman, 1972.

———. (ed.). *The Nature of Human Consciousness: A Book of Readings.* New York: Viking, 1973.

Owens, C. *Zen and the Lady.* New York: Baraka Books, 1979.

Parker, A. *States of Mind: ESP and Altered States of Consciousness.* New York: Taplinger, 1975.

Pearce, J. *The Crack in the Cosmic Egg.* New York: Julian Press, 1971.

———. *Magical Child: Rediscovering Nature's Plan for Our Children.* New York: Dutton, 1977.

De Riencourt, A. *The Eye of Shiva: Eastern Mysticism and Science.* New York: Morrow, 1981.

Ring, K. *Heading toward Omega: In Search of the Meaning of the Near-Death Experience.* New York: Morrow, 1984.

Savary, L.; Berne, P.; and Williams, S. *Dreams and Spiritual Growth: A Christian Approach to Dreamwork.* New York: Paulist Press, 1984.

Schwartz, G., and Shapiro, D. (eds.). *Consciousness and Self-Regulation: Advances in Research,* vol. 1. New York: Plenum, 1976. (t)

Siegel, R., and West L. (eds.). *Hallucinations: Behavior, Experience, and Theory.* New York: Wiley, 1975.

Shapiro, D. *Precision Nirvana.* Englewood Cliffs, N.J.: Prentice-Hall, 1978.

———. *Meditation: Self-Regulation Strategy and Altered States of Consciousness.* New York: Aldine, 1980.

Sugarman, A., and Tarter, R. (eds.). *Expanding Dimensions of Consciousness.* New York: Springer, 1978. (t)

Tart, C. *On Being Stoned: A Psychological Study of Marijuana Intoxication.* Palo Alto, Calif.: Science and Behavior Books, 1971.

———. *States of Consciousness.* El Cerrito, Calif.: Psychological Processes, 1983.

———. (ed.). *Altered States of Consciousness.* New York: Doubleday, 1971.

———. (ed.). *Transpersonal Psychologies.* El Cerrito, Calif.: Psychological Processes, 1983.

Taylor, J. *Dream Work: Techniques for Discovering the Creative Power in Dreams.* New York: Paulist Press, 1983.

Tulku, Tarthang (ed.). *Reflections of Mind: Western Psychology Meets Tibetan Buddhism.* Emeryville, Calif.: Dharma Publishing, 1975.

Valle, R., and von Eckartsberg, R. (eds.). *The Metaphors of Consciousness.* New York: Plenum, 1981.

Vaughan, F. *Awakening Intuition.* New York: Anchor, 1979.

Walsh, R., and Vaughan, F. (eds.). *Beyond Ego: Transpersonal Dimensions in Psychology.* Los Angeles: J. P. Tarcher, 1980.

Wavell, S.; Butt, A.; and Epton, N. *Trances.* New York: Dutton, 1967.

Weil, A. *The Natural Mind: A New Way of Looking at Drugs and Higher Consciousness.* Boston: Houghton Mifflin, 1972.

White, J. (ed.). *The Highest States of Consciousness.* New York: Doubleday, 1972.

_____. (ed.). *Frontiers of Consciousness: The Meeting Ground between Inner and Outer Reality.* New York: Julian Press, 1974.

Wilber, K. *The Spectrum of Consciousness.* Wheaton, Ill.: Quest, 1977.

_____. (ed.). *The Holographic Paradigm and Other Paradoxes: Exploring the Leading Edge of Science.* Boulder: Shambhala, 1982.

Zinberg, N. (ed.). *Alternate States of Consciousness: Multiple Perspectives on the Study of Consciousness.* New York: Free Press, 1977.

Zukav, G. *The Dancing Wu Li Masters: An Overview of the New Physics.* New York: Morrow, 1979.

APPENDIX B

Finding a Gurdjieff-Oriented Group

This appendix is addressed to those who have found the ideas in this book appealing enough that they want to find and work with a development group that specifically teaches Gurdjieff's work. I do not believe this is the only way of personal and spiritual development, of course, but it is a powerful system that can be very helpful to some of us.

I would like to give a long list of mailing addresses of such groups to make your task simple, but I cannot, for several reasons.

First, I would be implicitly approving groups on such a list, suggesting that they give an accurate and practical transmission of Gurdjieff's ideas and methods. Since my own understanding of the total range of Gurdjieff's ideas is limited, however, it would be presumptuous of me to approve or disapprove of groups teaching them.

Second, I have heard convincing arguments that no one can accurately teach Gurdjieff's ideas, as he did not unambiguously appoint anyone as a successor in his role of teacher. Perhaps all groups claiming to teach his ideas should be regarded as only partially qualified at best, or as simply mere imitators, and none should be recommended. On the other hand, Gurdjieff was a master of using ambiguity and deliberately failing to meet expectations in order to force people to awaken and perceive and think for themselves, so the fact that he did not publicly hand someone a scroll saying "X is awake and my official successor; take orders from X!" may be a great advantage. This lack of a clear lineage is not a problem in groups that simply claim inspiration from some of Gurdjieff's ideas rather than direct transmission. These kinds of groups need to be evaluated on their own merits.

Third, any development group whose teacher dies runs the risk of fossilizing, for the kinds of reasons discussed in Chapter 21. Transference-based attitudes that idolize the teacher and will stand for no change in anything he did, social needs that must be fulfilled by maintaining the social structure of the group, and the like tend to fix the group into a pattern of repeating the past, instead of waking up to the present. There are several development groups around that have a teacher who was a student of Gurdjieff or a student of a student of Gurdjieff. Does this give a genuineness of transmission that adds to the power of the group's work, or increase the probability of a fossilization of method? Is lack of innovation a sign of intelligent preservation of the essence of Gurdjieff's ideas, or a sign of insufficient understanding of them to adapt them to contemporary needs? I do not feel competent to make this judgment for others.

There are groups whose leader is "inspired" by Gurdjieff's ideas without having had much direct contact with the more orthodox groups: they are not in the "direct line of transmission," to use the terminology of spiritual systems that stress direct contact from teacher to teacher. Does this mean that the group is free of the fossilizing effects of orthodoxy and so more dynamic and alive, or that such "Gurdjieff work" owes more to imagination and inadequate understanding than to Gurdjieff's actual ideas? There are groups that have been around for a long time and groups that are quite young, about which the same questions can be asked. There are groups that are sincere and "orthodox," but which I suspect are probably fossilized to some degree. Yet you could learn a great deal by sincerely working with them. None of my own teachers, in the Gurdjieff work or other traditions, have been, to my perception, perfect beings or fully awake—indeed, they have sometimes had very clear character flaws—but I have learned enormously from them. There are other groups that are probably run by charlatans, using Gurdjieff's ideas and tough style as a way of exploiting people.

Ideally any development group should be judged by its fruits. A university, for example, may have impressive buildings and laboratories, dignified-looking professors and many libraries, and wonderful goals and plans. But it is ultimately judged on the actual scholarly and practical accomplishments of its faculty and graduates, not on its buildings and appearances, its plans, or its own opinion of itself. We have a general scholarly community that our society believes is competent to make such judgments. Some self-proclaimed spiritually advanced people have judged the Gurdjieff work, some saying it is outmoded and others that it is vital, but as our society has no generally accepted way of deciding who is capable in such matters, these judgments cannot be of much use to us. My own experience of meeting people from many spiritual traditions is that some people have indeed become more awake and mature, others use the traditions to fool themselves.

As individuals trying to awaken and grow, we must make our own as-sessments of a group and decide whether to give our energies to it, even while recognizing that our judgment may be distorted and inadequate. We can weigh in the opinions of others, but the final decision is our own. If we make a good judgment and grow from working with a certain group, fine. If we make a bad judgment and do not grow or are hurt in working with that group, fine—we did the best we could, and now we can try to understand why our judgment was poor and learn from it. The spiritual commitment contract discussion in Chapter 24 will be helpful for this.

Thus I do not point you toward any particular Gurdjieff groups, nor recommend nor warn about any particular ones. If you want to find such groups, use your everyday practical intelligence: write to publishers and authors of relevant books, talk to people in metaphysical bookstores, ask around among friends and acquaintances. Most major metropolitan areas will have one or more groups with at least some orientation to Gurdjieff's ideas. Once you find a potential group, use the suggestions throughout this book to see if it has heart for you.

As we have discussed earlier, groups are dangerous. Since we are so-cial animals, the power others have over us can easily deepen our sleep. They function as co-hypnotists with the culture, rather than as awakeners. Many of us are thus tempted to go it alone and avoid the dan-ger of others' influence, but we can't. We have already had the influence of the cultural hypnotist and many other groups programmed into us: psychologically we belong to many "cults." Working with any new group does entail risks, but also gives us an opportunity to wake up to group influences in a way that can let us undo the negative effects groups have already had on us. Remember, too, that *not* working with some de-velopment group does not mean you are safe.

Godspeed on your voyage of discovery!

NOTES

Chapter 1: *States of Consciousness and Enlightenment*

1. C. Tart, *States of Consciousness* (El Cerrito, Calif.: Psychological Processes, 1983; originally published 1975).
2. Throughout this book, when I use words like *his* and *he* (or sometimes *her* and *she*) in general examples, I intend them to be inclusive of both men and women.
3. Tart, *States of Consciousness*, p. 58.
4. Mild emotions can occur within various states, but when intensity goes beyond some critical point, there is a reorganization of consciousness into a discrete emotional state, a state different from that in which the emotion started.
5. If you are interested in a more technical and precise definition of states of consciousness, as well as some of the other topics in Chapter 1, you will find my *States of Consciousness* helpful.
6. Tart, *States of Consciousness*.
7. See Tart, *States of Consciousness*, chap. 7, for the general principles of inducing any altered state.

Chapter 2: *God and Reality*

1. An oral teaching attributed to the (mythical?) Sarmouni Brotherhood.

Chapter 6: *Living in the World Simulator*

1. The generally accepted contemporary scientific view is that mind is nothing but the activities of our brain, simulating our world, technically termed the psychoneural identity hypothesis. This is a useful theory for our purposes of understanding the ways in which we are asleep, but I do want to note that I am sure the total equation of consciousness with neural activity is wrong. The data of parapsychological research demonstrate conclusively that mind is much more than neural activity, and pragmatic considerations require us to be dualistic and see mind as partly neural activity and partly something more. I have elaborated such a theory elsewhere in "An Emergent-Interactionist Understanding of Human Consciousness," in B. Shapin and L. Coly (eds.), *Brain/Mind and Parapsychology* (New York: Parapsychology Foundation, 1979), pp. 177–200. Except for Chapter 20, I shall not pursue the parapsychological issue in this book, however, for it would unnecessarily arouse resistances in some readers and thus prevent communication of useful information. I can assure those

who don't like parapsychological ideas that most of the useful information in this book makes perfect sense even if you believe in the psychoneural identity hypothesis.

Chapter 7: *Emotions*

1. Tart, *States of Consciousness,* chap. 8.

Chapter 9: *Hypnosis*

1. Tart, *States of Consciousness.*
2. R. Shor, "Hypnosis and the Concept of the Generalized Reality Orientation," *American Journal of Psychotherapy* 13: 582–602; R. Shor, "Three Dimensions of Hypnotic Depth," *International Journal of Clinical and Experimental Hypnosis* 10: 23–38; also in C. Tart, ed., *Altered States of Consciousness: A Book of Readings* (New York: Doubleday, 1971).
3. I have also been selective in my emphasis as part of building up to the discussion of consensus trance in Chapter 10. Readers interested in a more comprehensive view of hypnosis should see my *States of Consciousness* and appropriate chapters in my *Altered States of Consciousness.*

Chapter 10: *Consensus Trance*

1. The consensus trance induction process probably begins before birth. The neurochemical balances of the mother's body may affect the fetus in some cases, reflecting emotional states. Recent research has also shown that speech sounds are heard very well in the womb, so the structure of the language of the culture, as well as the kind of emotional states reflected by shouting, excitement, etc., may have some effect on the fetus.
2. Sometimes in ordinary hypnosis the subject unconsciously projects his childhood attitudes onto the hypnotist. This is the transference dimension of hypnosis, which we discussed in Chapter 9. It definitely increases the hypnotist's ability to alter the subject's reality and control his behavior.
3. The reader will note that my white, middle-class conditionings show in this and other examples. For simplicity, I ignore class, ethnic, racial, and subcultural differences in the United States in this chapter.
4. As an interesting example of the semiarbitrary quality of our simulations of reality, I once trained several talented hypnotic subjects to simulate personal space in a different way. After explaining the concept to them while hypnotized, I suggested that they could then feel or perceive it in some way that was especially meaningful to them. This feeling/perception would stay with them when they returned to consensus consciousness, and they were then to go through their ordinary day with a notebook, making observations on personal space.

    The results were quite fascinating. Some subjects experienced personal space as an actual sense of touch, others as a dim light or fog around them. The implicit, the automatized and unconscious, became a "direct sensory" experience. It wasn't really a sensory experience of course, but was now being simulated that way, that was its internal reality.

5. This and the previous example of unconscious equations are simplistic, but the unconscious mind frequently works in a literal, simplistic fashion.
6. We won't deal here with so-called hallucinations that might have a certain reality, such as those conveying psychically or intuitively gathered information.
7. See J. Lilly and J. Hart, "The Arica Training," in C. Tart (ed.), *Transpersonal Psychologies* (El Cerrito, Calif.: Psychological Processes, 1983).
8. C. Tart, "The Hypnotic Dream: Methodological Problems and a Review of the Literature," *Psychological Bulletin* 63: 87–99.

Chapter 11: *Identification*

1. Tart, *States of Consciousness*, p. 130.

Chapter 12: *Identity States*

1. P. D. Ouspensky, *In Search of the Miraculous: Fragments of an Unknown Teaching* (New York: Harcourt, Brace & World, 1949), p. 59.
2. Ernest R. Hilgard, *Divided Consciousness: Multiple Controls in Human Thought and Action* (New York: Wiley Interscience, 1977) and "The Problem of Divided Consciousness: A Neodissociation Interpretation," *Annals of the New York Academy of Sciences* 296 (1977): 48–59.
3. Tart, *States of Consciousness*.

Chapter 13: *Defense Mechanisms*

1. Lilly and Hart in Tart, *Transpersonal Psychologies*.
2. For many people, a time-limited practice of deliberately and consciously lying can be very growthful. It is also very difficult. On several occasions I gave participants in my Awareness Enhancement Training group a "simple" assignment: tell five little white lies each day for two weeks. I specified that the lies were to be harmless, to have no real consequences for them or the people they were told to. Yet people usually found enormous difficulty and tension in carrying out this exercise, or resisted by consistently forgetting to try it.
3. Lilly and Hart in Tart, *Transpersonal Psychologies*.

Chapter 14: *Balance and Imbalance in Three-Brained Beings*

1. Although there is some modern evidence from neurophysiological research for the anatomical and functional distinctness of these three brains, it is their observable functional qualities that matter for our discussion. I shall continue to use the word *brain*, but don't be concerned with the anatomy of the physical brain. Gurdjieff used *centers* at times rather than *brain*, and also spoke of other centers and finer divisions of these centers, but that level of detail will not concern us here.
2. See Ouspensky, *In Search of the Miraculous*, p. 45.
3. We have no experimental data in parapsychology showing that the deliberate development of intense emotions increases psychic abilities, but dramatic, spontaneous

psychic experiences are usually connected with tragic events that arouse strong emotions. See my *Psi: Scientific Studies of the Psychic Realm* (New York: Dutton, 1977).

Chapter 15: *False Personality and Essence*

1. S. Spender, *Selected Poems of Stephen Spender* (New York: Random House, 1964).
2. See Ouspensky, *In Search of the Miraculous*, pp. 251–253.
3. C. Tart, *On Being Stoned: A Psychological Study of Marijuana Intoxication* (Palo Alto, Calif.: Science and Behavior Books, 1971).

Chapter 16: *Toward Awakening*

1. This is too limited a view of psychopathology but is enough for our purposes in this book.

Chapter 18: *Self-Remembering*

1. See Tart, *States of Consciousness*, for a more detailed discussion of stabilization processes.

Chapter 19: *Higher Levels of Consciousness*

1. Tart, *Transpersonal Psychologies*. See also C. Tart, *Hidden Shackles: The Assumptions of Western Psychology*, cassette tape, available from Psychological Processes, Box 37, El Cerrito, CA 94530.
2. Certain kinds of work with nocturnal dreaming can be quite valuable as part of the growth process. Proper analysis of dreams can give insights into the mechanisms and dynamics of false personality, for example. A special kind of *lucidity* can also be cultivated in nocturnal dreams which is similar to self-remembering in consensus trance, and can lead to very interesting developments. This book is not the place to develop this idea, but there are chapters on it in my *Altered States of Consciousness*; I have written at some length about it in issues 1, 2, and 4 of *The Open Mind*, vol. 1, and Stephen LaBerge recently published an excellent book on it: *Lucid Dreaming: The Power of Being Awake and Aware in Your Dreams* (Los Angeles: Jeremy Tarcher, 1985).
3. There are rare moments in life when a condition like objective self-consciousness just comes on us, even though we have made no preceding efforts at self-remembering. These states are blessings if used correctly. They can be very inspiring or quickly forgotten, depending on what you do. Accept them gratefully when they happen and try to learn from them, but don't depend on them. It is nice to find money lying in the street, but it's a very unreliable way to earn a living.
4. Tart, "States of Consciousness and State-Specific Sciences," *Science* 176 (1972): 1203–1210; Tart, *States of Consciousness*; Tart, *Transpersonal Psychologies*.

Chapter 20: *Spiritual Reality, Work, and Prayer*

1. C. Tart, "A Possible 'Psychic' Dream, with Some Speculation on the Nature of Such Dreams," *Journal of the Society for Psychical Research* 42 (1963): 283–298; C. Tart and

J. Fadiman, "The Case of the Yellow Wheat Field: A Dream-State Explanation of a Broadcast Telepathic Dream," *Psychoanalytic Review* 61 (1974): 607–618.

2. R. Stanford, "An Experimentally Testable Model for Spontaneous Psi Events: I. Extrasensory Events, II. Psychokinetic Events," *Journal of the Society for Psychical Research* 68 (1974): 34–57, 321–356.

3. Further information on psi may be found in Tart, *Psi: Scientific Studies of the Psychic Realm,* or in the very complete *Handbook of Parapsychology* by Wolman et al. (New York: Van Nostrand Reinhold, 1977).

4. C. Tart, "States of Consciousness and State-Specific Sciences," *Science* 176: 1203–1210.

5. Ouspensky, *In Search of the Miraculous,* pp. 300–301.

Chapter 22: *Problems with the Work Process*

1. Daniel Goleman, "Early Warning Signs for the Detection of Spiritual Blight," *Newsletter,* Association for Transpersonal Psychology, Summer 1985, p. 11. See also Dick Anthony, Bruce Eckev, and Ken Wilber (eds.), *Spiritual Choices: Recognizing Authentic Paths to Inner Transformation* (New York: Paragon House, 1986).

Chapter 23: *Compassion*

1. T. Gyatso (the Dalai Lama), *Kindness, Clarity, and Insight* (Ithaca, N.Y.: Snow Lion Publications, 1984).

Chapter 24: *Selecting a Spiritual Path*

1. Quoted in Ouspensky, *In Search of the Miraculous,* p. 364.
2. I. Shah, *The Sufis* (New York: Doubleday, 1964).
3. Lilly and Hart in Tart, *Transpersonal Psychologies.*

REFERENCES

Crabtree, A. *Multiple Man*. New York: Praeger, 1985.

Gyasto, T. (the Dalai Lama). *Kindness, Clarity, and Insight*. Ithaca, N.Y.: Snow Lion Publications, 1984.

Hilgard, E. *Divided Consciousness: Multiple Controls in Human Thought and Action*. New York: Wiley Interscience, 1977.

_____. "The Problem of Divided Consciousness: A Neodissociation Interpretation." *Annals of the New York Academy of Sciences* 296 (1977): 48–59.

Keyes, D. *The Minds of Billy Milligan*. New York: Random House, 1981.

LaBerge, S. *Lucid Dreaming: The Power of Being Awake and Aware in Your Dreams*. Los Angeles: Jeremy Tarcher, 1985.

Ouspensky, P. D. *In Search of the Miraculous: Fragment of an Unknown Teaching*. New York: Harcourt, Brace & World, 1949.

Shah, I. *The Sufis*. New York: Doubleday, 1964.

_____. *Tales of the Dervishes*. London: Jonathan Cape, 1967.

Shor, R. "Hypnosis and the Concept of the Generalized Reality Orientation." *American Journal of Psychotherapy* 13 (1959): 582–602.

_____. "Three Dimensions of Hypnotic Depth." *International Journal of Clinical and Experimental Hypnosis* 10 (1962): 23–38.

Spender, S. *Selected Poems of Stephen Spender*. New York: Random House, 1964.

Stanford, R. "An experimentally Testable Model for Spontaneous Psi Events. I. Extrasensory Events." *Journal of the American Society for Psychical Research* 68 (1974): 34–57.

_____. "An Experimentally Testable Model for Spontaneous Psi Events. II. Psychokinetic Events." *Journal of the Society for Psychical Research* 68 (1974): 321–356.

Tart, C. "A Possible 'Psychic' Dream, with Some Speculations on the Nature of Such Dreams." *Journal of the Society for Psychical Research* 42 (1963): 283–298.

_____. "The Hypnotic Dream: Methodological Problems and a Review of the Literature." *Psychological Bulletin* 63 (1965): 87–99.

_____ (ed.). *Altered States of Consciousness: A Book of Readings*. New York: Doubleday, 1971. (First published in 1969.)

_____. *On Being Stoned: A Psychological Study of Marijuana Intoxication*. Palo Alto, Calif.: Science & Behavior Books, 1971.

_____. "States of Consciousness and State-Specific Sciences." *Science* 176 (1972): 1203–1210.

_____. *States of Consciousness*. El Cerrito, Calif.: Psychological Processes, 1983. (Originally published in 1975.)

_____. *Transpersonal Psychologies*. El Cerrito, Calif.: Psychological Processes, 1983. (Originally published in 1975.)

_____. *Psi: Scientific Studies of the Psychic Realm*. New York: Dutton, 1977.

_____. "An Emergent-Interactionist Understanding of Human Consciousness." In B. Shapin & L. Coly (eds.), *Brain/Mind and Parapsychology*. New York: Parapsychology Foundation, 1979, pp. 177–200.

_____. "Lucid Dreams: Entering the Inner World." Part 1. *The Open Mind* 1, no. 1 (1983): 1–4.

_____. "Lucid Dreams: Entering the Inner World." Part 2. *The Open Mind* 1, no. 2 (1983): 1–5.

_____. "Lucid Dreams: Entering the Inner World." Part 3. *The Open Mind* 1, no. 4 (1983): 4–6.

_____, and J. Fadiman. "The Case of the Yellow Wheat Field: A Dream-State Explanation of a Broadcast Telepathic Dream." *Psychoanalytic Review* 61 (1974): 607–618.

Wolman, B., L. Dale, G. Schmeidler, and M. Ullman. *Handbook of Parapsychology*. New York: Van Nostrand Reinhold, 1977.

INDEX

Conditionees and conditioners, 65, 66, 67, 68
Conditioning, 10, 11, 16, 62ff, 95, 124, 254; classical, 62; human, 65; instrumental, 63
Conflict, x; with society, 254
Conscience, real, 202, 203, 217
Consciousness, four levels of, 210ff; fourth level of, 216, 217; nature of, 49, 50, 51; objective, 216, 217; of a computer, 48
Consensus consciousness, 11, 12, 16, 85ff, 237, 238, 239, 251
Consensus reality, 10, 81, 172
Consensus reality orientation, 81, 94
Consensus trance, 83, 85ff, 120, 124, 131, 132, 149, 176, 177, 184, 186, 202, 212, 214, 223, 251, 253, 255, 258, 259; content of, 96; continuing induction of, 105, 106; induction of, 91, 93, 94, 95, 96ff, 204, 205; parallels with hypnotic trance, 98, 100
Contradictions, inner, 130
Countertransference, 258, 259, 260
Courage, xii
Crabtree, A., 120
Crane/sorter analogy, 34ff, 41ff, 48ff, 106, 116, 117
Cultism, 245, 254
Cultural relativity, 86, 134
Culture, 86
Curiosity, 138, 204

Dalai Lama, x, xii, 276
Danger, of idea of awakening, 171, 172, 173; of the path, 289; of the work process, 251ff
Dead, people whose essence is, 166
Dealing with the unexpected, 35
Death of false personality, 166, 167
Decision making, 34
Defense mechanisms, 53, 54, 55, 130ff, 186, 191, 192, 248, 270, 273, 274, 295
Delusions, 251
Denial, 23, 145
Dependency, 245
Depression, 152, 153, 266, 267
deRopp, R., 297
Desire, 229; to help others, 267

Developmental tasks, 171
Deviance, suppression of, 96, 97
Discrimination, 296
Dissociation, 82, 94, 141
Distraction, 146, 199
Don Juan, 126
Dreaming, 299; lucid, 299; nighttime, 5, 210; nocturnal, 71, 212, 213, 214
Dreams, hypnotic, 6, 76, 103; nighttime, 4, 5, 103
Driscoll, J. W., 298
Duty, 97

Ego Plan, 60
Elitism, 245
Eliza, 24
Emotional states, 5, 210
Emotions, 57ff, 108, 154; as ends in themselves, 58; as motivators, 57, 58, 59; triggered by fantasy, 60
Empathy, 266, 267
Enculturation, 10, 11, 16, 30, 51, 66, 78, 82, 87, 88, 89, 90, 110, 113, 127, 128, 133, 138, 142, 154, 164, 166, 167, 171, 184, 185, 186, 188, 189, 244, 245, 254, 258, 269, 271, 272
Energy, 57, 59, 90, 107, 108, 113, 135, 163, 242, 258, 259, 260, 270
Enlightenment, 3ff; as a continuum, 7; available-states dimension, 12, 14, 18; dimensions of, 12; obstacles to, 3; problems in discussing verbally, 7; relative, 12; within-states dimension, 12, 13, 17, 18
Esdaile, J., 79, 80
ESP, see Psi
Essence, 10, 16, 88, 89, 90, 97, 98, 143, 154, 162ff, 214, 237, 252, 260, 270; development of, 145; nourishing, 279, 280
Evaluation, 81, 94, 149
Evolution, 34, 157
Existential neurosis, 151, 152, 176
Expectations, 53, 102, 103, 126
Experience and intellect, 295
The Explorer, 121, 122, 123, 124
Extinction, 65, 68
Extrasensory perception, 227; see also Psi
Eye closure in hypnosis, 75